Brian Mawhinney

This book combines two of the most all-consuming passions of those who are hooked. Hooked on football and, as with myself and Brian Mawhinney, hooked on politics.

No, this is not yet another autobiography about the minutiae of who knew what, when, and how. Instead, it is a reflection on the highest level of engagement in the glorious game and the highest echelons of political decision making.

As Brian so aptly puts it, 'Civic Britain is built around ordinary people volunteering their time and skills in volunteer fire brigades, hospital shops, driving the elderly and disabled to hospital, charity shops, running sport, church or political activity.'

From the dedicated fans on a cold winter's Saturday afternoon, to the unsung heroes pushing leaflets through doors, Brian Mawhinney pays tribute.

David Blunkett, Home Secretary 2001–2004

Brian Mawhinney is tough minded, big hearted and always compelling. Readers of this book will sit at the top table of politics, meet Prime Ministers, make peace in historic wars, and take a seat in football's royal box. This is a man who knows how to tell a story.

Daniel Finkelstein, *The Times*

Lord Mawhinney became the Football League chairman when it and many of its clubs were in crisis. He demonstrated a strong-willed determination and political skills, and actually secured solid improvements. That was striking in a sport where such leadership had previously been sorely lacking.

David Conn, *The Guardian*

I first knew of Brian Mawhinney's reputation when he was Secretary of State for Transport, universally described as tough and scrupulously honest. And so I found working with him in football: tough but always a good, wise friend; honest – I would rely totally on his word. Brian is exactly the person you want at football's top table, a huge success leading the Football League and a principled and practical influence on the FA.

Lord Triesman, Chairman of the Football Association 2008–2010

Football should have found Brian Mawhinney thirty years earlier. He brought the game a bit of tough love and saw through its self-obsession, and, when he left, the Football League lost an outstanding leader.

Patrick Barclay

Brian Mawhinney is the only Ulsterman to reach the top of British politics in the 1980s, but he never forgot his Ulster roots. The sections in this book which deal with the Northern Ireland problem are striking and original. They contain new insights and information which will surprise even the most accomplished experts in the field. As a result this book is a major contribution to the history of the Irish question, as well as being an important political memoir.

Paul Bew, Professor of Irish Politics, Queen's University Belfast

In his eight years as chairman of the Football League, Lord Mawhinney made miraculous progress by restructuring the Football League. Using his expertise in so many different fields, he enabled the Football League to rapidly progress and prosper on and off the field with the governance and financial deals that he put in place, which kept many Football League clubs in existence.

Barry Fry, Director of Football, Peterborough United FC

Just a Simple Belfast Boy
BRIAN MAWHINNEY

To Joan and David

with every good wish

Brian

Biteback Publishing

First published in Great Britain in 2013 by
Biteback Publishing Ltd
Westminster Tower
3 Albert Embankment
London SE1 7SP
Copyright © Brian Mawhinney 2013

ISBN 978-1-84954-532-7

10 9 8 7 6 5 4 3 2 1

A CIP catalogue record for this book is available from the British Library.

Set in Caslon and Bulmer

Printed and bound in Great Britain by
CPI Group (UK) Ltd, Croydon CR0 4YY

With love
to
Joanna, Sarah, Noah
Ethan, Daniel, Mary
Imogen, Esther, Lois & Anna
and to
Betty
who binds us all
together.

Contents

Jesus said:

'Everyone who hears these words of mine and puts them into practice is like a wise man who built his house on the rock. The rain came down, the streams rose, and the winds blew and beat against that house; yet it did not fall, because it had its foundation on the rock. But everyone who hears these words of mine and does not put them into practice is like a foolish man who built his house on sand. The rain came down, the streams rose, and the winds blew and beat against that house, and it fell with a great crash.'
Matthew 7: 24–27

Mark Twain:

'Always do right! This will gratify some people and astonish the rest.'

1

Dear Joanna, Sarah, Noah, Ethan, Daniel, Mary, Imogen, Esther, Lois and Anna

Grandparents are hard to get to know when you are young, apart from cuddles, treats and high fives. You see them only occasionally and learn about them mainly from your parents. They seem old, loving, maybe wise and often soft-hearted but definitely living in a different world to you. Sometimes they can be allies when mum or dad needs to be persuaded to do what you want to do. Often grannies seem more approachable than grandpas.

This book is written with you in mind – to help you understand your grandpa a little better. When you were young I read you stories which you liked. These are my stories, and I hope you will enjoy them. Perhaps they will persuade you to learn a little more contemporary British history. I am writing now because by the time all of you have developed your own curiosity I may be in heaven or simply no longer able to remember.

My maternal grandfather, Andrew Wilkinson, died when I was six. I cannot really remember him but know he owned a large garage and car dealership in Belfast, where he held the Riley and Singer franchises. My grandmother, whom I well remember, lived into her ninetieth year.

My paternal grandfather, Fred Mawhinney, died while I was at university. He was an imposing man with a strong personality. I knew little of his business life except that, I believe, he imported the first

Rolls-Royce into Ireland – to sell rather than drive, I hasten to add. His business did not make him prosperous. He taught me to drive in his old Vauxhall Fourteen. You never need to drive faster than 60 mph, he told me, in the days before speed limits or motorways.

I remember him and my grandmother sitting together in church on Sunday mornings. My grandmother, with his encouragement, used to make me repeat the contents of sermons after church so she could be sure I had been listening.

My parents carried on their conservative Christian tradition. We were taught regularly that though the facts and values of the Christian gospel could be transmitted between generations, its transforming power had to be accepted and experienced personally. My life changed fundamentally when, as a teenager, I accepted that truth for myself.

I said 'we' because I had a younger sister, Coral. She was not as academically inclined as I was but was enormously gifted musically. She could hear a song on the radio for the first time and then sit down and play it on the piano. Coral tragically died of a brain haemorrhage when she was twenty-eight. This effectively killed my father, who died eight months later 'of a broken heart', disguised as a coronary.

Our loving parents shielded us, as far as they thought sensible, from bad news and the more unattractive aspects of the worldliness around us. We went to church three times on Sundays and read our Bibles, on which we were examined. This form of Christian lifestyle made us 'different' from school friends but we all learned to cope with the occasional awkwardness our 'difference' created. One natural consequence was that our friends tended to be those who shared our Christian experiences.

My grandfather Mawhinney dropped dead of a coronary on a Belfast street while a passerby, who recognised him, knelt beside him on the footpath and quoted Psalm 23, 'The Lord is my shepherd...' He was in his early seventies. A coronary also killed Grandfather Wilkinson – in his bed – and, as I said, my own father in a hospital bed. Both of them were in their sixties.

While I could add some 'colour' to the above, you can see that my knowledge of my grandfathers does not amount to much. I remember my grandmothers better because they lived longer.

My father consecutively managed several small businesses. He was a pillar of our local church and a lay preacher. My mother, in today's parlance, was a homemaker and very good at it. We never experienced real need, though equally we never lived extravagantly. My father ran a small car, though its repair bills sometimes constituted a challenge. While we did not actually count pennies, money was always carefully handled. And we only had what we could afford to buy or rent. We did not 'do' debt, other than a mortgage, as far as I am aware. Considering today's world, that was a good early habit to learn.

My grandfathers and indeed my father were good and honourable men. They created employment for others. Their opinions were sought and they were respected and influential in the circles in which they moved, the common everyday ones which characterise most in our society.

My circles turned out to be more far reaching than I or my family ever imagined would be the case. That reality never signified that I was better than them. I was just different. They knew, and I have learned, it is a mistake to think that fame, celebrity, power or money are appropriate substitutes for good character, integrity or loving your neighbour as yourself, as Jesus encouraged us to do.

Like all parents, mine had aspirations for me. My mother wanted me to become a judge, my father imagined me as a doctor. In that spirit they both were adamant that I should be the first Mawhinney to go to university, although they could have made good use of some part of any salary I might have brought into the house. Later, when I was a university teacher, my friends thought I might one day become a professor; others saw me ordained into church ministry.

All very respectable.

Instead, after years as a university teacher, I wound up in politics and football administration – in public esteem, not nearly as exalted as law, medicine or learning! But to me they were stimulating and fulfilling, not least because they both required me to broaden my mind, my experience and my skills. And to the surprise of many people, including friends, I turned out to be passably good at both.

Some of that surprise probably lay in the fact that although they are public pursuits, I am a private person and have a somewhat introverted personality. Indeed, a number of political journalists used to delight in labelling me a 'dour Ulsterman'. No doubt some of the 'differences' of my Christian youth have become embedded, in a more mature form, in the way I live. On the other hand, my face in repose does not look cheerful. People comment regularly that I am looking glum when, in fact, I am feeling perfectly relaxed and unpressured.

On the plus side, I have always had a reasonable intellect, a well-developed curiosity (though not about mechanical or electronic devices), a willingness to work hard, a natural gift for public speaking and a combination of sensitivity to people coupled with a tendency to be unorthodoxly blunt in speaking my mind. I seldom do, or appreciate, 'political correctness'. During my public service my bluntness occasionally rocked boats but never, I hope, to the point where any important ones capsized. I once told Prime Minister John Major, in the company of other MPs, that at heart he was little more than a Chief Whip. The former sensitivity to people helped to make me a good constituency MP. Making decisions was seldom, if ever, a major problem; right or wrong.

I suppose in everyone's life there are moments of lasting importance. They cement intentions, change directions or shape the future. I am no exception.

During my final year reading physics at Queen's University Belfast I had no idea what I wanted to do next. While some had encouraged me to do a physics PhD, I knew in my heart that my maths was not strong enough. Then, some weeks into that final year, I got into conversation with a doctor at a Christian student conference. She introduced me to the subject of medical physics and radiation biology, through which I could apply my physics knowledge to direct human benefit. This idea attracted me though I knew relatively little about the subjects.

Only days later, while walking through the university, I spotted a notice inviting final-year students to apply for the Michigan exchange studentship. This was a graduate exchange programme, one student each way each year, between Queen's and the University of Michigan, USA. Exchange students were not charged tuition fees, and low-level living and travel scholarships were possible. The advertisement included a long list of subjects on offer. For the first time in my life I saw the printed words 'radiation biology'.

Without discussing the possibilities with anyone – perhaps at times I am too private – I became one of the twenty-one pending graduates who applied. They included some of the university's best-known students. Few knew me.

To cut a long story short, there were two interviews, after which I got a letter telling me, to my great surprise, that I had been chosen. All that was left was to obtain a good honours degree (2:1) to complete the qualification.

Now I had to tell my parents. My father was nonplussed and annoyed that I had done this without telling him. He insisted that he could give me no financial help. Mother was distraught at the thought of me leaving home for a year. Friends, I think, were a little envious. To me, the idea of a year away in America was surreal and certainly courageous.

After the transforming change that committing my life to Jesus entailed, this turned out to be the second fulcrum moment in my life. My year in the US was both hugely enjoyable and educational, and much flowed from it that has shaped the rest of my life.

I completed a master's degree in radiation biology in two semesters, which subsequently smoothed the way for my PhD in radiation biology through the University of London.

My Michigan supervisor, Professor Claire Shellabarger, put me in touch with Professor Bill Osborne at the University of Iowa Medical School and out of that emerged my first academic job, after my PhD had been completed. Our second son, Stephen, was born in Iowa City and probably owes his life to the special skill which the academic hospital doctors exercised in diagnosing and curing an early lung problem.

I joined the Michigan (University) Christian Fellowship (MCF). At its first social gathering a gorgeous blonde student approached. She apologised for not having picked me up at the airport to bring me to Ann Arbor (Christian friends had organised a ride to the campus to ease my transition to the university). My pique at being left standing at the airport for three-quarters of an hour and then having to get a cab I could not afford was a thing of the past. Anyway, she sounded sincere and was very charming so her apology was accepted and we moved on. Two years later we were married. Betty was easily the most important consequence of my American adventure. She was a native of the Detroit suburb of St Clair Shores and was to graduate as a nurse. Marrying her was the third crucial moment of my life.

Our graduation ceremony was more than personally important. The guest of honour was President Lyndon Johnson, who made his famous 'Great Society' speech. Originally President Kennedy had accepted the invitation but he had been assassinated in Dallas the previous November. All those experiences, and many others, turned me into a lifelong admirer of the USA and a firm supporter of the transatlantic special relationship.

As President of the MCF I helped organise Billy Graham's first ever university mission. This, in turn, laid foundations for Christian service and mission for the rest of my life, as well as establishing links with the Billy Graham organisation.

During my Michigan year I travelled from Toronto to Miami and New York to California and learned to exist on a daily allowance, excluding rent, of three dollars a day, financial carefulness which later became part of my nature.

The final fulcrum moment which shaped my life occurred in Blyth in Northumberland. A church friend, Brian Griffiths (now Lord Griffiths of Fforestfach), had been selected as Conservative candidate in Blyth for the 'three-day week' general election in

February 1974. There were and are few Tories in Blyth, so I offered to spend a couple of days supporting him.

On the Saturday morning, while giving out leaflets in the marketplace, I got into conversation with a passing lady who showed interest. Her name was Joan Reeve and she was the party's senior organiser in the north of England. She had come incognito to observe Brian Griffith's political skills. Over coffee, she encouraged me to think about standing for Parliament. I told her I did find it interesting but was pretty ignorant of politics and would not be interested in the 'boot licking' (my phrase) which I told her I thought would be involved. Before parting company I promised to send her my CV.

We spent the month of July with Betty's parents in Detroit. On our return, a number of letters were waiting for me from Conservative constituency associations in the north of England, regretting that I had not been selected for interview to be their parliamentary candidate. Puzzling.

At ten o'clock that evening the phone rang. 'My name is Armitage', a voice said, 'and I am chairman of the Stockton & Billingham Conservative Association. I am ringing to tell you that we want to interview you to be our prospective parliamentary candidate.'

'Mr Armitage,' I said, 'I am honoured but was not aware that I had applied.'

'Yes, you did. I have your application in my hand!'

Joan Reeve, bless her, had been peddling my credentials around the seats for which she had responsibility. She was the first person to have confidence in my political ability, and the whole of the rest of my life was rooted in her judgement. Thank you, Joan.

The rest is quickly told. I became Stockton & Billingham's Conservative candidate and did well in the October election in 1974, losing by a mere 18,000 votes! Only one memory of that election day stands out. My opponent – the Rt Hon. William Rodgers, then Labour's Secretary of State for Transport – made a prediction in his winner's speech. He told his constituents that on the basis of his majority that night, he would be their MP until the end of the century. Within a few years he had left the Labour Party and the House of Commons. Whoops!

Subsequently I was put on the party's central candidates list and was selected, in August 1975, to be the prospective parliamentary candidate for Peterborough.

After the Stockton adventure, back in my job lecturing in medical physics at the Royal Free Hospital School of Medicine, Betty and I analysed what this wholly unexpected and unplanned episode in Stockton might mean. Others might have calculated whose friendship to cultivate in order to build a political career. Being 'different', Betty and I prayed that if God wanted us to change our lives then we would like that made unambiguously clear, please.

Some months later, ninety-three people applied to become the Conservative candidate in Peterborough, which at that time was represented by a Labour MP, Michael Ward – a good man. Originally about sixteen of us were invited to attend the first round of interviews.

Having found Peterborough on a map (I had never heard of the city, much less visited it), I took an early train so I could get a feel for the place before my interview. Seeing the cathedral in the city centre (it was hard to miss), I abandoned political thoughts and went to explore. The huge building was empty. As I sat quietly I 'heard' a voice saying, 'This is where I want you to be.' My faith was so strong that I did not tell a soul – except Betty, some time later.

In 1979 I was elected Peterborough's MP with a majority of over 5,000 – part of the swing to the Conservatives which put Margaret Thatcher in No. 10.

On my first day in Parliament I wrote my first letter on House of Commons notepaper.

Dear Joan. See what a fine mess you've got me into now.
Warm regards, Brian.

She wrote back,

Dear Brian. Serves you right for picking up strange women in the marketplace.

Sincerely, Joan.

The rest is a matter of public record.

Two other decisions helped direct my life – becoming a government minister and being elected chairman of the Football League. Both are dealt with in detail in other chapters.

Overwhelmingly the two factors which have shaped, defined and underpinned all my adult life are my Christian faith and my family. They have contributed enormously – beyond description – to the 'good' part of Brian Mawhinney. The less good parts are my fault.

Those are the main pillars of my story, the seminally important things to happen to me. I say 'me' but in fact I was part of a team. Betty, as a 23-year-old, thought she was marrying a scientist and university teacher. We looked forward to raising our family in a campus context. Boy, did that turn out to be a miscalculation for both of us.

Together we entered uncharted political waters, without political background, experience or skills. We just had each other and a real sense of Christian purpose.

Betty never wavered. Threats of terrorist violence; having to assume major responsibility for bringing up the family; being on her own so much; having to read about and hear of me being vilified (sometimes unfairly) – she took all these in her stride and with her typical grace. She was strong and she was never diverted from her faith, her family or me. She had told Peterborough Conservatives, at my selection meeting, that these were and would be her three priorities. That 'speech' earned her a standing ovation. She never ceased to encourage and support me in public. Her private criticisms and advice were always helpful and constructive. And she gently reminds me from time to time that Christians are never perfect, just divinely forgiven.

The credit for the fact that our children, David, Stephen and Alison, turned out to be fine, happily married Christian adults and parents lies overwhelmingly with Betty. She is not easily persuaded that this is true – but it is. She is the one who binds us all together.

The facts of my public service are straightforward. I was a Member of Parliament for twenty-six years (1979–2005), standing down of my own choice. I was made a life peer two months later and since then have been a member of the House of Lords as Baron Mawhinney, of Peterborough.

I had no political background. My father never voted in his life (for religious reasons), nor, I believe, did his father.

For eleven-and-a-half years I was a government minister, rising through the ranks to Cabinet level under John Major. I am told that, in 1996 when Conservative Party Chairman, I was the second most quoted person in the UK media after the Prime Minister. While this may be an interesting statistic, it is not necessarily an important one; I was only doing my job as I saw it. It is not how much you say but *what* you say that is important in life. However, all those words did make me a controversial public figure from time to time.

I worked hard and for long hours (often too long) over many years. In that sense I 'earned' what I achieved. As for public recognition, a certain level of that is normal for someone in the jobs I have held. But it is of limited value. To some, people in the public eye have a sort of 'celebrity' status. Strangers smiled at me, sought to engage me in conversation and nudged each other when they saw me on the street. The boldest approached. Strangely, the larger proportion said something like, 'You're not who I think you are, are you?' Recognition is often only skin deep.

In the front of my diary I have written the words 'Doing your best is always good enough'. It is not a bad mantra. Nor is 'Love the Lord your God with all your heart, soul, mind and strength – and your neighbour as yourself.' Being recognised for these qualities seems to me to surpass being thought of as a celebrity.

I have a secondary reason for telling these stories. The public have a low opinion of politicians generally. They rank them in public esteem with journalists and estate agents at the bottom of repeated polls of public judgement. (Though, interestingly, people have a higher regard for their own MP than they do for the genre.)

Frequently this low regard stems from a commonly held belief that politicians do not give straight answers to straight questions; that they are not honest. When that is true, for sometimes it *is* true, it simply reflects how, occasionally, we all behave towards each other. The trait just seems more noticeable in MPs because they get questioned in public – and usually by people who have strongly held views on what the answers should be or what answers they want to hear.

The truth, of course, is that many questions cannot be answered helpfully, or even truthfully, with the simple 'yes' or 'no' most people want. To convey accurate information, answers often need to be qualified, as they are by all of us in everyday, one-to-one conversations. How much more true is this likely to be if the politician's answer is supposed to cover the range of different assumptions represented by 60 million people?

For whatever reasons, politicians are seldom revered. Their public personae are often reduced to little more than House of Commons votes, speeches, press releases, media or email sound bites (usually negative), photo opportunities, civic functions and constituency visits. In my experience, while some MPs behave badly, the majority, in all parties, work hard and diligently. They care about aiding their constituents in ways which seldom receive appropriate recognition.

I hope these stories will help to redress that imbalance – if only by a little.

In my twenty-six years as an MP, I did not hold those 700 surgeries or write the 400,000 letters to boost my ego or profile. They were genuine public service. As were the hundreds of thousands of conversations, or the actions that helped 'ordinary' people make better sense of their lives. Only those involved in each individual incident knew about it, and it shouldn't be otherwise. MPs of course want to impress their constituents but, for the most part, that happens 'below the public radar' on an individual basis.

In short, most people have little insight into the ordinary and sometimes extraordinary events which constitute the lives of MPs and ministers. I hope this book draws back the curtain just a little.

Political commentators, and historians, will find here some new information which will add to and maybe enlighten the existing published literature. This, in turn, should lead to a more informed and less ambiguous historic record. I hope the same will be true for those who have a passion for 'the beautiful game'.

I am privileged. Unlike many of my generation, I have stories to tell within two public frameworks. Politics touches all of us in that we each have a right to vote and the responsibility to pay taxes, and it shapes every aspect of our lives. Football, on the other hand, is voluntary. Yet millions 'volunteer' each week of the season – criss-crossing the country to support their team, yelling encouragement, obscenities and judgement on referees' birthrights and eyesight. Others settle in front of the television or radio – watching or hearing about great skill, tactics, effort and cheating – absorbing knowledgeable punditry, and sometimes prejudice dressed up as punditry, which occasionally appears deliberately to undermine referees (sometimes with the aid of electronics unavailable to the refs). But then, the 'beautiful' in 'the beautiful game' has always been mainly in the eye of the beholder.

Each week, crowds at local football grounds represent the largest expression of 'community' in scores of cities and towns across the country. And as that understanding has taken root in recent years, local professional football clubs have become increasingly important social providers to local people.

All this activity needs organising, funding and regulating – a governance framework – to ensure that all clubs in any league play by the same rules, thereby protecting the integrity of competitions; this is where bodies like the Premier League, the Football League and the Conference League come in. Their job is to undertake these three primary functions on behalf of their clubs and independent of them, which all three do admirably and for the common good. With others, I fulfilled that function for the Football League for over seven years.

This book's chapters on football are not meant to constitute an in-depth analysis, much less a comprehensive survey, of the current state of the game. As in the reflections on my political life, they are stories which illustrate how a few of the big issues of the day were handled behind the scenes. In both pursuits, choosing which stories to tell has been difficult. Many good ones had to be omitted. Still, I hope you find these few stimulating and informative.

It will be clear to all that my experiences are being reflected through the prism of my Christian faith. I realise that my pre-suppositions will not necessarily be widely shared. But every book reveals something of the author's values. In that sense this one is no different. I can only hope that these stories are a worthwhile read in their own right.

2

Peterborough People Are Normal

Getting married. Holding your children and grandchildren for the first time. Your children's weddings. Graduating. Your first pay cheque. Giving your life to Jesus Christ. All are life-altering experiences – and so is becoming a Member of Parliament. It affects how you live and see life. It also changes how people see you. As a public person you sacrifice an element of your privacy. Whether you should or not is beside the point. You do.

The job generates relatively little public praise and lots of criticism. Sometimes it is deserved and sometimes it stems from the fact that it is impossible to please most of the people most of the time. This is never pleasant. Occasionally it can be hard to take, especially for the family and particularly when it derives from ignorance, lies, prejudice or personal animosity. Interestingly, at least to me, the same credit imbalance characterises football.

MPs have little direct power though they can exercise 'power' by influencing events through persuasion, obstinacy, challenge and through the media. One of the great privileges of the job is that you get to see the best and worst of human behaviour – the selfless and selfish; the good, the bad and the bizarre.

The greatest privilege of all is being invited into the personal lives of thousands of people. They tell you things which sometimes they will not share with anyone else. They need help and choose to turn to you for it. What an honour.

I was not one of those who decided at an early age that he was going to become an MP no matter what. Ambition is good, although less appealing if it becomes the driving force in life. Others are elected MPs because friends and colleagues encouraged them to get involved, having identified in them a commitment to people and the ability to do the job. I am one of those.

I did not join the Conservative Party until I was thirty, by which time I had my university degrees, was in my second professional job and our sons David and Stephen were already part of our family. I joined mainly because I was interested in current events. Throughout my twenty-six years as an MP I saw myself as a public servant – a mantle which should sit easily on any Christian. Jesus, the Gospels tell us, came to earth in the form of a servant: not to be served but to serve.

During those years as an MP, always in and around the city of Peterborough, I dealt with many people's problems and concerns. It tells you something depressingly significant about our world that the very act of helping someone, by providing information, arguing their case or demanding action on their behalf, was welcomed by so many.

I have been asked often what an MP does apart from the obvious – voting; making speeches; issuing press releases; attending civic functions; making countless visits to businesses, schools, hospitals, fetes and voluntary groups; not to mention attending working breakfasts, lunches and dinners. In this chapter I will try to give a sense of the answer to that question.

During my twenty-six years, I dealt with people caught up in murder; bereaved by sudden and violent death; charged with incest, child abuse and rape (and their victims); threatened with violence by thugs; blackmailed; burgled; burned out by arson; and many people who claimed to have been jailed wrongly or who claimed, sometimes with cause, that someone else should be put in jail.

I was asked regularly to help constituents obtain visas – too often requests which turned out to be fraudulent – to expedite extraditions and to facilitate arranged marriages. Sometimes I had to explain to distraught people why I could not or would not help and, even worse, why I did not really believe them.

People who had no legal right to be in this country asked me to press government to regularise their presence. Sometimes I tried to help, especially in what seemed to be legitimate asylum cases; on other occasions I refused. Indeed, in some cases I gave the Home Office solid information so that people could be deported. The Home Office virtually never acted on this information, which was a disgrace. It is no wonder so many people are so cynical and so upset by the failure of government immigration policy – under both parties. If they are truthful, many MPs have become despairing and cynical too. Government control of immigration and asylum cases has nearly broken down, particularly over the past fifteen years. Even worse, if you make this failure public, too often you find yourself branded as racist or xenophobic by the liberal politically correct brigade. The Blair government did us all a major disservice by promoting or condoning the idea that public discussion of immigration policy was driven overwhelmingly by racism.

In fact it was often driven by real social concern about the pressure created on jobs, housing, schools, GPs and social services – though I admit an element of racism sometimes lurked in the shadows. Governments seldom perform a public service when they use the threat of guilt by association or accusation by innuendo to stop people talking in the public square about what they tell each other in the pub.

I was asked to help people get jobs, keep jobs, move house, change sex, get moved to more family-convenient prisons, obtain university places, receive protection from neighbours (often by having them evicted). People came for legal advice (after all, MPs make the law, was their argument) and for medical advice (after all I was *Dr* Mawhinney). People came for advice or guidance on how to start a business, grow a business, rescue a business or make a business behave more fairly to its employees. They wanted to know how to join the police, the civil service, a trade union (and how to leave one), become an MP or councillor, get a council house, sue their neighbours, the government, the European Union.

My constituents complained about the council, the government, the Church, law and order, unemployment, immigration, supermarkets, pornography, drugs, violence, the price of stamps, the BBC licence, the state of the roads, the railways, the weather, politicians, immorality, the NHS, schools, Peterborough United's football team and the cost of just about everything. Too often their favourite phrases were 'it shouldn't be allowed' and 'somebody should do something about it'. In other words, Peterborough people are normal.

Nothing was too big, too trivial, too old or too complicated to bring to the MP. The more rational of my constituents understood that I would not necessarily know the answer, but they expected me to find it. The rest just gave me their problem and told me to fix it. It was a privilege to help them.

Overwhelmingly people needed assistance to sort out their relations with bodies whose primary job was to serve them. One recurring theme was that government and council departments would not answer letters (in my pre-email age) or phone calls, especially when it came to benefit payments. People with reasonable incomes have no idea how soul-destroying and, at times, life-threatening being dependent on a government- or council-paid benefit can be, especially when the benefit is not paid on time or is reduced without warning. Easily the worst body I had to deal with was the Child Support Agency (CSA). It was a national disgrace. Gordon Brown's tax credit administration was not far behind, though it has now improved.

We, a Conservative government, set up the CSA. Its sound basic principle was that parents, even if split from each other, retained responsibility for their children. As a consequence the so-called 'absent' parent (usually the father) should continue to make payments towards the upkeep of his children because they remained his. In financial terms this was amendable only when the children had a stepfather.

The principle was good but its application was far too complicated and the whole thing was poorly run. We badly underestimated the effect that broken and discordant relationships would have on parents' willingness to pay and willingness to demand payment. The absent parent too often saw the payment as 'bailing out' his former partner, seldom an attractive prospect to him, rather than supporting his children. Many resented having to continue to pay when they started a second family and that resentment was often stoked by the second wife who wanted her husband's income devoted solely to their children. And enforcement of payments was a legal and logistical nightmare.

The result was hundreds of thousands of children deprived of income to which they were legally entitled, queues at MPs' surgeries and a huge increase in aggravated human relationships causing incalculable damage. But the principle remained right.

On my constituents' behalf I wrote tens of thousands of letters to government departments. These covered benefits of all kinds, as well as tax, education policy, hospital waiting lists, driving licences and speed cameras, food hygiene, animal welfare, trains, buses, television programmes, Europe – and what it was doing to us as a nation – strikes, public services (the Post Office was a favourite focus of complaint, and rightly so), farmers' incomes, law and order issues including too many yobs and too few police, war and nuclear deterrence. I became an 'expert' in things as widely disparate as potato rot and UFOs.

I also wrote repeatedly to local councils and learned how to plot a course through their bureaucracies. Often their actions (or lack thereof) affected people's lives more intensely than did government departments. Of course my constituents should have taken up these concerns with their locally elected representatives – councillors – and many did. But many did not and many were dissatisfied with the responses they received (or did not receive) from their councillors, so they came to me. Assuming the workload of an 'honorary' councillor became increasingly onerous during my twenty-six years. Some came to see me because they had heard only of their MP but knew nothing about their councillors, not even their names. Some had heard that the MP would pay attention and often 'fix it'. Successive council chief executives and I became pen pals and sometimes friends.

The questions never ceased.

Why were there never enough council houses? Why were the rules for getting a council house so 'unfair'? (They were always 'unfair' when an individual constituent did not qualify.) And why were all the council houses going to immigrants? (They were not.)

Why couldn't my child get into the school of my choice and why were 'they' letting my child be bullied in school or on the streets?

Why were there never any police walking the streets when you needed them? And why did they not show up when my house was burgled? (I often wrote to Chief Constables as well.)

Why were there no buses on my road and why would the council not fill in the potholes? (I have particular sympathy with this latter, justified complaint.)

Why could I not have planning approval especially when what I wanted to build was perfectly reasonable?

Why did someone not do something about the yobs hanging around my house, my street, the city centre?

Why did the council not have a sensible car parking policy, taxi policy, clean environment policy, anti-litter policy, attracting investment and jobs to the city policy?

Why did the street lights not work, bin men not arrive? Why were those living in the city given more and better services than those who lived in the villages?

Why was the council tax so high? What idiot dreamed up the poll tax?

Why did government not do something about ... any subject you like?

The list was comprehensive, instructive and, at times, seemingly never-ending.

These were the issues that affected people's lives, so they became the issues on which MPs focused.

For most of my time in Parliament, emails were not a regular means of contact, thank God, but I was not hard to contact. My PA, Judi Broadhead, was based in the constituency. I wrote letters – my estimate is up to 400,000. I saw constituents in about 850 to 900 surgeries. Coupled with multiple phone contact points in both the Commons and the constituency, and with, for many years, a pager, I was relatively easy to get hold of – even urgently.

All this contact with real life changed me permanently in at least one trivial respect. I never watch so-called reality programmes on TV, or indeed soaps. Having been privileged to deal with the lives of real people, I do not find at all attractive 'celebrity' egomania or personal humiliation on television.

I have used the word 'privilege' several times. It is the right word. It was a privilege not just to offer help but also to see people at their best and most selfless. So many good people. They cared for the young and old, the disabled and the disadvantaged, often for no reward other than helping those less fortunate than themselves. And when they worked for the state, on my behalf and yours, they were never paid what their care, commitment and devotion were worth.

Thousands in my constituency worked hundreds of hours each year for charities and good causes. Some worked through churches and faith groups. They and others helped strangers by organising and attending fund-raising events, by rattling collection tins on street corners in sunshine and rain, by baking, sewing, making and selling. And, what was even more remarkable to me, they invited me and Betty to their events because they valued our appreciation and support, which we gladly gave, involving ourselves with them in 'doing good'.

Like any MP worth his or her salt, I ate with my constituents and for them. I bought literally thousands of raffle tickets and hundreds of cakes and second-hand books. I could not count the number of fetes I opened and the many, many more I attended. And I learned the religious and wedding rites of many countries through being a guest at the weddings of my constituents.

Civic Britain is built around ordinary people volunteering their time and skills: in the volunteer fire brigade, hospital shops, driving the elderly and disabled to hospital, charity shops, running sport, church or political activity, keeping villages tidy, through the St

John Ambulance, Red Cross, Salvation Army and the like, arranging treats for underprivileged children. The list is endless, for all of it is as expansive as human generosity, which recognises no boundaries. Doing good to and for others is or should be a normal part of human behaviour. It responds to the fact that men and women are created in the image of God, and that there are always needs to be met.

These people were an inspiration in my daily life as an MP. They helped to 'balance' the less attractive aspects of human behaviour I saw and the complaints I had to deal with.

The Bible encourages Christians to love their neighbours as themselves. In reality most people love themselves more and focus on their personal needs first. Over my twenty-six years, tens of thousands of people made a case to me for help or justice. I responded to the best of my ability. The number who told me the truth, the whole truth and nothing but the truth was much smaller. I do not mean that most set out deliberately to deceive – though some did. They just believed they had been wronged and presented their case in ways which they thought would maximise their chances of persuading me to help.

To me, however, it was not the eloquence of selective presentation that was persuasive. I responded because I wanted to love my neighbour, though I seldom explained this to them in those words. They thought I was simply doing my job, and they were right.

The need to respond to each person equally was a hard lesson to learn. It is human nature to warm to those who warm to you and vice versa. At times it was difficult to treat everyone the same, especially those who made it clear that they did not like me personally – or my party.

Initially, as a new MP, I took people at face value and believed what they told me. On reflection I think that was because I had been brought up to believe that people should tell the truth. I am grateful to the many officials who patiently taught me reality. I soon learned how to assure constituents that I would look out for them without committing myself to believing everything they told me.

Month after month, the agenda of meetings with constituents was similar, even routine. Surgery cases followed patterns for me even though they were unique mega-disruptions in the lives of constituents. Sometimes I had to guard against responding too quickly to their requests. I had to learn that for constituents, a valuable part of seeing their MP was that he should listen and give them the opportunity to be heard. Too quick a response on my part made me sound like a smart alec who was not taking them seriously.

While it was possible to group cases under headings (tax, health, housing etc.), the truth is that each case was different because each constituent was different. Some were full of bravado; some had the air of defeat and desperation. Some were barrack room lawyers who had researched their issue thoroughly and 'knew' they were in the right or had been wronged. Others felt so threatened and overwhelmed that they could not easily explain even the basic facts of their problem.

Some demanded that I personally sort it all out. Others said they doubted I could help. Many were angry and blamed the government, the council, their neighbours – seldom themselves. Many were at the end of their tether.

Depressingly few of them appeared to believe that coming to see me really would help. Thankfully, that number decreased as the years went by. An encouraging, though small, number wrote later to say thank you.

Courtesy usually prevailed in our meetings – but not always.

Most of the thousands of constituency cases were not memorable except, perhaps, for the individual involved. Perhaps a few of the memorable ones would help illustrate the diversity of my life 'in the patch'.

It's the police that's the problem

Our dependence on public services is probably most sharply defined when we become involved with the police. Usually some illegal act has been committed, so sinned against or sinning, these memories stand out.

One such surgery case definitely stands out. The man in question was a villain. He told me he had been in prison frequently, on charges which contained the word 'violence' too often for my liking. He must have weighed twenty-plus stone – all muscle, very little fat – and had a fully shaved head before this was fashionable. His hands were huge.

He had come, he said, to complain about the Lincolnshire police – and the Cambridgeshire police. From time to time people did complain to me about the police, but to complain about two forces at one sitting was a new one.

We started with his unhappiness with the Lincolnshire Constabulary. I proceeded carefully, using simple arguments and non-threatening words. Eventually he was persuaded, reluctantly, to drop his concern without it being seen as a police victory.

He then turned to the Cambridgeshire Constabulary, the force that looked after Peterborough.

At which point I made a big mistake.

I still do not know what I did wrong. I may have relaxed my guard, conveyed the impression that he was wasting my time or stopped treating him with the exaggerated respect he thought he and his problem deserved. Whatever – I got it wrong, big time.

Suddenly he let out a roar, jumped to his feet, lifted up his side of the desk that was between us, pushed it into my body and came over the top to get me.

I was scared. Really scared. Had he got to me, he could (and I think would) have beaten me badly. He obviously saw me as part of the 'Establishment' with which he was at war. And he was bigger and tougher than I was. Much bigger and much tougher. When people are really frightened, they sometimes say or do strange, even irrational things. I did. In my fear I yelled at him in a purely instinctive reaction. 'You can't do that,' I shouted. 'I'm a Member of Parliament.'

As you read these words in a calm setting they sound silly, even pompous. And they are – both. When I tell the story to friends, they always laugh at my instinctive stupidity. But I was frightened.

Then the most remarkable thing happened. He froze, stared at me, put the desk back on the ground and sat down. I gathered myself, while trying not to show too much discomfort, and told him he would have to leave unless he behaved himself (which I knew was a bluff). I would not help someone who threatened me. Eventually he calmed down and told me of his complaint against the Cambridgeshire police. It sounded implausible but I told him I would look into it.

I wrote to the Chief Constable. A few days later I received a very irate phone call from a senior policeman. What did I think I was doing siding with a known serial violent offender against the police? Was I not supposed to support the police and promote law and order?

I did not appreciate either his attitude or his response, especially given what I had experienced at the hands of my constituent. My view was simple. The police should never be above criticism, though in order to sustain public confidence in Peterborough I never once criticised them in public in my twenty-six years as the local MP (though I did in private).

I told the officer rather sharply that I was not 'taking sides'. Allegations had been made against the force and I was seeking its response. Only when that was received would I make a judgement. And, I added, I am the MP for all of my constituents not just the socially acceptable ones and certainly not just the ones who have police approval.

He did not like that last remark and, additionally, gave no sign of either understanding or agreeing with the constitutional imperative. The conversation ended in a frosty impasse. A more measured reply arrived later. On this occasion my constituent's complaint owed more to prejudice than substance.

This big, threatening constituent returned to other surgeries with other complaints. Each time, I had a male member of my association in the room with me. One serious scare was enough and one big mistake was nearly one too many.

Mr Peterborough

Politics is about people, and their elected representatives come in many varieties – good, bad and forgettable. One Peterborough man is an outstanding example of 'good', though initially he and I had little in common.

Charles Swift is, probably, the best-known politician in Peterborough. He has served as a councillor for more than fifty-five years and remains the youngest mayor ever to have been elected in the city. Like me, he is proud to be a Freeman of the City.

Charles was a train driver, a strong trade unionist, a passionate Labour man and an ardent supporter of the Salvation Army. He was the political thorn in the flesh of my Conservative predecessor, Harmar Nicholls. In his youth he often got himself thrown out of hustings meetings by robust Conservative stewards for his over-enthusiastic heckling!

Charles watched me from afar during the nearly four years I 'nursed' Peterborough as a prospective parliamentary candidate. Once I was elected, however, Charles became very vocal. He did not want to share his city with a political opponent so he found reason to criticise much of what I said and did. I responded in kind. Local residents were entertained or bored by the struggle. On a daily basis our back and forth added little value.

Given our responsibilities Charles and I often attended the same local meetings. Whoever spoke first, the other disagreed. We were in danger of becoming an unseemly and disagreeable sideshow which diminished the importance of the public offices we held. We were both competitive people and we both shared the blame. Engaging with Charles did help me to understand that the letters MP after my name were not some sort of magic potion. They might give me a right to be heard, but not the right to be believed. They certainly did not give me the right to be respected. That had to be earned.

One night at a community meeting with representatives of the increasingly large Asian immigrant population in Peterborough we were at it again. I said something. Charles disagreed disagreeably.

I retaliated. While the meeting continued I realised my behaviour was not very Christian. I should have realised this sooner, but I did not; my competitive instinct was too strong. On a scrap of paper I wrote 'Churchill said jaw jaw is better than war war', leaned forward and handed it to Charles. He tells me he still has it.

Thus started a friendship which continues to flourish thirty years later. We rarely have even occasional disagreements. Our friendship is solid and by working closely together we have improved our city. Indeed we offered so much joint leadership locally that our duality – Conservative and Labour – itself became an issue. Most people approved; though, given our personalities, they could not understand how we did it. When, some years ago, Charles needed to recuperate after a period of illness, he and his wife Brenda stayed with us in our home in Barnet.

Charles and I did not just seek to build a better Peterborough by attracting investment to the city. We fought to improve public services and, with the Salvation Army, initiated a number of socially beneficial programmes. And together we walked the streets in support, and sometimes defence, of our immigrant communities when that was necessary.

Eventually Charles's enemies in the Peterborough Labour Party used our friendship as an excuse to oust him. There was no justice in the way the Labour Party handled it. Socialist political jealousy knew no boundaries. Subsequently his beloved North Ward voters repeatedly re-elected him as an independent to the council.

Today, the Labour Party in Peterborough hardly exists as an electoral force, while Charles's standing as an elder statesman is beyond argument, as is our friendship.

My Lord Bishop
During my twenty-six years as MP Peterborough had three bishops.

When I was elected in 1979 the incumbent was Douglas Feaver – a tall man with a beaky face which was seldom much bothered by smiles. For a bishop, Douglas was remarkably and unimpressively reclusive. In the nearly four years I nursed the seat, prior to my election, I met virtually every significant local person except the bishop. He was never to be seen.

Douglas Feaver had another claim to fame. He was among the most aggressively undiplomatic people I have ever met. His reputation for bluntness, up to and beyond the point of rudeness, was formidable. Not for nothing was the Peterborough diocese known in those days as the Dead See.

In July 1979 Betty and I were invited to a lunchtime reception in the city. Across a crowded room I spotted the bishop holding forth. It was time we locally influential Christians met, I thought, so I made my way across to where he was standing.

I did not push in or interrupt. Others in the group around him saw me and acknowledged my presence. Douglas ignored me as I stood silently waiting for him to finish. Eventually he turned towards me. As I did not know him, though I knew his reputation, I proceeded with propriety and caution.

'My Lord Bishop,' I said, 'please permit me to introduce myself. I am the new Member of Parliament for Peterborough, Brian Mawhinney.' I extended my arm to shake hands with him. He looked at me without a word then stiffening his back, abruptly crossed his arms against his chest, ignored my outstretched hand and in a loud and penetrating voice said, 'I never shake hands with members of the Lower House.'

I was not the only one who was stunned. I nodded and rejoined my wife.

Douglas liked to shock. I think he found it fun. Unfortunately the majority of people who observed and listened to him drew their own conclusions about his personality and, more importantly, his Christian faith. They were not impressed. Neither was I.

Unlike with Charles, Douglas and I never became friends though we maintained civility. Had we been able to, the common good of the city might have been enhanced.

Betty's hat

Politics is about both truth and, often more importantly, people's

perception of the truth. Frequently the latter can be much harder
to handle and more powerful in its influence. Perception can be
important even on seemingly trivial issues, as Betty and I discovered.

The redevelopment of Peterborough – a third-generation New
Town – had at its heart a large, new shopping mall in the city
centre. It was scheduled to open in the early 1980s and the person
chosen to perform the task was Queen Beatrix of the Netherlands.
She was on a royal visit and stopped in on her way to Lincolnshire's
tulip fields.

On the day before her visit to the city, Mrs Thatcher held a
formal lunch at 10 Downing Street in the Queen's honour. Betty
and I were invited because the visit to Peterborough formed part of
the Queen's itinerary. The usual phone call was made to the Prime
Minister's office. As this was a royal occasion did my wife have to
wear a hat? The reply was encouraging. The Queen would be wearing a hat. Out of respect, so would the Prime Minister. Other ladies
were excused.

Betty was pleased. Hatless we enjoyed the royal lunch.

Next morning we set off for Peterborough for the official opening
of Queensgate (the name given to the shopping mall). Fortunately
we were early. When we went into the shopping mall some guests
had already arrived including senior councillors and Development
Corporation officers. All the ladies were wearing hats.

At that moment I understood an important truth. The provinces
are almost always socially more conservative than London.

Instantly a second truth dawned. No explanation, even with
reference to No. 10, and no matter how plausible, would persuade
local people that it was acceptable for my wife not to wear a hat. We
would be labelled by my constituents either as ignorant of protocol
or as arrogantly superior. They would think we believed we were
too important to follow the hat 'requirement' that everyone else had
adopted. And all politicians know that relatively minor issues like
this generate long memories.

Personally I was starting to get used to people having all sorts
of odd and untrue perceptions about me (it goes with the political

territory) but I would not allow them to have a negative perception of my wife. Any explanation about not having to wear a hat yesterday would cut no ice with these important and, in some cases, self-important Peterborough people. Above all, I did not want my wife to be embarrassed.

Urgent remedial action was required. We dived into British Home Stores, the closest clothing store, before anyone spotted us.

Betty likes to shop deliberately and with plenty of thought. She likes to compare and choose. As she says herself, she is not an impulse buyer. She takes her time.

Not on this occasion. We did not have time to shop around for fear of being seen. BHS, on the shopping mall's main square, was our only option (because that was where we were) and we had to be quick.

Five minutes later we emerged immaculately attired and beyond reproach, my wife with her new hat on. Peterborough's standards had been met.

'I could have been attacked'

Being an MP can sometimes be a risky business. I am not just talking about terrorist or violent threats, like the villain I mentioned earlier, or even the book bomb once sent to me in the post. Every day you do business with strangers. Many are under stress and some have violent tendencies. Occasionally MPs are attacked; it goes with the job. Those who work with MPs can also be vulnerable, which is always a worry.

In my case, those who have worked with me have been fortunate, although the constituency secretary who took receipt of the book bomb from the postman had exceptionally good instincts which saved her from serious injury. My PA has also had her moments. She more than anyone else came face to face with my constituents.

During my years as an MP I was helped by a full-time secretary in the Commons, by my PA, Judi Broadhead, who handled the constituents and others who tried to contact me in Peterborough, and always by my wife.

For over thirty years Judi has been crucially important. Often I could not easily drop everything in the Commons, or when a minister, and rush off to Peterborough whenever a constituent demanded urgent help. Usually, if really necessary, I could rearrange my diary within twenty-four hours and few constituents needed my help more urgently than that. Most of these really pressing and so-called urgent cases could be handled by my telephoning the constituent and then the appropriate statutory authority asking it to contact the constituent directly. Very occasionally I needed someone I could trust to pay an interim visit on my behalf.

On one such occasion we got a desperate plea for help from a man who had benefits problems. He said he had no money. I spoke to him on the phone but that did not suffice. He could not explain his problems properly that way, he said. Someone needed to come to see him. If not then, given his personal circumstances, there was little point in his 'going on'. He was by no means the only one to threaten suicide, to me, and I always found it a serious challenge to gauge how real any such threat was.

I asked Judi to visit him. 'Just listen,' I said, 'and get the facts, including the name of the official who has been dealing with his case. Give him my apologies and tell him I will get to work urgently, as soon as I hear from you.

'Be cautious,' I added, 'he sounds agitated.' When she expressed concern about going I told her she would be fine, adding unhelpfully that there was no point in crossing bridges before she got to them. This is one of my 'favourite' sayings and one that invariably seems to irritate her.

The man turned out to be mentally ill. He circled his room talking to Judi in a disjointed way which was abnormal and sounded threatening. To protect herself Judi also kept moving to ensure that he was never between her and the door. She definitely felt threatened. Fortunately he took no action.

'How could you?' she demanded, more than once, when we next spoke. 'I could have been attacked and John [her husband] would not even have known where I was.'

Judi has never forgotten the incident. Legally, as her employer, I owed her a duty of care which probably was breached, albeit in good faith. I let her down. Thereafter, when I could not attend an 'urgent' case myself I sought interim help from the statutory bodies directly. And Judi did do more 'blind' calls for me. But every time we met constituents, a risk existed.

As I recall, the man's problem proved to be unsolvable.

What a difference a good chief executive makes

One of the strongest memories I have of a council-related issue involves a constituent who lived in New Road, Peterborough. New Road consists of neat, semi-detached houses with small front gardens. It was built before cars were a regular feature of everyday life and certainly before most of New Road's residents owned one.

New Road is just wide enough to allow two cars to pass carefully. Too often, when cars are parked on the road outside residents' houses (there are no driveways), they get sideswiped by careless passing motorists.

My constituent, I will call him Mr Jones, came to my surgery and told me his parked car had been sideswiped several times. He was fed up and had decided to pave his front garden to enable him to get his car off the road. The garden was just big enough so that the car did not protrude on to the pavement if parked parallel to the house.

The problem which brought him to me was simple. His application for planning permission to make the change had been refused by the council. Please would I help?

In my view there was a compelling logic in what he wanted to do but, despite my entreaties, the council refused to budge. Eventually I explained to Mr Jones that I had no power to make the council behave as he and I would wish (how often did I repeat that truth to constituents over the years?). I was sorry but there was nothing more I could do. As his councillor was not interested his only other recourse was to consult a solicitor.

Eventually he left my office grateful that someone had taken him seriously, but disappointed and mad at the council.

Weeks later Mr Jones reappeared. He had seen a solicitor; had appealed against the council's planning refusal in court; had lost, and now, on top of everything else, he owed the council £750 towards its legal costs. He was understandably upset.

In this conversation he mentioned something he had not said previously. He told me he could not understand why the council had a problem with his application when they had let so many of his neighbours pave their gardens for parking.

I said I would look into it. After he left I drove down New Road, carefully.

Gillian Beasley was the council's chief executive. She was and is good at her job and usually sensitive to people's needs. We happened to have a lunch pending. I rang her office and said I would arrive thirty minutes early because I wanted us to go for a walk before lunch. She agreed.

When I arrived at the Town Hall she asked where we were going.

'New Road,' I replied.

'Do I need to bring the file?' she enquired.

'No.'

We parked at the end of New Road, walked down one side and back up the other.

If my memory serves me right there were about 180 houses in the road, forty or more of which had paved front gardens being used as car parking spaces. We stopped outside Mr Jones's gate, which was near the end of our walk.

'So what is the problem?' I asked Gillian. 'Forty-plus people have done it, why not Mr Jones? Are you not guilty of discrimination within public policy by refusing him planning permission?'

Gillian is a friend as well as a good chief executive. She defends her council appropriately and sometimes legalistically but can be honest about its failings.

'It is worse than that, Brian,' she replied. 'None of these houses has planning permission yet clearly at least some of those garden parking areas have been in use for years.' If that use, albeit illegal i.e. without planning permission, has been for more than two years, and the council has taken no action (which it had not), then they are legally 'deemed' to have planning permission.

'So', I said, 'Mr Jones is being punished for being law-abiding. Others, who may not have applied for planning permission yet have had the benefit of safe parking for years, are legally protected. How can that be right?' I asked.

Gillian said she would 'sort it'.

She was as good as her word. Within days Mr Jones received a cheque for £750 to cover his outlay in meeting the council's legal costs. Gillian found she could not change the planning refusal administratively. So a new application was shepherded through the council's system under her eagle eye. Eventually Mr Jones was given permission to pave his front garden. He was delighted and agreed not to seek compensation.

On this occasion the chief executive righted a wrong and, maybe, registered a warning to her staff about undertaking and then defending sloppy work. Not wishing to admit you are wrong and to say 'sorry' is a human frailty. We are all guilty of it from time to time. It is a reality which is much too prevalent in government – national and local.

The case of Mr Jones taught me again the importance of perseverance and of checking facts myself. Over the years my experience has been that if you always rely on others for crucial information occasionally you will miss a key fact which you recognise as important even when others do not. This experience is more significant than many are willing to acknowledge.

It was also my experience that sometimes, when I got things wrong, I found it hard to admit my error and even harder to say 'sorry'.

The A1(M)

Sometimes a minister's job gets entangled with his constituency responsibilities. This happened to me once when I was in Transport.

For years the A1 road had been becoming increasingly congested, especially at Alconbury and at the Norman Cross roundabout near Peterborough. Both became serious traffic black spots. Cars could take forty-five minutes just to get past Norman Cross on a Friday evening.

My department received numerous complaints and eventually decided to make that stretch of road into a motorway. One day my Permanent Secretary, Patrick Brown, came to my office. 'Secretary of State,' he said, 'I have here the plans for the new A1(M) in Cambridgeshire. Before I give them to you to decide whether to proceed, I have to ask if any of this proposed route goes through your constituency. If it does then your vested interest would disqualify you from making the decision. Another minister would have to do so.'

'Permanent Secretary,' I replied, 'I have no idea how much of the proposed new road goes through my "patch" but I think not much. Nevertheless as we both want the procedure to be beyond criticism, I suggest you write to Mr Bill Samuel [then chief executive of Peterborough City Council]. He will be able to give you the definitive answer.'

'I will,' said Patrick, gathering up the plans and taking them with him so that I could not even sneak a preview.

About a week later Patrick reappeared in my office. 'Secretary of State, only about 100 yards goes through your constituency. Legally we consider that "de minimis" so you can make the decision.' This time he left the plans.

I decided the road should be built.

In the following months the Boundary Commission reported ahead of the implementation of new constituency boundaries for the 1997 general election. My constituency was cut in two.

Some time later I was selected to stand in the North West Cambridgeshire constituency, which included 44 per cent of my old Peterborough seat. I am still grateful to Mary Jones and Stephen Froling, senior local Conservatives, for their advocacy on my behalf.

Ironically my new seat also included about ten miles of the approximately thirteen miles of the new A1(M). At least, at every stage, every decision was taken decently and in order.

†

Thinking back I learned a lot during my years as MP. I learned that, although I was an MP, I was dependent on the help and support of others to do my job properly.

I learned that integrity is important, as is defending it in the face of ignorance, scepticism or special pleading. And that an important component of integrity is not making promises which lie beyond your power to keep – and keeping the promises you do make.

I learned it was important to take time to listen. Thousands of constituents came to see me, many with real problems. But many just needed someone to listen and to sympathise. Figuratively they needed a hug. I tried to fulfil that figurative role. And I learned that my constituents deserved to be 'heard' robustly at Westminster.

Who you are in yourself – your values and beliefs – and how you behave in public and towards others can be at least as important and often more so than what you know intellectually, can do practically or afford to buy. The combination of who you are, what you believe and how you behave helps to define your real and potential role and effectiveness in society. And, at least in my case, it was a reflection of my Christian faith, always remembering that Christians are not people who are perfect but people who are forgiven.

Finally I learned that first impressions are hard to erase. You cannot have a second chance to make a first impression.

I still find it hard adequately to convey the privilege I felt at being allowed into the lives of thousands of people. Politics is a worthy vocation if carried out responsibly and, when appropriate, confidentially. People are grateful for your help, though often guarded. Their appreciation of their own MP usually far exceeds their views on the collective species – and that is how it should be.

3

Out, Out, Out

'What are we going to do about the Irish?' has plagued British politics from before 1171, when Henry II took a formidable army to the island to emphasise to Irish barons that he was their ruler. Since then, hatred, lack of trust and respect, duplicity and violence have ebbed and flowed between the two nations and peoples. In the past 200 years, memories of former 'wrongs' outweighed any instinct towards genuine political reconciliation.

In the past fifty years, largely republican-driven violence took an unbelievably heavy toll in lives, broken bodies and ruined property, but democratic government did not crack, at either end of Ireland.

This chapter heralds the start of a seismic change in British–Irish politics and relations. It is an apparently mundane story of how the impossible became doable, how politics prevailed over violence, how 'love your neighbour' finally pushed in the direction of at least partial accommodation for the common good. In every sense of the word, this is a 'big' story, when such are very hard to find – particularly in Britain's dealings with the Irish.

†

The signing of the Anglo-Irish Agreement (AIA) caused much disruption in Northern Irelands's normal political process. What I find intriguing, however, is how much Margaret Thatcher 'moved' politically in the two years which preceded the Agreement. Perhaps this story will help shed some light on that significant period.

In April 1980 Garret FitzGerald TD (leader of Fine Gael), Charles Haughey TD (leader of Fianna Fáil), Dick Spring TD (leader of the (Irish) Labour Party) and John Hume MP (leader of the (NI) Social Democratic and Labour Party) set up a cross-party group called the New Ireland Forum.

The first paragraph of its report states: 'The New Ireland Forum was established for consultations on the manner in which lasting peace and stability could be achieved in a New Ireland through the democratic process and to report on possible new structures and processes through which this objective might be achieved.'

The group's report did not find much favour with Margaret Thatcher or her government. As she said in the House of Commons on 20 November 1984 (Hansard col. 154) in a reply to David Winnick MP,

> The hon. gentleman ... is well aware that the proposals in the New Ireland Forum were rejected by the Secretary of State for Northern Ireland very quickly after they were published, when he made it clear in a statement that he rejected reunification, the federal solution and the joint authority proposals.

Fourteen months later she had signed the AIA with its widely perceived, albeit misconceived, elements of a 'federal solution' and 'joint authority' which she had so roundly rejected. In my view the former was a baseless concern. As was the latter but it needed to be watched.

My memory is that Northern Ireland's Unionist parties made no formal submissions to the Forum, although several prominent Unionists did so in their personal capacities. Nor did the Forum canvass opinion beyond the shores of Ireland. So no one should have been surprised when its outcome was of an Irish nationalist/ Republican bent. 'They would say that, wouldn't they' seemed to be a general response to the report except, of course, for Unionists who were 'outraged' – as though the document was as important as, for example, an Act of the Westminster Parliament.

The Secretary of State's earlier rejection of the Forum conclusions was not an earth-shattering news event even at the time. Much more politically seismic was an answer the Prime Minister gave at a press conference on the day before her statement in the Commons. This news conference followed her Anglo-Irish summit meeting at 10 Downing Street with Dr FitzGerald, the Irish Taoiseach (Prime Minister).[†]

Question: Prime Minister, you said that you want political stability within Northern Ireland, within the United Kingdom. Could I ask you, in your view, does Dr FitzGerald therefore accept that what you are both working towards is an internal solution within Northern Ireland, within the United Kingdom, and by implication, does that mean that the British government has for the foreseeable future ruled out the three main options within the Forum report?

Margaret Thatcher: I have made it quite clear – and so did Mr Prior when he was Secretary of State for Northern Ireland – that a unified Ireland was one solution. That is out. A second solution was confederation of two states. That is out. A third solution was joint authority. That is out. That is derogation from sovereignty. We made that quite clear when the report was published.

Northern Ireland is part of the United Kingdom. She is part of the United Kingdom because that is the wish of the majority of her citizens. The majority wish to stay part of the United Kingdom.

The Forum report indicated that they realised that any change in the status of Northern Ireland could only come about by the consent of the people of Northern Ireland, so we are dealing with a situation where Northern Ireland is part of the United Kingdom because the majority of her people wish to be part of the United Kingdom and we have a minority community. That is the situation we are presented with.

---

† I rely on the CAIN web service for the extract of that press conference below. http://cain.ulst.ac.uk/

Anyone reading the New Ireland Forum report and the Anglo-Irish Agreement will easily see the differences and certainly note the different political tone the British government adopted to the two documents. So what changed, you may ask?

The answer probably involves Douglas Hurd MP, who went from being Northern Ireland Secretary to Foreign Secretary; Sir Robert Armstrong, the Cabinet Office's most senior civil servant; and Foreign Office mandarins who set out to reshape British–Irish policy. They decided, and persuaded Margaret, to usher in a new era. And, just possibly, I played a small part in Margaret's transformation.

The Irish were greatly distressed by Margaret's 'Out, Out, Out'. They believed their report deserved a more considered response. I knew this because I had a good friend in the Irish Embassy in London who kept telling me so; though, diplomatically, they kept most of their anger out of the public domain.

How could your Prime Minister be so dismissive of so much hard work – and well-intentioned work? We were genuinely trying to challenge the historic deadlock, they said. It was this spurning of what they believed were their good intentions that upset them most.

The Irish view, namely that Mrs Thatcher was impossible to work with (or words to that effect!), was repeated often in my hearing. I tried to explain that, style apart, the substance of her response accurately reflected the views of her government, her party, most of the people of the UK and a majority in the Province.

These indisputable facts did not seem to impress embassy staff. They and their political masters had too much invested in the Forum to simply turn away from it. They all thought that Margaret had simply 'dissed' their work, totally failing to recognise the one-sided impression the report gave.

Some weeks after this press conference my friend rang me at the Commons. His tone had changed. Senior politicians in Dublin had concluded – on what basis I could not tell – that Margaret must have rejected the report because she did not really understand it or its possibilities. They also believed that she was never going to be persuaded by the Irish to change her mind. What the Irish needed, he said, was for someone of good faith to come to Dublin to see whomever he wanted, to ask any questions he wished and then to report back to the Prime Minister his views – without the Irish having sight of that feedback. In other words, they were willing to trust the chosen intermediary to behave honourably. The Irish hope was that such a process would cause the British government to reflect more constructively on the report. I responded that that might indeed be the outcome but, on the other hand, the proposed process might just reinforce the British position. That risk was acknowledged by my friend. It was a risk, he said, the Irish were willing to take.

Their chosen envoy had to meet two criteria, my Irish friend continued. He or she had to understand the politics of Ireland, north and south. Secondly, whoever came had to have sufficient standing in Mrs Thatcher's eyes so that the report would be accepted as being as near to objective as, politically, it was possible to get. He or she had to have the Prime Minister's confidence.

He told me that, after much consideration in Dublin at the 'highest' level, he had been instructed to ask if I would undertake the task. I was genuinely surprised.

'For how long do you want me?'

Twenty-four hours.

'Who would organise the visit?'

The Irish government would – travel, accommodation and meals would be arranged, subject to my approval.

'Who would I be seeing?'

Garret FitzGerald himself; Dick Spring, the Tánaiste (Deputy Prime Minister); Brian Lenihan, the deputy leader of Fianna Fáil; and Peter Barry, the Irish Foreign Minister. My friend was certainly right. If all these men across the three main Irish political parties had been lined up to see me, and on one day, then the strategy had indeed been cleared at the highest level.

Why was I not seeing Charles Haughey, the leader of Fianna Fáil and the official opposition?

'That has nothing to do with you personally,' I was told. 'For his own political reasons Mr Haughey is not willing to have in his diary a meeting with a British Conservative MP – and definitely not at the moment. But he has agreed for you to see his deputy because he wants Mrs Thatcher to get a unanimous report from across the Irish political spectrum.' Knowing Haughey's reputation this explanation sounded genuine. And anyway I knew (and liked) Brian Lenihan from previous meetings.

I also knew, and liked, Garret FitzGerald. He was an impressive politician and, more importantly, he was a man of integrity as was Brian Lenihan. I did not then know Dick Spring or Peter Barry.

I told my Irish friend that I would reflect on his invitation and get back to him.

I arranged to see Jim Prior, the Northern Ireland Secretary of State, and told him about the invitation. I had decided that the risks of my accepting it without 'official' British cover were just too great. Throughout my conversations with the Irish I had become very aware that I was a mere backbench MP and that there was a real danger that I might get 'crushed' between the two governments, who were finding it impossible to agree. The political fallout of this initiative could be considerable. In retrospect I realise that I had in mind negative political fallout. However, I also realised that if I went with British government approval there was more chance my government colleagues would take my report seriously. I needed to establish if I did indeed have Margaret's confidence.

Jim said he would think about my invitation and get back to me, which I assumed meant that he too wanted to take advice, presumably from the Northern Ireland Office, the Foreign Office and No. 10.

When we met some days later he said it might be helpful if I went. My sense was that he did not wholly share Margaret's antipathy to Irish efforts to break down decades of political deadlock. That we did not agree with the Forum's analysis or conclusions was clear, but he seemed more impressed than Margaret that the Irish had been willing to examine historic issues. Jim suggested some questions I might ask and wished me well. He said he would like to receive a copy of the report he expected I would write for Margaret. I took this to mean that No. 10 had been alerted.

I asked if I could I tell the Irish I was going with his approval. He replied that I could. At no point did he suggest or even imply that I could say that I was going with No. 10's approval. From my point of view this answer was crucial. I was 'covered'. I told no one other than my wife and my PA. My friend at the embassy was pleased to hear my acceptance. Flights were confirmed. I would stay at the Shelbourne Hotel.

A couple of days before the trip started my Irish contact called again. There had been a new and slightly bizarre development.

Apparently Charlie Haughey had had second thoughts. Whether he had been pressured or not was never explained but now he was willing to see me. However, there would still be no trace of me in his diary. The plan was that he would call in on Brian Lenihan while I was with him, pretending that he had thought Brian was alone. Brian would introduce us and we would have a short chat. Charlie would reinforce his support for the report's findings. There would be no record of the meeting.

Bizarre indeed. I believed then, and still do, that my Irish contact was acting in a personal capacity and was not supposed to tell me of this development. It was meant to come as a 'pleasant' surprise. I think he told me out of friendship and because he did not want me, afterwards, to doubt his good faith.

I flew Aer Lingus to Dublin in a reserved front-row seat and was met at the aeroplane steps by two Irish Special Branch officers. We drove into the city in their unmarked car.

We were early for my first meeting so the officers asked if there was anything I would like to do to 'kill' an hour. In my youth I remembered going to Bewley's in Grafton Street, famous for its coffee and cakes. I said I would like to refresh those memories by visiting Bewley's.

We parked the car and set off on the short walk to Grafton

Street. One of the officers took my small overnight bag out of the car to carry it. I told him I had no need of the bag but he insisted on carrying it.

'Actually, sir,' he said, 'we would prefer to keep your bag with us. The truth is that there is an epidemic of car thefts in Dublin at the moment. There is a real possibility that our car will not be here when we return. In the circumstances there would not be too much of an official fuss if we lost the car. There would be an enormous fuss if we lost your bag; we would prefer to take it with us.'

Bewley's coffee was excellent.

The meetings went well, every one courteous and friendly. Dick Spring was clearly under diary pressure though he made an obvious effort to slow down and gave me sufficient time to understand his views and ask my questions.

Peter Barry appeared to be the one least comfortable with the process. But then again I think he was the one who would always have been less comfortable being relaxed and affable with a British MP. Unlike Dick Spring (he and I had talked rugby too) Peter did not indulge in any small talk. He stuck to the business at hand – as he did in my later ministerial dealings with him. He was clear, succinct and cool.

It was good to see Brian Lenihan. We had met on a number of occasions and always got on well. He could not have been friendlier and seemed genuinely pleased to see me. I reciprocated. Our style together was a bit 'cramped' because he had with him one of Charlie Haughey's closest advisers, a somewhat intense and seemingly humourless 'republican' whose antipathy to all things British we believed to be deep and wide. Whether this perception was fair or unfair is not for me to judge – though I do have a view. My immediate reaction on seeing him was that his presence was to ensure that Brian's friendship with me would not lead him into becoming indiscreet. Today, I imagine he attracts more respect in the wider Irish political firmament, as a former government minister, than he had back then.

In the middle of our conversation, as predicted, the door suddenly opened. In walked Charlie, in shirt sleeves with his tie hanging down, looking a bit shop soiled. He looked up from the sheaf of papers he was carrying which he purported to be reading. Feigning surprise he said, 'Sorry, Brian, I didn't realise you had a guest.'

'Hello Charles. You know Brian Mawhinney, don't you?'

'Of course. Good to see you again, Brian' (we had never previously met).

'I was just telling Brian about our Forum report...'

Charlie stayed about ten minutes, gave me his messages about how important the report was and how equally important it was for 'you British' to take it very seriously etc. etc. – and left. I kept my face straight throughout and played along but the meeting had elements of pantomime farce. At any moment I thought someone might go 'I say, I say, I say.'

After he left, Brian Lenihan, with a similarly commendable straight face, resumed our conversation as if nothing significant had happened. He rose even higher in my estimation. His companion remained poker faced throughout.

Garret FitzGerald's chief adviser, Michael Lillis, took me for a meal in Dublin before we went to Garret's home for our conversation. Michael told me the Prime Minister had been out politicking (in Donegal if I remember correctly) so he would be tired. He was looking forward to seeing me but his wife was not well (she would be in bed in the next room) so I should stay for no longer than forty-five minutes. 'I know you and he are friends but he needs his rest.' I agreed immediately.

Garret greeted me warmly and we sat in his living room, talking about politics, Ireland and the work of the Forum. After precisely forty-five minutes I stood to leave. He refused to let me go. He said he appreciated my personal thoughtfulness but he was enjoying our chat, it was good to see me again and the Forum report really was more significant than we British realised. Michael Lillis did not say a word. I sat down while Garret checked that his wife was comfortable.

After two hours I left for the hotel. The rest of the visit was uneventful as was my return trip to Westminster.

I wrote a report for Margaret explaining my meetings and the importance the Irish attached to the report, with emphasis on progress through agreed democratic structures and on our giving it positive long-term consideration. I reported that I had told the Irish that my personal view about the report's three possible ways forward coincided with hers. What the Irish really wanted, however, was for us to engage with their analysis – if not their conclusions – in the hope that out of joint examination of the differences new, mutually acceptable political arrangements would emerge.

I added that, for the Irish, the real significance of the report was that it should be seen as a signal that they were willing to work with the British government constructively about the future of Northern Ireland and its place in a United Kingdom context. The North was also part of the island of Ireland and this too needed to be redefined. They wanted us to accept that their report represented historically new thinking on their part. And it did. They also wanted us, in return, to be willing to understand their three proposals not with a solid commit- ment to any one of them but as an expression of their willingness to open a genuine dialogue. Whether this amounted to a watering down of their aspirations in light of Margaret's public stance I cannot say.

They hoped the British government would respond with opening proposals of its own. They also hoped we would recognise, whether we liked it or not, that the Irish had an interest in the North that they would continue to pursue. It would not go away.

I copied my report to Jim Prior. Neither Margaret nor Jim responded in substance beyond a 'thank you'. I made no report or comment to the Irish subsequent to my visit beyond a 'thank you' to my friend. To this day there has been no public reference to my visit, which I continue to believe was bilaterally helpful.

It is a matter of record that, within months, Garret and Margaret signed the Anglo-Irish Agreement. I cannot prove 'cause and effect' but my personal view is that the two papers – the New Ireland Forum report and the Agreement – do bear some relationship. That relationship probably lies more in symbolism and the process of agreement than it does in shared substance.

Did my report make a significant difference to government thinking? Did it help usher in a historic change in UK–Irish relations? I do not know, not least because no one has ever told me officially (though Jim Prior was appreciative and hinted that Margaret would be less so).

My considered view is that, taken in isolation, the report was unlikely to have changed Margaret's mind. But in the hands of some of her ministers and officials who were seeking to persuade her to write a new chapter in the history of these islands, it may have turned out to be more influential than I had realised at the time. And, of course, the AIA did get signed.

Let me digress. I had got into Margaret's bad books years earlier. As a new MP, and the only one from Northern Ireland in the Conservative Party, I was not overly impressed by the government's Northern Ireland policy, nor by Humphrey Atkins MP, the then NI Secretary of State, who was handling it. Humphrey was one of Margaret's favourites but he found the Province's complexities challenging. John Carson, a former Ulster Unionist MP and a friend of Margaret's thought so too, labelling him 'Humphrey Who?'

Eventually, perhaps in frustration that no one was paying any attention to my ideas, I wrote an article for *The Guardian* setting out an alternative policy (and in the process incurring the wrath of my whip, David Hunt MP). Anyone who understands British politics and/or Margaret will quickly deduce that such an initiative on my part could reflect only naivety or antagonism. For the record, the former is much closer to the truth. I remain grateful to Julia Langdon, a *Guardian* journalist and a friend, for facilitating this initiative which led to a change in government policy and a new future for Northern Ireland.

My proposal was simple and novel. Irish nationalists, for many reasons, would never give their full allegiance to London. Ulster's Unionists would never give their allegiance to Dublin. So what I thought was needed was an elected assembly in Belfast – very different from the 'old Stormont' – to which, over time, both groups could learn to give their allegiance.

Initially, it would be difficult for the assembly to agree on much, if anything, so at the beginning only easier non-controversial matters should be devolved to it. As confidence and structures developed more could be devolved until everything – other than those matters which had to remain with the sovereign government – had been handed over, with security policy probably being the last to be devolved given its contentious nature.

Thus so-called 'rolling devolution' was born.

I sent a copy of my article to Margaret. I still have her reply. My ideas were interesting but we already had a policy with which she was content. In other words – thanks but no thanks; and probably a black mark for me!

On this too she changed her mind. With the help of Jim Prior, my ideas were eventually legislated. Today, Northern Ireland is run as I envisaged should be the case twenty years ago.

Sometimes in politics, and indeed in human inter-relations, hope lurks in even the most unlikely circumstances. Saying 'Out, Out, Out' to the Irish initiative did not seem, on the face of it, a likely basis on which to build a wholly new, constructive inter-governmental relationship. But by and large that is what happened.

Less than two years after 'Out, Out, Out' the same Prime Ministers were signing the Anglo-Irish Agreement. Today, differences, sometimes serious differences, remain between the two governments but their relations are incomparably better, probably better than at any time in history.

I believe that 'Out, Out, Out' had one truly historic consequence which, without Mrs Thatcher having used those words publicly, might have been much more difficult – if not impossible – to achieve. The Irish finally understood that no lasting settlement of 'the Northern Ireland issue' would result unless they gave up their constitutional claim to the Province being part of a united Ireland. Of course they had heard those sentiments expressed by many politicians over many years. They had heard them from me. Sometimes, however, it is the way that the familiar is stated that finally catches people's attention. That is an enduring and fundamental political reality. Good politicians never neglect presentation.

All three of the New Ireland Forum proposals were based on the assumption that the Irish constitution applied and would continue to apply in some way to the North. I explained 'Out, Out, Out' to the Irish in those constitutional terms during my visit. Perhaps unnecessarily, I made it clear that I could not speak authoritatively about what lay behind Mrs Thatcher's robust analysis. But knowing her views and those of her party (of which I was a member) I told them I was certain the Irish constitution had to change before any 'new' relationship could be cemented. For us British that was a given. To be fair the Irish received my restatement of this reality calmly.

The Anglo-Irish Agreement did not include a specific constitutional change. But it left open the possibility. More, it paved the way for the Good Friday Agreement, which did include the mechanism for this necessary, historic change in the Irish constitution.

'Out, Out, Out' forced the Irish to face up to the, to them, unpalatable fact that the status quo was not compatible with their policy objectives, with respect either to Northern Ireland or to improved relations with the British government. There had to be change.

There had to be change, too, in British government thinking as we came to terms with the fact that the Irish had to be taken with a new seriousness. I was privileged to be part of that process, as I will tell you elsewhere.

I was just a small cog in these historic changes, but perhaps a significant one. The fact that I played any role was not because I had the power to demand involvement or to deliver change. Ultimately it was because others took the view, after watching me over a period of years, that I had the ability and the integrity to make a positive difference, which was flattering. I hope I did.

4

No. 10 Calling

'The Prime Minister has appointed new ministers.' This is the bald media statement the public hears. In fact each appointment is different and personal. So each minister's report on his or her 'elevation' will vary in the detail. For many years an impending reshuffle was signalled by the sight of ministers trudging up Downing Street to be told by the Prime Minister that their services were no longer required. It was often a brutal human drama.

More recently Prime Ministers have changed this procedure. Often they see departing ministers in the PM's room in the Commons, or ministers have gone privately and without fanfare to No. 10, through the Cabinet office inter-connecting corridor or even received their marching orders the day before. In such cases the deed has been done away from the media gaze: altogether a more civilised approach.

I went through the appointment process five times. On the first occasion I knew my appointment was pending – though it is never 'real' until it actually happens. On the morning in question I was at my desk in the Commons office I shared with John Townend MP. The phone rang. A man said he was contacting me on behalf of the Prime Minister. She would like to speak to me sometime during the afternoon. Could I be free? I could.

We arranged that I would be available on my Commons number between 2.00 p.m. and 6.00 p.m. (the Prime Minister had a busy schedule, he said, so it was not clear when she might be able to get to the phone).

I called my wife and told her – otherwise no one. At 5.55 p.m. the phone rang.

'Brian, I would like you to become an additional Parliamentary Under Secretary in the Northern Ireland Office.'

'Thank you, Prime Minister. It would be an honour.'

'You may tell your wife but please do not mention this to anyone else at the moment. I have other appointments still to make. I would be grateful if you would wait until you hear the announcement on the media before commenting.'

That was it. Brief and to the point. I told Betty, who was pleased and, therefore, typically supportive in her own quiet way. She never mentioned the associated physical risk to me, her or the children. If she had security concerns or unhappiness about the disruption my appointment would cause at home – with the extra responsibility that would fall on her – she kept them to herself. I was and am more grateful that I can convey for her attitude, which never wavered throughout my six-and-a-half years in the Northern Ireland Office (NIO). As for me, I was delighted. Had Margaret given me my choice I would have chosen the NIO. It would be a privilege to put something back into the society which had given me so much.

There was no announcement on the 7 p.m. news, so I went down to dinner. The first person I bumped into was Nick Scott MP, a friend, who was also Tom King's deputy at the NIO. To my surprise his first words were, 'Congratulations, I hear you have joined the team.' I thanked him and explained that the promotion had not yet been announced by No. 10. We went into dinner where we were joined by Michael Heseltine. There was some irony in this group because the day's minor ministerial reshuffle had been delayed for weeks while Margaret and Michael had disputed a helicopter contract. In reality the disagreement was only the most recent manifestation of a more fundamental dispute between the two of them over attitudes and policy towards the USA and Europe. Finally Michael had left the Cabinet, on a matter of principle, just a few days earlier.

At 8.55 p.m. I excused myself saying simply that I wanted to see the nine o'clock news.

'He's been made a minister in the NIO,' Nick Scott told Michael and several other MPs within hearing range. 'He wants to know if he can talk about it!'

After hearing the news, I could.

My second appointment was totally different. It took place while I was in Belfast as duty minister. Earlier in the week John Major had been appointed Prime Minister in succession to Margaret Thatcher, having defeated Michael Heseltine in a poll of Conservative MPs.

When my last afternoon meeting finished about 6 p.m. my private secretary told me the new Prime Minister wanted to speak to me as soon as I was free. Because I had been in Northern Ireland for some days there had been no opportunity to speak to John but I had written to congratulate him. My immediate assumption on getting the message was that he was ringing to thank me for my note. So I dialled No. 10 myself to ensure that my private office did not listen in on the conversation.

'Brian,' he said, 'I want you to remain in Northern Ireland and I am promoting you to Minister of State in recognition of your work there. It is for Peter [Brooke – the Secretary of State] to decide the allocation of portfolios but I do want you to take the new and significant Anti-Terrorism Bill through the Commons. It starts in Committee next Tuesday.'

'Thank you, Prime Minister. I am delighted to be staying and will do my best for you.'

'Congratulations again. And well done. You deserve it.'

The phone went dead.

I called Betty, then our children David, Stephen and Alison followed by John and Judi Broadhead in Peterborough. They were then, and still are, our close friends.

By the time these calls were completed the news had been announced and officials were coming into my office to offer their best wishes.

I had been in the NIO since January 1986. My nearly five years working on education had been controversial (see Chapter 7); Northern Ireland people can be persuaded to change, but often not easily. Yet both civil servants and those at the further education college that evening where I gave a speech were generous in their appreciation. They assured me they shared the Prime Minister's view that my time in the Province had been good for local people and that I deserved my promotion.

My third ministerial appointment created a dilemma. I went into the 1992 general election as Security and Political Affairs Minister in Northern Ireland. My security brief was not complicated. Peter had told me to toughen up the security message and get a firmer grip on presentation. Public confidence required a more robust security stance.

Within a few days of taking over the brief from Lord Belstead, and following some tough anti-IRA messages which the media had projected widely, I was given full, i.e. 24-hour, personal security cover. My excellent driver, George, took lessons on how to drive an armoured car and the (then) Royal Ulster Constabulary (RUC), the Metropolitan Police (in London and Barnet) and the Cambridgeshire Constabulary (in Peterborough) took control of my life outside the confines of home, Parliament and Stormont. They forbade me from doing *anything* unless they were accompanying me.

I am probably the only person in Peterborough's history who canvassed voters out of the back of an armoured car – with four Special Branch officers looking on day by day. But they never took part in the electoral process.

A couple of days after the election, I was relaxing at home reading the morning papers when about 11.00 a.m. the phone rang. 'The Prime Minister would like to see you. When can you get here?'

I needed time to get dressed and to summon my Special Branch officers who were thirty to forty-five minutes away. How about 2 p.m.? No good, was the reply. 'The Prime Minister wants to make further changes to his government (the Cabinet changes having already been announced), and he cannot make progress until he has seen you.' The implication of that statement was that I was to be offered a senior Minister of State job back in England. Good.

I made a quick decision and said I would be there by I p.m. Clearly I was still going to be a minister, but not in the NIO, so what did it matter if I took a risk by breaking the protection 'rules' in order to help the Prime Minister? Anyway, as everyone knows, unpredictability is one of the best protection policies against terrorist attack. I drove myself to the Commons and, before going to Downing Street, called my NIO office and asked them to tell my Special Branch minders where I was.

'I want you to become Minister for Health,' John said when we met. 'Virginia Bottomley will be your Secretary of State and she is looking forward to working with you. You will make a good team. The Health job is one of the most senior and important Minister of State jobs in government. You deserve it.'

'Thank you for your confidence, Prime Minister,' I replied, and started walking across Whitehall into Richmond House to find my new office and boss.

Happily, George transferred from the NIO with me but his services were not required that first night. I had to drive my own car home. As I walked to the Commons parking area, totally by coincidence I bumped into my two former minders. They took it upon themselves to tell me off for what I had done and left me in no doubt that they thought my judgement had been poor.

My transition from the NIO to Health had an additional immediate effect. My full personal security was withdrawn there and then. The Metropolitan Police kept a continuing eye on our house, as did the Cambridgeshire Constabulary when I stayed in the constituency, but the close protection was withdrawn. Allegedly the IRA lost interest in me as soon as I left the NIO. Whether life, or the IRA, was that straightforward is a matter of conjecture. Certainly no one asked me what I thought.

During the Health years, which were good ones, I revamped the country's GP services; developed GP fundholding, in collaboration with appropriate BMA leaders; enhanced the role of nurses; and, more controversially, handled the amalgamation of the main teaching and specialist hospitals in London – two by two – to improve patient services. After two years in Health I was 'translated' into the Cabinet.

The skills Virginia and I possessed proved complementary. Using different methods of reasoning we usually arrived at the same conclusions. In our two years she had to read too many mischievous and speculative media stories about who was really running the Health Department (I was never in any doubt) but none of those stories were sourced by me and I worked hard to convince her of my personal loyalty. Virginia was professional in her leadership and in her personal working relationship with me. Years later, rather brutally, I was made to understand that those stories might have started a process of undermining her confidence in my affirmations of support but at the time she was very appreciative.

Anyway, immediately prior to the 1994 government reshuffle there was much media speculation that my promotion to the Cabinet was in the offing. This was the first time I'd been mentioned in connection with a Cabinet post and it was not always easy to handle. Party colleagues joined in, which was kind of them – and appreciated – but it did complicate relationships in Richmond House.

About 9.30 on the morning in question my private secretary told me that ministerial changes had begun. She and I had talked briefly about the possibility of my leaving the department; some of the speculation had been that I would be promoted to Secretary of State for Health – in place of Virginia – and this too had complicated working relationships.

At about 11.00 a.m., and with a discernible air of disbelief, my private secretary came into my office to say that there had been no word from No. 10. As my natural instinct tends to look first to the downside, I said that probably the speculation was wrong and I would be staying at Health. She was encouragingly sceptical.

Another hour passed during which my conviction that I had been bypassed strengthened. I went for a walk down the corridor. As I wandered back to my office my private secretary came to meet me. 'Can we have a word in your office please, minister?' she said.

We went in and closed the door.

'You are to go to No. 10 immediately. There has been a mess-up. You were supposed to have been one of the first summoned, but one official thought another was contacting you – and vice versa. The whole reshuffle is stalled until you get there.'

It was a short walk. Before entering No. 10, I stopped in Downing Street for a chat with Stephen Dorrell, who, like me, was to enter the Cabinet that day for the first time.

'Brian,' John Major said, 'I want you to join the Cabinet as Secretary of State for Transport.' My first and instant thought was – Transport? What do I know about Transport? In my previous appointments, I had known something about Northern Ireland and Health. Transport was new territory. Indeed, for the first two minutes of our conversation I was so fixed on the idea of Transport that I forgot to be pleased about this ultimate political promotion – to the Cabinet.

John gave me two specific instructions. First, the privatisation of British Rail had slowed – maybe even become bogged down. Get it moving again. Although controversial, it was a very important part of our legislative programme.

Secondly, I was to get a grip on the department and the way it performed. Its reputation and working practices needed to be sorted and strengthened. That was made a priority.

'One other thing,' the Prime Minister added. 'I am reducing the number of your departmental ministers from five to four. Steve Norris will be the only remaining minister. Your Minister of State, John Watts MP, and Lords Minister, Viscount Goschen, will both be new to government. Can you handle this?'

Within me a voice said, five ministers down to four, two of those are new ministers and I am a brand new Secretary of State – what does he think he is doing? Where do I go for experienced advice?

Outwardly I thanked the Prime Minister for the honour: whatever team he decided was fine with me. I was politically sensible enough to realise that questioning the Prime Minister's judgement would not be a good start to my Cabinet career. And, anyway, I supposed his new format was a sort of vote of confidence.

Out I went into Downing Street. I ignored the media's shouted enquiries about which portfolio I had been given. However, my appointment was soon 'announced' on TV. Apparently the smile on my face, which is usually more dour, signified that I was pleased with my conversation with the Prime Minister.

On my way back to Health I bumped into Virginia.

'Where are you going?'

'Transport.'

'Are you pleased?'

'Yes.'

It was not until my private secretary told me that Virginia had been moved to National Heritage, and was very unhappy at the prospect and the implied demotion, that I understood why the atmosphere of our conversation had been strained and perfunctory – and why she had not waited for me to enquire about her future.

I called the Transport Permanent Secretary, Patrick Brown, and explained that I would not be going to the department that afternoon. The Prime Minister had asked me not to go until he had had the opportunity to tell existing ministers that they would be moving. I invited Patrick to come over for a 'getting to know you' drink with me and my wife. I had, of course, called her first and asked her to join me on the House of Commons Terrace. I did not tell Patrick about my Prime Ministerial instructions.

My time at Transport did not last long, though solid progress was achieved. The national rail strike was settled. Rail privatisation made real progress, transatlantic aviation policy was liberalised, our first privately designed, built and financed road was commissioned and ferry safety was considerably enhanced.

The following summer John Major resigned as party leader and following his re-election, I was one of the early invitees to No. 10. I found Lord (Robert) Cranborne in the State Room thumbing through a list of peers.

'I have been offered the job of Leader of the Lords,' Robert said, 'but I don't approve of the PM's choice of Chief Whip there, so he sent me away to come up with an alternative suggestion.' I was amazed. In my naivety I had thought Prime Ministers were all powerful. In reshuffles they are not (as Tony Blair and Gordon Brown amply demonstrated). Still, I had learned something about both John and Robert.

'Thank you for your help in my re-election,' the Prime Minister said when I entered the Cabinet Room. 'Now I want you to be Party Chairman. Many people, including parliamentary colleagues, tell me I need an articulate, streetwise toughie to do this job and a good manager to prepare the party for the general election. Your name crops up more frequently than any other. Will you do it? I need not stress that, given our poll standing, this will be a significant challenge.'

I had a single question. 'Will I still be a member of the Cabinet? I believe I need to be, in the run-up to an election.'

'Of course,' he replied. 'You will be Minister without Portfolio and will have an office in the Cabinet Office. Incidentally,' he added, 'you need to understand that this job will have a profile far higher than any other you have had. This is the job by which you will be remembered in future.' (Fifteen years later John has been proved only partially right. To the extent that anyone remembers, I am associated first with Northern Ireland. Maybe my accent is a factor in determining that order.)

'Michael Heseltine will be the new Deputy Prime Minister and I want you two to work closely together. He also will have his office in the Cabinet Office and you will both have direct access to me.'

Michael and I were closer friends than I think John or the media realised. The latter were licking their lips at the prospect of these two 'big beasts' fighting for the Prime Minister's ear. However, I was delighted at the thought of working with Michael and accepted John's offer without hesitation. I spent no time thinking about how difficult the political and management task would be. Maybe I should have.

†

Being invited to become one of Her Majesty's ministers is a great honour. But the truth is politics and political advancement is really very Darwinian – it is the survival of the fittest. The only problem with that sentence is that no one has adequately defined what it is the fittest need to be fit for. For most people there is also, probably, an element of good fortune in a promotion – being the right person in the right place at the right time. And, of course, all appointments and disappointments are subject to events, over which the individual minister or potential minister has no control.

As Harold Macmillan once famously said, 'Events, dear boy, events,' when describing the most challenging aspect of being Prime Minister.

The ministerial process is about skill and judgement, understanding, confidence and instinct. It is about intellectual capacity and personal values as well as human relations and emotions. It certainly feeds egos. That's politics.

The best advice I got was to remember that becoming a minister should never be an end in itself. It is what you do with the power, or often more correctly 'influence', which is important. Becoming a minister should only ever be a means to an end. The real 'end' is service – doing what is best for tens of millions of British people, with a special emphasis on helping the poor.

That latter point is primarily a reflection of the influence of the Christian faith on our democracy.

By the way, being a minister also means hard work, long hours, lots of criticism and too few plaudits. It is stressful and demanding as well as challenging and stimulating.

It is also fun – most of the time – and a great privilege – all the time.

In addition to 'how did you get into government?' and 'what did the PM say?' the question most frequently asked is how I got to the point of being considered for government in the first place. Everyone's story is unique, which adds to the political interest. This is mine.

MPs are not randomly picked for the honour of stepping on to the first rung of the ministerial ladder. Many are chosen from the ranks of the parliamentary private secretaries (PPS). These are

MPs who work unpaid to assist senior ministers. In doing this they get an insight into ministerial life. Their job is to maintain contact between their minister and members of the House of Commons, especially government backbenchers on whose support the minister relies, and, occasionally to offer political advice, privately, to their minister in the department.

I was selected from the ranks of the PPSs. Initially I had a short stint at the Treasury working for John Wakeham and Barney Hayhoe. Most of the time I worked for Barney because John was recovering from the injuries he received as a result of the IRA bomb explosion at the Conservative Party Conference in Brighton in 1984. Barney is a gentle man, an astute politician and one of the best political analysts I ever met. He taught me a lot. My friendship with and appreciation of John blossomed as we got to know each other. For years he has been one of the country's most influential parliamentarians.

I then served as Tom King's PPS at the Department of Employment for about fifteen months while he was Secretary of State. Previously I had not known Tom personally but we established a good relationship which grew stronger over time. He helped me understand ministerial life and allowed me to attend 'top of the office' meetings with ministers and senior civil servants. Eventually he trusted me enough to ask me to set up the very private one-to-one, monthly meetings he held in his London flat with senior trade union leaders. These usually took place over early evening drinks.

Margaret Thatcher's government had very strained relations with the trade unions. This stemmed in large part from our rolling legislative programme to 'reform' the unions and 'to give them back to their members'. Nevertheless, despite the public rumpus, both 'sides' realised that maintaining contact was important. So it suited both parties to meet, but only in private. Had the existence of the meetings become known, neither party could have sustained them in the face of what would have been considerable 'political' opposition. I never asked Tom but my guess is that only the department's Permanent Secretary knew of the meetings.

These encounters were undoubtedly helpful. They kept open channels of communication and some element of goodwill at a time of fundamental political disagreement and considerable tension over unemployment. Personally, they helped me to understand that serious differences did not have to be a bar to dialogue, if both parties could see a possible – even if at times unlikely – common good. Tom and I developed this thought further in Northern Ireland.

I am a great admirer of Tom King, the man and the politician. His dedication, political intuition, common sense and personal courage are impressive. They always outweighed his poor time-keeping! Tom was invariably late, though not because he was lazy or discourteous. Quite the contrary. Frequently he was just too enthusiastic for his diary. He always had to fit in one more quick meeting before he left the office, even when the clock said 'no'. As a result it became my job to open the flat to the trade union barons, pour their drinks and keep them occupied until Tom arrived. It was good experience to hear differences being discussed and explained courteously and in a civilised manner. I learned from both parties.

Tom King was good to me. I tried later to convey my appreciation by asking him to be one of my two formal supporters when I was introduced into the House of Lords.

In September 1985 Margaret appointed him Secretary of State for Northern Ireland. I rang that afternoon to congratulate him. His response was typically positive and enthusiastic. But he went on to say that, having spoken to the Northern Ireland Office (NIO) Permanent Secretary, the department wanted him to get a new PPS.

Civil servants did not want me anywhere near the Office. The reason they gave was that, as I was from the Province, I would not be seen as unbiased by Ulster's competing political tribes. I was a Protestant with Unionist inclinations. This was a matter of record and, as such, was not acceptably even-handed to the civil service. (Had I been a Catholic with nationalist tendencies that too would probably have been unacceptable. It was the 'home grown' they did not like.)

Tom could not have been surprised when, in response, I adopted the Ulsterman's habit of calling a spade a spade. I told him he was not being given the real reason for civil servants' opposition. Their primary concern was not that I might be, or even be thought to be, biased. Had there been any such perception or reality it would have been a 'political' problem for Tom to solve, not the civil servants. No – what really concerned them was that I had detailed knowledge of, contacts in and experience about the Province, which, to put it kindly, they would not be able to control. They saw me simply as a probable dilution of their influence. That was their real problem.

Having told Tom this, and added that my local knowledge could be an advantage to him, I said I would not step down at the behest of NIO civil servants. If, after reflection, he thought I should resign because my being there would make his job more difficult then, out of respect for him, I would go quietly.

He rang the next day and asked me to remain.

But the NIO officials were not finished. As Tom's PPS it was part of my job to spend time in his Belfast office. After all the Province was where the main action was. But I was made an outcast in Stormont. Perhaps officials thought that by freezing me out I would quit.

'Sorry, Dr Mawhinney, we have no office available for you – we are short of space' … 'No, unfortunately, there is no telephone number you can use for contact purposes' … 'Regrettably we cannot let you see the Secretary of State's diary – security reasons. I know you will understand.'

I did not understand. And said so.

What I did understand was that officials did not want me there and were doing their best to discourage me. I mentioned my treatment to Tom but he was preoccupied and not concentrating on my problems. Clearly my circumstances were a low priority and were for me to resolve. Perseverance became the order of the day.

Within days of his appointment, and solely on officials' advice, Tom made a serious political misjudgement. His taking office predated, by a couple of months, the signing of the Anglo-Irish Agreement (AIA). At that time it was being negotiated with the

Irish in a very hush-hush environment. The Prime Minister had decreed that knowledge of its conception and contents were to be on 'a need to know' basis. Even some Cabinet ministers had no need to know, so a PPS definitely did not.

In what was, in effect, a political vacuum in Northern Ireland, officials persuaded Tom to make an early visit to Dublin to meet Irish ministers. I learned about the visit from the BBC, having been barred from seeing his diary and thus offering independent political advice.

A problem quickly emerged. Before going South Tom had not had time to meet the leaders of all the political parties in Northern Ireland. He should have met those provincial leaders first if only to assess their political sensitivities and priorities and recognise their status. Only 'non-political' civil servants could have thought otherwise. If the NIO or the Foreign Office had had enough sense to include Sir Kenneth Bloomfield – an Ulsterman and Second Permanent Secretary in the NIO – in the negotiations, he would not have agreed to Tom's premature visit to Dublin. Ken would have insisted on getting the order right. Maybe those instincts were what worried the British negotiating team.

Ian Paisley was one of those who had not met Tom. He made his unhappiness about Tom's trip abundantly and loudly clear. Tom was upset. He understood immediately his political faux pas and that it resulted from official advice. He asked me, privately, what I thought he should do to help retrieve the situation.

I offered to talk to Ian, whom I knew through shared Christian contacts, to see if we could find a way forward. Tom agreed. Ian said he would be happy to welcome me to his home for a chat. I was early. He was delayed. And Eileen (now Baroness Paisley of St George's) made me afternoon tea. I approached Ian as a fellow Ulsterman and Christian friend, not as a political opponent.

When Ian arrived he was a bit tense. He was clearly affronted by Tom's action and rather nervous about me, having quickly understood that, with an Ulsterman in or near government, the local political parameters had to be adjusted.

Anyway, we soon settled into a calm conversation spiced with a little of his typical banter. Ian's public profile is larger than life, strident, at times unforgiving. Unless you knew him well in those days you could fail to appreciate his infectious sense of humour.

I told him straight out that I thought Tom had been given poor political advice and that I had not been involved in the decision to go to Dublin. There had been no intention to be discourteous and Tom really wanted to repair the damage and start building bridges. Eventually Ian was persuaded to take a phone call from Tom, who, I promised, would regret the misunderstanding. A meeting between the two would be arranged. I thanked Ian and Eileen for their hospitality and left.

Tom was hosting a reception at Hillsborough Castle that evening so I went there. After it was over Tom took me, and two civil servants, into the main State Drawing Room. Mark Elliott was the more senior. He was on secondment from the Foreign Office and handled, behind the scenes, issues of security, politics and the developing Anglo-Irish Agreement (AIA). John McConnell was head of the political development office of the NIO. At that time he knew little, if anything, about the AIA.

I reported my conversation with Ian, my positive reception and the satisfactory outcome. Mark and John were extremely angry. They berated the Secretary of State for sending me to see Ian in a way which, at that stage of my career, both shocked and bothered me. I thought they were out of line – as well as wrong.

Why had he used his PPS, not officials, to make such a sensitive approach?

Why had he not told officials before my visit?

What excuse would the office use when Ian went public and revealed the whole 'mess', as assuredly he would?

Was the Secretary of State prepared to blame me for taking an unauthorised initiative?

Tom too was shocked by the reaction. Not knowing the people involved he began to wonder if he had made a mistake. I weighed in, expressed distaste for the way the Secretary of State was being treated, told Tom that Ian would not make the matter public and that, far from it being a 'mess', potentially the issue had been resolved. If there was a 'mess' it arose from official advice to go to Dublin, not from my initiative. Tom could safely disregard the officials' response. I twisted the knife a little by adding that their ire owed more to their being cut out of the loop than it did to the merits of my meeting.

The civil servants were even less impressed by me. The meeting ended in strained circumstances.

The phone call was made. Regret was expressed and accepted. The meeting took place. And to this day there has been no public knowledge of the mechanism of reconciliation. I behaved as I thought a Christian should. So did Ian. My relationship with Mark never fully recovered. More than twenty-five years later John is one of my best friends.

Days later the Conservative Party Conference started in Blackpool. Tom had a small ministerial office in the Conference hotel – to handle government business – otherwise our days were spent in the world of politics. He asked whether we could meet on the Wednesday afternoon for a private chat.

So that afternoon, which was cold, overcast and windy, we went for a walk on Blackpool beach. We had it to ourselves apart from the two Special Branch men who trailed us.

'I am not supposed to tell you,' Tom started, referring to Margaret's 'need to know' edict. 'I have inherited a policy, already well developed, to which civil servants and the Foreign Office are committed. I feel I need to hear some external political reaction to it, to test its foundations, to pick your brains, before any final decision is made. Could we please talk in complete confidence?' We could – and he knew from experience that he could trust me to keep my word.

He then proceeded to tell me about the fledgling Anglo-Irish Agreement and its contents. After he had talked for some time and in some detail he sought my reaction. We walked a further fifty yards in silence while I marshalled my thoughts.

This was certainly a historic proposal, I said. It would probably enable the two governments to improve relations, which was positive – even overdue. However, I thought there were some potential political pitfalls associated with the proposal.

If I had understood Tom correctly the AIA would make no provision, either initially or over time, for the removal of Articles 2 and 3 from the Irish constitution. These articles were the basis of the Irish claim to jurisdiction over the Province, to a 32-county Ireland. This omission meant that the proposed agreement would be seen as seriously deficient, even dangerous, especially by Unionists.

Secondly, the proposed Anglo-Irish inter-governmental conference, which was to be co-chaired by the Northern Ireland Secretary of State and the Irish Foreign Minister – in which I was to take part later as a minister – would be seen by most in the Province as a form of joint governmental authority over Northern Ireland or, at least, the beginning of that process. Nationalists would welcome this. Unionists and many Conservatives would not. And Tom should remember that Margaret had ruled out joint authority after the New Ireland Forum report had been published. This public perception would take her and the government into sensitive political U-turn territory, at the very least.

Thirdly, the agreement proposal for a secretariat in Belfast would probably be seen by some as the Irish intervening in internal Northern Ireland affairs. This 'interference' would evoke the same reactions as would joint authority. In both cases an argument could be made in support of the initiatives but it would need very careful handling.

If the Irish wanted a presence in the Province our government would be asked why they should not open a consulate following well-established diplomatic procedure. They could not do that, Tom said, because to them constitutionally Northern Ireland was part of Ireland and they could not and would not open a consulate in their own country.

Finally, Tom confirmed that neither Unionists nor senior NI civil servants had been involved in the discussions; not even the formidably impressive Sir Kenneth. This was a mistake, I said, and would prove to be a liability.

I gave him a summary. The AIA would be historic. It would open new relationships with the Irish and new political opportunities and realities in Northern Ireland. The Unionists would hate it. They might even feel betrayed. It was a radical strategy with merits but its handling would be very demanding. Looking at the Irish Sea I told him choppy water lay ahead.

Tom was genuinely surprised. 'Civil servants are not telling me this,' he said.

'Well,' I replied, 'I may be wrong. But you asked for my immediate reaction and that is it.'

I never forgot Tom's comment – civil servants are not telling me this.

Tom and I made our way back to the hotel. He gave me no further reaction to what I had said. Then or later. And I told no one – not even my wife.

Incidentally, for those who want a balanced and erudite account of the more recent history of Ireland, the relationship between the two governments and the AIA I recommend *A Tragedy of Errors* by Sir Kenneth Bloomfield.[†] He deals with these issues excellently and puts them in a wider context. I am encouraged that, twenty-five years after the event, his analysis of the AIA is similar to my immediate reaction on Blackpool beach.

Life returned to normal after the Conference. Tom was still preoccupied. Now I knew why, even though I could not do anything about it.

A couple of weeks later Tom called me into his Stormont office and shut the door. He only had two minutes, he said, before he had to fly to London for a Cabinet Committee meeting.

'Remember what we talked about in Blackpool?' he asked. 'I would like your quick reaction to a development on one of the proposals we discussed. This morning's Cabinet Committee has to decide the location of the Secretariat. The Irish and our Foreign

---

† Bloomfield, Kenneth, *A Tragedy of Errors: The Government and Misgovernment of Northern Ireland* (Liverpool: Liverpool University Press, 2007)

Office propose that the office should be here – in Stormont Castle or in Stormont House. What do you think?'

There was no time for diplomacy. 'If you agree to that you are dead – finished,' I replied. 'You will *never* convince anyone, including the Unionists here and the House of Commons, that this arrangement does not amount to joint authority. You may retain your job and title but your influence and standing will be gone.'

'Thank you,' he replied, as he rushed out to the helicopter – late – having again sworn me to silence. It is a matter of record that the Cabinet Committee turned down the proposal to place the AIA Secretariat in Stormont. It was located a couple of miles away. Tom King deserves credit for this decision.

One evening in December, Tom and I were chatting in his Stormont office when he said, 'I have a problem and so do you. Your initial judgement about whether you should remain my PPS has turned out to be accurate. This job needs political advice as well as advice on policy and diplomacy. And the best political advice still comes from politicians. As time goes by I am relying more on your advice than I think is sensible, especially when your contribution does not agree with advice I am getting from civil servants. This is constitutionally wrong and dangerous for both of us. Eventually something will go wrong. The present arrangement cannot continue.'

My immediate thought was that I was for the chop. Instead I was in for a major surprise.

'After reflection,' he said, 'I have decided that your advice is valu-able – not least because of your local knowledge and perspective. So instead of looking for a new PPS I have decided to ask Margaret to appoint you as an additional minister. Then whatever advice you proffer can be scrutinised by officials in the normal way. My "up front" reason for asking for an additional minister is that the work-load in the NIO has increased considerably following the signing of the AIA,' which it had.

I was genuinely surprised and pleased. I thanked him and said I would be delighted and honoured to join his team and would await further news. The following week he told me Margaret had agreed in principle to the appointment and hoped to make an announcement at the turn of the year. I told Betty but no one else.

In January the media was focused on the developing row between Margaret Thatcher and the Secretary of State for Defence, Michael Heseltine, about that helicopter order for the armed forces. As mentioned, this superficially 'trivial' issue masked a much larger one – should our defence capabilities be tied more closely to Europe or to the USA? These two formidable Conservatives had fundamentally different philosophical and political views.

Tom told me that no ministerial announcement would be made until this row (which subsequently would also involve the Attorney General and the Home Secretary, Leon Brittan, who resigned) had been resolved. After all, he said, it would be very embarrassing for the Prime Minister if, having just announced government changes, she was forced to make further changes because a senior minister had resigned. His comment gave me a first indication of how important was the dispute that lay behind the media reports of the row.

I have never known whether Tom's comment was a statement of the obvious or a signal that he had some insight into Michael Heseltine's intentions. In due course came the fateful day when Michael abruptly walked out of Cabinet, announced his resignation to the reporters outside No. 10 and stormed off along Downing Street.

The overwhelming Unionist reaction to the signing of the AIA was outrage. By and large their arguments reflected those I had rehearsed with Tom. They withdrew their willingness to talk to or work with British ministers.

To underline this opposition all Unionist MPs resigned their seats in the House of Commons. The fourth Thursday in January was the date appointed for the multiple by-elections. When re-elected, the Unionist MPs claimed they had a democratic mandate to oppose the working of the agreement.

For the first and only time since he had raised my proposed

appointment, I went formally to see Tom. I stressed that I had not been pressing him – which he acknowledged – and that I did not want to do so now, but I owed him my best political judgement.

Every day my appointment was delayed in the present circumstances reduced its political credibility, I said. If it was delayed until after the by-elections it would be seen as a panic-driven, token reaction with all the political consequences that would then flow.

Tom told me he shared my analysis, thanked me for it and got in touch with the Prime Minister. I was made a minister the day before the by-elections were held.

In the event the timing of my ministerial appointment turned out to be less important than the appointment itself. Nationalists did not – indeed would not – welcome a local appointee, mainly because I had grown up in the Unionist/Protestant tradition, which tells you more about them than about me. Unionists also condemned my appointment, fortunately taking no solace in my background. To them I was worse than all the other ministers because, as an Ulsterman, I should have known better.

Eventually both sides mellowed towards me, though it took time, patience and a scrupulous determination on my part not to be politically biased. My accent, local knowledge and contacts, as well as my known Christian values, also helped.

And that is how I wound up waiting for No. 10 to call.

5

Jaw Jaw Is Better than War War
– with Apologies to Churchill

If the first half of my ministerial service in Northern Ireland was dominated by education reform, the second half focused on trying to re-establish 'normal' political dialogue. This had collapsed following the signing of the Anglo-Irish Agreement.

Unionists in the Province were genuinely angry with an agreement that had been negotiated over their heads. To them it smacked too much of governance by joint authority, a danger against which we did have to guard, especially in the early days. Their outrage was enhanced because they believed, probably with cause, that the Irish government had not excluded the nationalist SDLP from the preliminary consultations in the way the Unionists had been left in the dark by the British government.

On the day the agreement was signed Hillsborough was 'invaded' by Unionists. The main square was packed with protestors watched by a significant police presence. Those who were invited to the castle for the ceremony entered either through one of the estate's minor entrances or arrived by helicopter. With Tom King's permission Nick Scott (Minister of State) and I (Tom's PPS) arrived by RAF chopper.

Amid the protestors' noise the Rev. Ian Paisley's booming voice stood out. He had not seen the agreement but was irrevocably opposed to it anyway. The crowd took their lead from him.

Inside the castle tension abounded. The senior BBC editors John Cole and John Simpson argued vigorously about whether the agreement was a major political event, in which case John Cole would lead the news, or a diplomatic one, when John Simpson would front the BBC reports. Eventually John Simpson prevailed though I wanted John Cole to do so. After all, as an Ulsterman, this day was all about his heritage even if he was too professional to allow himself to be swayed by such a thought.

We guests were shown to our seats in the 'ballroom' before Tom King appeared, followed by Margaret Thatcher and Garret FitzGerald.

One thing immediately struck a number of us. Neither Margaret not Garret looked even a little bit pleased. Their voices said 'historic', 'new beginning' etc. etc.; their body language suggested concern or unhappiness. And there was little conversation between them.

Years later Margaret made clear her reservations about the agreement. Apparently she thought it owed its existence more to Foreign Office influence than it did to No. 10. Still, she signed it.

Apparently Garret was concerned about the political opposition he would face back home in Dublin. Charles Haughey, then opposition leader, might be tempted to try to persuade Republican Ireland to believe that Garret had achieved too little and conceded too much. And FitzGerald's political position was much more vulnerable in the Dáil than was Thatcher's in the Commons.

Nevertheless on the day the rhetoric was rock steady and positive, even though everyone seemed surprisingly downbeat. Subsequently Charles Haughey did not launch a major assault on the agreement – which surprised a lot of people. I believe his acceptance of it should be traced back to Ian Paisley. Ian was so uncompromising in his Unionist opposition that Charlie was persuaded that the agreement must have merit from Dublin's point of view. After all, if Paisley was so against it then there could be little political justification for a Haughey attack. The premise was simple: anything Paisley opposed Haughey should support and vice versa. Visceral politics. The agreement was saved.

In my view, if Paisley had acclaimed the agreement it would have been at considerable risk in Dublin. Had he praised this historic achievement, had he claimed that 'de facto' it heralded the beginning of the end of Irish claims to a 32-county constitution, had he lauded Margaret as the liberator of Northern Ireland and the defender of their UK aspirations then Haughey would have had to oppose it. Had Paisley added that while he had full confidence in the lady who had broken the historic all-Ireland claim of successive Irish governments and affirmed his belief that she could be trusted to ensure that no joint authority took place, nevertheless he and his colleagues would keep a close watch on NI ministers to ensure that they followed Margaret's lead, then in my view the agreement would probably have foundered in Dublin.

Such an approach by Paisley, though out of character at that point of his career, would have been more politically astute and enhanced Unionist influence in Belfast and Westminster. It would also have edged everyone closer to reality. Any suggestion that the Prime Minister who had reclaimed the British Falkland Islands would 'give away' part of the United Kingdom was so preposterous as to be just plain silly.

For Paisley to have taken this approach he would have required a constructive political mindset which then he did not possess. Years later he showed enormous and principled flexibility and Province-wide leadership to become Northern Ireland's First Minister, but that was after he had undergone a major and extended course in political realism.

Unionist MPs projected their anger against the agreement by refusing contact with Northern Ireland ministers and by resigning their parliamentary seats, thereby forcing a popular judgement on the hated agreement. In a favourite protest phrase of the time, they would have no dealings with those who had 'sold them down the river'.

Most Unionists followed their leaders' example and stopped talking to us. MPs would not even write to us on behalf of their constituents. They chose, instead, to write to the departmental Permanent Secretaries – a supreme example of gesture politics, or even hypocrisy, for they knew perfectly well their letters would go to ministers. Despite my contrary advice, ministers connived in this silliness.

Some rank-and-file so-called Unionists were out of control. We were attacked physically as well as verbally, in some cases with what appeared to be deadly intent. I do not exaggerate. An attack on Tom King finished up as a court case. The only reason others did not was ministerial restraint and forbearance.

The worst attack on me occurred at the Slieve Donard Hotel in Newcastle, County Down. I had been invited to attend a teachers' union annual conference, to give the keynote address at the end of the morning session and stay for lunch. On the eve of the conference the invitation to come early and stay for lunch was withdrawn. I could still speak but would then be expected to leave immediately. I was warned that I would be received, heard and dispatched in total silence.

Ministers spent a long time debating how we should respond to such discourtesies. We all agreed that if we kept our level of conduct above that which was being targeted on us, and behaved 'normally', then a return to traditional political relations was more likely to happen sooner rather than later. Some of us believed that nothing was going to change in a hurry. Ulster people – I speak as one born in the Province – can be very stubborn. If you are interested in a personal reflection, it was difficult 'to turn the other cheek' in the provocative face of a bunch of thugs.

Psychologically there was another factor at work. Most ministers were Englishmen who, before becoming ministers, knew little about the Province and its people. They understood they were there legitimately but sometimes seemed to give way to an almost subconscious instinct to defer to local people on contentious issues because, after all, this was their country. The inference that they were in some way unwelcome interlopers undermined their ministerial authority. It also questioned the reality of the United Kingdom, to which both ministers and Ulster Unionists were so committed. Understanding local people better, I was probably less inclined to deference, but more empathetic to what my countrymen really wanted and needed.

Anyway, my proposed presence at the teachers' conference was leaked. A large and aggressive crowd gathered round the gate to welcome me. After being warned by local police we entered the hotel by a side entrance. The crowd heard of our arrival and, as we walked the last fifty yards to the door, they broke through the police cordon at the gate and charged up the drive to get me, armed with pieces of wood, hockey sticks and, bizarrely for Unionists, hurling sticks. TV cameras recorded my arrival.

I absolutely refused to run for the shelter of the hotel door. So TV viewers saw what to them should have been the alarming sight of armed men and women intent on braining a government minister. I was protected by local police, Special Branch officers and hotel staff who, in some cases, were literally rugby-tackling those who got too close to me. It was very ugly and, truth to tell, frightening. Sometimes the veneer of human civilisation can be remarkably thin. Without my protectors I would have ended up in intensive care or worse. To their shame not many TV viewers seemed particularly concerned.

Having failed to maim or kill me these so-called Unionists vented their anger on innocent others by driving nails into the tyres of most of the cars in the hotel car park. Some belonged to hotel guests. Others belonged to conference delegates. None belonged to our party – though that appeared irrelevant. The mob's attitude seemed to be that it served the owners right for being in the same hotel as a government minister. Talk about vindictive and irrational.

For many months, ministers' travel around the Province was difficult and dangerous. On occasions the police advised us not to cross protest lines on the grounds that public order might break down. Sometimes we took their advice. More often we insisted on fulfilling our engagements. One of the ironies of this unhappy situation, completely lost on Unionists, was that the police, who were enforcing our legitimate democratic mandate, were taken away from protecting them against terrorist attacks.

Some 'Unionists', who allegedly were too law-abiding to contemplate anything like direct action against ministers, appeared to have no hesitation in tipping off others who were not so scrupulous, or perhaps I should say 'self-righteous'. One particular incident illustrates this attitude. It was not the most dangerous evening in the protest but because it involved my family it was the nastiest. My contempt for those who were involved remains undiluted even though, for example, I now serve on a British–Irish parliamentary body with at least one of those who was significantly involved.

In those days one government minister was 'on duty' in the Province at all times. The rota, including weekends, was established months in advance so that ministers could plan constituency and personal diaries. As I became a minister towards the end of January, my first weekend duty was over the extended Easter break – Good Friday to the following Wednesday.

The major advantage of weekend duty was that we stayed in Hillsborough Castle and could be accompanied by our families. So as Easter approached we embarked on my first weekend in the Province in nearly twenty years – all of us: my wife, our children and my elderly widowed mother, who lived with us in Barnet.

On the Friday evening, after I had completed ministerial business with the Chief Constable at Stormont, we went to see a musical at a theatre in the centre of Belfast. This seemingly innocuous decision was significant at the time. Ministers did not 'go out' much given the general hostility of Unionists. In my naivety I had assumed that good manners and common sense would prevail and that no one would bother us as we were clearly a family and not on ministerial duty. Wrong.

During the show's interval my Special Branch officers warned me that a few members of the audience had recognised me and were planning a demonstration. No sooner had they done so than a couple of 'upright' citizens came over and offensively remonstrated with me about the AIA. I had separated myself slightly from the family so that they would not be directly involved in case any nastiness broke out. Even so it was unpleasant for them to see people shouting at me.

When we returned to our seats a few people stood up and in loud voices denounced me and the agreement and shouted that I should leave. I ignored them. The musical recommenced.

Towards the end of the show my minders warned me that during the interval someone in the audience had rung a local radio station, told them where I was and, with the aid of the station, was encouraging Unionists to come down to demonstrate, to tell me I was not welcome in my home country. By doing so, they explained, they could convey Unionist anger – as if I would be cowed by their intimidation. The radio station, of course, was simply creating a news story for itself, unburdened by any obvious value system. Another case of populism and money trumping democracy.

My Special Branch officers suggested that we leave the theatre early to ease the handling of our exit because, by doing so, we would be separated from the exiting crowd. I refused. I knew the family were enjoying the show and was not willing to deprive them of the climactic ending.

More important, I was not willing to create the public impression of running in the face of bullying. I would not give a Unionist mob nor the radio station that satisfaction. And I was confident that the police could and would protect us. However, in a compromise to ease the pressure on the family and the police, I did agree that we should move as soon as the audience stood to applaud the actors. This would put us ahead of most of the crowd and make it easier to get safely to our cars.

Outside there was quite a large howling and jeering mob being held back by police. Their language was at times foul though fitting for the mindset of people who would threaten an old age pensioner and young children.

Normal police procedure was that minders ensured the safety of their 'principal' by getting the minister into the car first. For the only time in my six-plus years in Northern Ireland I broke that rule. I saw my wife and one of the children into our car then escorted the other two children plus my mother to theirs. In this small way I showed my contempt for the crowd.

It was thoroughly unpleasant. Despite the shock, our teenage children behaved superbly and we were very proud of them. They, in particular, found it scary. They could not understand why people were mad at their dad, having always been perceptive children.

My mother simply could not comprehend how anyone could behave so badly towards her. She was a Northern Ireland girl who had spent the first sixty-five years of her life in the Province. She was, and is, a gentle woman who never did a bad thing to anyone. Why were so many with similar backgrounds to hers behaving in such a disgusting manner towards her or indeed her son?

For me the experience was a foretaste of things to come. This crowd of so-called Unionists was right in one respect. Their protest did influence me long beyond its duration, though not in their favour.

Not all the pressure on ministers was of the mob variety. Sometimes the offensive protest was personally delivered. My diary for my third day in the Province provided the Unionist leadership with its first opportunity for an attack against the agreement, this time for the benefit of TV cameras. I was scheduled to speak at a European Union event in the Great Hall at Queen's University. My civil servants were nervous about the talk of threats and incidents of protest. Was I sure I wanted to go? Yes, if only to avoid the perception that would have followed a refusal: namely that all ministers were weak.

I would not be scared off by threats, especially not at my first event. Had I ducked out, no excuse would have been good enough – or believed. My reputation and effectiveness in the Province would never have completely recovered.

Initially everything was calm and those present were courteously welcoming. Then the Rev. Ian Paisley and John Taylor made their grand entrance. They had been invited as this was a European event and they were both MEPs.

At the beginning they ignored me while each did an anti-government, anti-minister tirade for the benefit of the TV cameras. Clearly, however, the drama of the moment required confrontation so eventually they headed in my direction. John Taylor and I were, and continue to be, acquaintances, originally in the Commons and now in the Lords. I doubt if either of us would claim our relationship amounts to genuine friendship.

On the other hand, Ian Paisley and I were friends – and remain so. That friendship is rooted in our love of Northern Ireland but grounded more in our relationship with Jesus Christ than it is, or was, in politics. Our mutual respect remains to this day as do periodic differences in our political views.

John left most of the talking to Ian – not that he had much choice. Ian berated me for agreeing to join this terrible government and for betraying my fellow countrymen, and told me that I was worse than all the other ministers because, being from the Province, I should have known better. He expressed his opposition to the AIA in strident language.

Apart from calling him 'Brother' (in the Christian sense) and saying in a loud voice how good it was to see him again, for the benefit of the other guests and the media, I had little opportunity to say anything else. As soon as Ian had finished he and John walked out. It was then my turn to face the cameras.

I determined to present a contrast to Ian so I smiled warmly into the camera and said simply 'It *is* good to be home.'

That was all. But the effect was electric and the response of the guests enthusiastic.

That short sentence did me, and the government, more good than would have been generated by the winning of months of argument. This was the first high-profile clash between a minister and the re-elected leaders of Unionism. It set the tone for all too many months of useless confrontation.

Some people genuinely thought these protests were important. They seemed to believe that government in general and Northern Ireland Office ministers in particular were attracted by the idea of some sort of joint authority with Irish ministers to govern the Province. I have absolutely no reason to believe that this assumption was valid inside government at ministerial level (though honesty requires me to add that I would not have wanted to vouch for every senior official in the Foreign Office).

Margaret Thatcher was certainly not attracted by any concept of joint authority and would have been offended at the very suggestion. Neither was Tom King. And such an idea never entered my head. Indeed, within the ministerial team, I was the one who most rigorously questioned why specific issues were being referred to the Anglo-Irish Secretariat for consultation. And I was the last minister to agree to socialise with the Irish and British civil servants in the Secretariat. They were good people but they were just not going to edge us in the direction of joint authority while I was a minister, though to be fair I am not aware they ever tried. That was also my colleagues' view. What attitude prevailed under New Labour is for others to describe and defend. My personal suspicion, without access to hard evidence, is that some element of defence might be in order, particularly when Mo Mowlam was in charge. On the other hand Peter Mandelson was a good, fair and robust Secretary of State.

My attitude was not anti-Irish per se. I thought then, and think now, that the AIA, properly handled, was in the best interests of all the people of Ireland – North and South – and of both governments. Improved relations and trust between the two countries were needed and have benefited both, culminating in Her Majesty's visit to the Republic of Ireland. Apart from normal political differences I have never held prejudiced views of the South, other than resenting their claim on my constitutional birthright.

The simultaneous state of aggressive threatening and ignoring of ministers by Unionists continued throughout 1986, 1987 and 1988, though the strength of their protests waned over time.

In the latter part of 1988 Tom King and I, together with senior NIO officials, including John McConnell, the excellent head of the Political Affairs Bureau, began examining how we might reintroduce more normal political dialogue into the Province in the hope of attracting Unionists to discuss and eventually negotiate a sustainable political future.

The main nationalist party, the SDLP, and its leader, John Hume MP, were also not much interested in exploring the political future at that time. In the aftermath of both the New Ireland Forum

report and the Anglo-Irish Agreement, they were in close fellowship with the Irish government and content to let the Irish lead the
conversations with the British on behalf of the island's nationalist
community. John accepted the obvious: that the Irish government
had more clout with the British than did the SDLP. Later, when
he discovered that the Irish were believed to be in private dialogue
with Gerry Adams, the leader of Sinn Féin, 'behind his back' he
changed tack, investing his energy in seeking to convert both the
British and the Irish to his political aspirations.

At that time the IRA were bombing and shooting people regularly so there was no prospect of us talking to Sinn Féin, the IRA's
political persona. During those months loyalist violence also took
place but its perpetrators had no political party advocating their
'position', as the IRA did, so the question of engaging politically
did not seriously arise.

After much talking and considering of multiple policy papers –
on a restricted 'need to know' basis – our 'top of the office' group
agreed early in 1989 that the time was right for Tom King to launch
a political exploration. Even if Unionists said 'no' at least we would
be seen to be trying to get a political debate started, which
would count as progress.

The group also decided that, given the considerable uncertainty
associated with this initiative, it should be led by a junior minister not the Secretary of State. Thus Tom's position was 'protected'
against any failure to attract the Province's political leadership into
meaningful dialogue. As I was the minister in charge of political
development and media relations, and a member of the senior
group, Tom asked me to take the lead.

The proposal was launched in a St Valentine's Day 1989 speech
by the Secretary of State. Before that, however, the other ministers
and senior officials in the NIO who had not been involved in the
planning had to be briefed. The only significant query came from
Richard Needham MP, the minister responsible for the Province's
economy. His view was that, as MPs wanted more investment and
jobs in their constituencies, the economic route, with him in the

lead, was the one more likely to break down political barriers. He wanted to front the initiative but his view did not prevail.

Tom King's speech on 14 February included an explanation of why he thought the time was right to try to revive political dialogue. He told the Province that he 'was asking Brian Mawhinney to explore, with the Northern Ireland parties, the possibility of making political progress'. With hindsight, this signalled the start of the process which culminated in the Good Friday Agreement many years later.

As anticipated, Tom's speech generated a lot of interest and media comment and, perhaps, a similar amount of scepticism. No one seemed inclined to respond positively. Messages into the NIO indicated that Unionist leaders were looking forward to hearing from Brian Mawhinney so they could snub him.

I remained publicly silent. In private, John McConnell and I spent hours debating how to find a way forward that would not give the Unionist leaders a veto or indeed the satisfaction of being able to rebuff me.

Soon my public silence started to work in our favour. Unionist MPs began wondering what was happening. They had not been approached and had heard nothing. Was something going on behind their backs? – and if so what?

With John's help I devised our strategy. Given the MPs' hard-line attitude there was little point in going straight to them. I needed allies to persuade them to become engaged, people to whom they would listen even while they were not listening to me; a form of third-party endorsement.

Our first decision was to concentrate on the Ulster Unionists, who, while belligerently anti-government, were less so than Ian Paisley's DUP. Without any hint of secrecy I talked to nationalist and Alliance Party leaders, though initially these talks were more about style than substance. Understandably they were not inclined to take me seriously until they saw some Unionist movement. And there was no public sign of that.

Behind the scenes, however, John McConnell was working his magic. He had the best set of political relationships across the

political spectrum of anyone in the Province, which is still probably true even though he retired some years ago. And being an
Ulsterman, I had long-established friends to whom I could talk,
away from the public gaze.

John and I decided to concentrate on people who were politically
inclined. They would have a better understanding of the changes
that were needed than would Unionist business people, church
leaders or party employees. In reality this meant we had to talk to
councillors. So the question became, which Ulster Unionists could
be persuaded to talk to me, in circumstances of complete secrecy,
and who would believe our assurances that we would not unilater-
ally tell anyone that they were doing so?

To enhance the confidential 'protection' we offered these councillors, Tom King agreed that I should not circulate, within the NIO,
details of what I was doing or to whom I was talking. This greatly
reduced the prospect of leaks occurring. Instead I briefed him
verbally with only John McConnell and the two NIO Permanent
Secretaries invited. My ministerial colleagues found this frustrating
but only Richard Needham complained.

The other strategic decision that John and I took related to the
conversations themselves, often conducted over meals. We decided
that, initially, I would not put pressure on my guests to change their
views. Instead I invited them to explain how they saw the present
political scene developing and to what end point. Then I would
use my wits to probe the political consequences of their own freely
stated positions. These were almost invariably negative and insular,
offering no hope of success for them, their party or the Province.

It was only after they had accepted the negative logical consequences of their own positions, sometimes after a number of
discussions, that I asked them in what areas of political life they
might be persuaded to accept changes that would enhance the
prospect of more hope for them and Northern Ireland.

Obviously we conducted a number of these conversations in
parallel and the level of mutual trust increased the more we talked.
The talks were 'unrelated' because the individual councillors did not

want their party colleagues to know that they were breaking the anti-ministerial embargo. I salute each of them for their political courage. While they had political loyalty to their leader and their party, they also had a commitment to the good of their constituents and the common good of the Province. Despite the risk of embarrassment or worse they did not flinch from doing what they believed was right.

Clearly these stories are primarily about events and experiences rather than personalities. In this case, however, without some of the personalities there would have been no story. It was they who persuaded the Unionist political leadership to reopen dialogue with government. I just facilitated the return to 'normal' service.

Among the most influential were:

- Chris McGimpsey, who, with his brother Michael, had legally challenged the Irish constitutional claim to jurisdiction in Northern Ireland. He was very influential in the party and one of the first to realise that the then Unionist position offered no future hope.

- Robert Coulter, a councillor in Ballymena, which lies at the heart of Ian Paisley's constituency. He was a close confidant of James Molyneaux MP, the leader of the Ulster Unionist Party. Robert had a good sense of rural Unionist opinion. We met in his home, with its magnificent picture window looking on to the back garden, eating delicious homemade apple tart.

- Reg Empey, subsequently a Lord Mayor of Belfast, knighted for his services to the Province and now a member of the House of Lords. A scheduled meeting over a Chinese meal provided one of the few lighter moments in the process. We were to meet in Newtownards. John McConnell and I sat waiting in one restaurant, Reg in another. As is always the case in such communication breakdowns, and between good friends, each blamed the other!

- And Ralph Brown, who lived in Dungannon. He too had a good feel for what mainstream Unionism was thinking. It was in his wife's restaurant, closed to the public for the evening, where eventually we brought all the councillors together.

After many weeks I told John McConnell the time had come to
bring all the conversations together into one. Not for the first time
he told me I was mad. He maintained that councillors would refuse
to reveal their secret involvement with me to each other. My analysis was that the individual talks had gone as far as they could. It
was time to take a managed risk to try to move to the next stage.
We might fail but, if so, we would have to realise that we had taken
this part of the process as far as it could usefully go. Without the
next step we would have achieved little because Unionist leaders
were still no closer to talking to ministers. We needed to bring the
influence of all these councillors together in order to make progress.

In addition I had great faith in John's persuasive powers and the
trust the councillors had in him. Finally I had to 'require' him to
approach all of them with a view to a joint meeting around another
dinner table. That faith in John was justified. All of them, without
exception, agreed to attend a communal meal, though still in confidence. Tom King was pleased.

John and I went early to Dungannon that night so that I could
welcome each councillor as he arrived. The first thirty minutes were
great fun. Each of them looked round the gathering, about seven
or eight strong, with staring eyes and open mouths, uttering inane
comments like 'you mean *you* were talking to him', 'I didn't know
you were having secret conversations' or, the most inappropriate
comment of them all, 'you never said'. Nevertheless, the presence of
their friends settled people and this, in turn, stiffened resolve.

By the end of the meal *they* had decided that they would go to
Jim Molyneaux, tell him what they had been doing and say forcibly
that the time had come for the party to re-engage with government. They believed, and I agreed, that if Jim decided to re-engage,
Ian Paisley would have to join him. And they insisted that as they
were taking the initiative, not me, I had to agree to do nothing,
with respect to Jim and Ian, until I had heard from them again. I
agreed. Predictably Ian and Jim insisted on talking to the Secretary
of State, as well as me, and proper dialogue commenced.

The rest is history. The Ulster Unionist Party edged back into dialogue with ministers and they were joined in this by the DUP. The first meetings were characterised by considerable suspicion and tension but slowly political development followed on the back of incrementally increasing trust.

Initially no detail was too small that it could not be presented as a barrier to progress, or at least a stumbling block. But Peter Brooke, who had succeeded Tom King, patiently edged everyone forward. Eventually the first political round-table talks for sixteen years, between the four constitutional Northern Ireland parties and ministers, were convened – after a mega-row about the shape of the table, including who would sit where, and the spending of many thousands of taxpayer pounds to build a new table especially for the talks so that no party would be thought by the others to have a psychological or positional advantage!

The talks took place at Stormont and lasted ten weeks – Monday to Thursday each week. Jim Molyneaux led the Ulster Unionists, Ian Paisley the DUP, John Hume the SDLP and John Alderdice the Alliance Party. Peter Brooke and I represented the government. Sinn Féin joined later talks, after the 1992 general election, following a significant reduction in IRA violence.

Peter Brooke was outstanding. He facilitated the holding of the talks during the countless hours of 'negotiating' meetings we held with the parties. Our objective in each meeting with Jim and Ian was to identify, among the raft of aggressively anti-government rhetoric, one small item on which we could all agree. Over multiple meetings these accumulated into a basis for the formal talks. The two Unionist parties came to meetings together, the others separately. Peter was skilled and sensitive with his sharp mind, historical perspective and genial charm fixed on progress. It was a privilege to support him through all the meetings, preliminary and formal. Government whips were understanding, excusing us from Commons voting so that Peter and I were able to be based in Belfast during the week.

No one limited the purpose of the talks either in advance or while they were taking place. I think we all agreed that they had three primary objectives and that these were more likely to be attained if we minimised restrictions. So, in part, we 'made it up' as we went along. We aimed:

- to get NI politicians used to listening to political views with which they disagreed, sometimes strongly, without losing their tempers or walking out. This process was increasingly successful. Their reaction to things they did not want to hear, and did not believe, moderated as time passed.
- to require local politicians to set out coherently what they believed and wanted, with some regard to priority. This too proved to be an evolving process.
- to seek general consensus on which issues were so outside the realms of early possible agreement that they could safely be set to one side – at least as far as these particular talks were concerned. They could be dealt with later. This increased the chance of some element of agreement on other less contentious issues.

Those people, including those in the media, who thought we were embarked on a mission to find – in ten weeks – a comprehensive solution to Northern Ireland's historic, deeply rooted antagonisms were simply parading their ignorance.

The talks were not easy. By that I do not mean to imply that they were conducted in a particularly hostile or aggressive atmosphere. Most of the time they were not and the atmosphere improved as the weeks passed. Sometimes a party, or its leader, would become impossible on an issue. But with an element of goodwill, some persuasive arguing in the corridors and Peter Brooke's political skill and soothing words we overcame even these testing moments. Initially the Unionists kept repeating that they were talking to us under protest, but that mantra too abated with time.

Those side 'corridor' meetings became very important. I chaired a sub-group – one from each party – whose job ostensibly was to determine the agenda for the next day's plenary meeting. Often, however, we would stray into negotiating issues of substance. From time to time we were able to identify a way forward after the larger forum had stalled. Eddie McGrady MP (SDLP) and Peter Robinson MP (DUP) were particularly helpful in that process. Afterwards we would return to our individual 'parties' to persuade the leaders and colleagues to take the same line. Peter Brooke never second-guessed me.

Speaking of Peter Robinson, who went on to become Northern Ireland's First Minister, reminds me of another aspect of those talks about which no one knew except us two, Peter Brooke and the Permanent Secretary. The main talks concluded each week on a Thursday afternoon. This left Fridays and weekends for the politicians to do constituency work and for officials and advisers to draft papers to guide the following week's talks.

Unfortunately the main talks fell into a sort of unhelpful pattern. On Thursday afternoons one of the party leaders, often Ian Paisley, would raise the temperature on an issue so that when we broke up we did so in a state of tension. We often adjourned our discussions in a form of political cul-de-sac, so that even contemplating next week's business became far more challenging than should have been or ever needed to be the case.

Peter Robinson and I have been friends, though not particularly close, for a long time. He is a skilled politician and while he could be as partisan as anyone in Northern Ireland politics he had a sense of political realism and an understanding of the 'big' picture not shared by many of his peers. He and I often disagreed but I respected his integrity of mind and purpose and this respect seemed to be reciprocated. He is not the easiest man to get to know but he was then, and remains, an impressive political operator who understands the importance of delivering good outcomes for people, not just for 'his' people.

Over the first few weeks of the formal talks Peter and I would occasionally reflect together on our progress or on the blocks preventing progress. Peter had been the DUP's deputy leader for a long time so he spoke with authority. As such he was then one of the few who could influence Ian Paisley's thinking and he had the skill and know-how to predict how much flexibility could realistically be introduced into any DUP position. We both agreed that for the talks to be successful we needed to instil an element of political flexibility into all those matters of 'principle' so beloved of the Province's politicians.

I cannot now recall precisely how it happened, but one week Peter and I agreed that we should set aside some private time for a serious conversation about how we were getting on and how we might move progress forward. Diaries made the holding of such a conversation difficult because at weekends he was in Northern Ireland and I was in England. And there was virtually no freedom of individual movement during Mondays to Thursdays due to media scrutiny. It was just too risky. Had we been 'discovered' the political conspirators would have had a politically damaging field day – including some around the table.

It was my practice to fly back to Belfast on Sunday evenings, ahead of the Monday meeting, so we decided that if we were to get together it had to be late on Sunday night. Understandably Peter did not feel like leaving his home at ten o'clock or later so I went to his house, which had the advantage of shielding us from prying eyes. His wife Iris made us coffee and sandwiches and we sat in the kitchen identifying ways to extricate ourselves from Thursday's cul-de-sac and make progress in the coming week. Frequently after midnight I would be driven to Stormont House for a short night's sleep. This became our weekly routine.

For obvious reasons neither Peter nor I wanted the existence of these talks, much less their substance, to become known – and they never were. But they proved enormously helpful. Now, many years later, I pay tribute to the significant contribution which Peter made. He helped us understand where the real Unionist boundaries lay and by doing so improved all our chances of reaching a successful outcome. Monday solutions to Thursday conundrums became easier to achieve. For the removal of doubt, Peter never asked for any favour for sacrificing his Sunday evenings – nor did he get any.

Bearing in mind their limited objectives, the outcome of the main talks was positive, even successful. Inter-party political dialogue moved on to a new footing. A lot of ground clearing was accomplished and new ideas and relationships were established, explored and nurtured. We laid the basis for the more expansive talks which were later to take place, by which time Peter Brooke and I had moved on.

Our contribution to the 'peace process' was to transform the impossible into the possible. The process which would lead eventually to the Good Friday Agreement was soundly established. Each participant and political commentator will have personal views on what were the most important foundations on which the final agreement was built. I offer two.

Dispute resolution requires people to feel they can trust the other person's integrity and understand their point of view, no matter how unpalatable it may be.

Secondly, dispute resolution requires developing the skill to think 'outside the box' – to find new and innovative solutions to what appear to be old, insoluble problems – and then be willing to settle for less than ideally you would like in order to achieve resolution.

In 1992 I left the Northern Ireland Office, but I never forgot that, initially, I was not welcome in the land of my birth. Indeed I was not made welcome even when I returned to worship in the church in which I was raised. Some ostentatiously ignored me, others literally hissed. As I have said elsewhere, Christians are not perfect.

Nor have I forgotten what we were able to achieve, not least in bringing people closer together, or the improved relationships which made those achievements possible.

6

Hats Off

John Parkes had been the Permanent Secretary in charge of Northern Ireland's Department of Education for some time before I arrived. A good man, he ran the department competently having enjoyed an easy time with my predecessor. Nick Scott MP was a fine, left-of-centre Tory – which was the preferred Conservative Party genre in Northern Ireland – and relatively easy going. During the latter part of his ministerial tenure Nick had become increasingly involved in security and Anglo-Irish issues, which meant he spent most of his time at Stormont Castle, in Belfast (the Education Department was located in Bangor). While he still received education papers and made the big decisions, he left most of the others and the day-to-day issues to John Parkes and his colleagues.

My appointment came as a shock to their system. Initially I had no responsibilities other than those covered by education (which included sport, arts, libraries and community relations) so I was around the department much more than they were used to. It did not take John Parkes long to decide that, on the whole, he did not appreciate me nor like me much. That judgement deepened with the passage of time. I was told he complained to his senior colleagues about me and my 'style'. He said he could not 'control' me. He told them that the two of us were not 'compatible' – which I took to mean that I was not as 'smooth' as he was – and that I insisted on taking the decisions (that were constitutionally mine to take). To be fair to John he was not the only civil servant who did not warm to me. Ministers who challenge the status quo and implement necessary politically driven change can count on the loyalty and active support of only some – the best – civil servants.

John gave his most senior NIO colleagues a 'clue' of his views of me at one of their regular top of the office meetings. I am indebted to two of those present for the following, albeit alleged, account. Sir Kenneth Bloomfield, the most senior of the NIO civil servants, had asked his colleagues to persuade their ministers on a certain course of action. All agreed, apparently, except John. He said he was not confident he could persuade me. When asked to explain, and in case his answer might be interpreted by his colleagues as weakness, he is supposed to have said: 'Let me put it this way, my minister and I are not compatible. I am a Scorpio and he is a shit.' Only now will John become aware that I knew this was his view.

There is no prior training available for newly appointed ministers, which helps explain why good ministers often emerge from the Parliamentary Private Secretary (PPS) ranks of MPs because PPSs get to watch their senior ministers in action. You learn to be a minister largely by doing the job and by making mistakes in the process. I did, which occasionally must have been tiresome for others.

On my first day in office all I knew was that, constitutionally, I was in 'charge' of this area of government policy – answerable to my Secretary of State – and that I was the one who was supposed to make the decisions. In trying to put this into effect I soon found that such ideas were too simplistic. Senior civil servants had to make decisions every day. There was no way every decision could or should be referred to me. So I had to learn two difficult lessons: how to decide policy and strategy without personally implementing all of it, and how to determine when to intervene and when to keep quiet and let others make decisions within the agreed policy framework. The latter is a particularly difficult lesson for any eager minister to learn, especially one with an interventionist tendency who thought he knew as much about Northern Ireland as his advisers. On that too I was not always right.

Clearly some departmental officials did not appreciate having the first-ever Ulsterman minister, born, bred and educated in Northern Ireland, in their department. They spent far too much time speculating about my sources of information, why I had asked specific questions or who had been talking to me about the delivery of our policies. In other words they acted out their real concern, that they could not 'control' their minister. For clarity's sake 'control' means controlling the flow of information, which is what adds weight to officials' advice.

Perhaps one example will illustrate their problem. One year Belfast Royal Academy (BRA), an excellent grammar school, was experiencing real resource problems. Bill Sillery, its excellent headteacher, asked if a formal delegation, led by him and the chairman of governors, could meet me to present their case for extra money. Bill knew I was sympathetic but did not have any spare cash in that year's budget. He told me the real point of the meeting was to convince his school governors, as well as me, that he really was serious about raising extra resources and to put in an early bid for the following year.

We met in Stormont Castle's big reception room, sitting around the large rugby ball-shaped table once used by the Unionist government's Cabinet. I and my officials sat on one side, the BRA delegation on the other. When each one was at his or her place I went in. I walked as if to my place but continued past it around the top of the table and behind half of the governor delegation to the chairman. Then, without saying a word, I gave her a kiss on the cheek. Still without speaking, I continued around the rest of the table and took my place, inviting everyone else to sit.

Bill Sillery finally broke the silence. Well, he said, that effectively wrecks this meeting. How can we have a serious discussion about resources when the meeting starts with the minister kissing the delegation leader?

Our daughter Alison's second name is Coral. She was born in the year after my younger sister, Coral, died when a blood vessel burst in her brain. One of her best friends was Sandra Glass (née Shannon). Sandra was especially kind to and supportive of my sister during the episodes of serious ill health which preceded her death. It was only sixty seconds before the meeting was due to start that I learned that Sandra was the chairman of BRA's governors, by which point all my senior officials were already with the delegation. I explained the connection and we then proceeded with the meeting.

In one respect Northern Ireland's civil servants had an easier job than did their colleagues in Great Britain. The civil servants were local while ministers, overwhelmingly, were transient Englishmen who knew little or nothing about the Province and would be gone in a relatively short time. So NI civil servants controlled the flow of relevant information to ministers in a way that could never be the case in GB. This control was strengthened by the security realities which restricted ministerial movement. And if the worst came to the worst they could play an issue 'long' knowing that in due course a new, neophyte Englishman would be sitting in the minister's chair.

I presented them with a unique challenge. As a local boy, I had lots of friends and even more acquaintances and old school, university and church ties, not to mention family. It was impossible for them to 'control' my information flow.

All the above led to some early tension which made the development of trust between minister and senior advisers harder to achieve. I found it difficult to trust some who I judged would have preferred not to have had me as their minister. For their part they did not know how to deal with this first local boy 'made good'. Sometimes they bristled when, in an informed way, I questioned the 'why' of their recommendations. To be fair, over time most officials became more resigned and then positive about having a 'local' minister.

I do not want to give the impression that there was no trust. There was plenty. Many of these men and women were very good at their jobs. As I learned to appreciate this fact my trust in them increased. Their trust in me and my competence also grew. Sometimes I was right to question what I was told. At other times I should just have trusted and kept my mouth shut. But, as I said, you only learn by doing. At least none of us were confused about the importance of our roles.

The Province's chief executives of the five Education and Library Boards (ELBs) were important and influential men. It was not until my second year that I came to understand that my somewhat scratchy relationship with them was a reflection of the department's attitude to the ELBs and had little to do with me personally. They were not answerable to civil servants, though they had to work with them, and these two facts set the tone of the relationship as far as the chief executives were concerned. ELBs did not always agree with departmental policy which, ironically, was sometimes less of a problem for me than for some civil servants. I came to realise that I should have been more politically astute and less dependent on civil service advice as I developed my own links with the ELBs. Had I done so I would not have had to spend so much time later repairing dented relationships.

One of my greatest sources of personal satisfaction, during the nearly five years I spent at Education, were the five genuine friendships with ELB chief executives which blossomed after that scratchy start. The 'thank you' dinner they gave me when I left Bangor for Stormont will live long in my memory.

As well as with the chief executives, I worked closely with many fine educationalists. Sister Genevieve stands out. She was the principal of St Louisa's – the largest girls' school in Europe – with 2,500 pupils who lived in the IRA heartland on the Falls Road.

As well as being an educationalist, Sister Genevieve had to be a deeply spiritual toughie, for her girls often saw and got caught up in violence. Fathers and brothers were killed, sometimes in their living rooms in front of the family, or had to be visited in the Maze Prison. Teaching at St Louisa's was hard not least because it served too many people with little hope.

Sister Genevieve commanded immense respect. Her Christian faith shone through whether she was criticising government, distancing herself from her bishops, defending her girls, combating the IRA or working for prisoners.

We worked well together and she was particularly helpful on my plans to reform Northern Ireland's education system, though she

tended to have the same sort of strained relations with my officials
as she did with her bishops. Neither group understood why I was
impressed by her sometimes unconventional clarity of thought and
analysis, not to mention her occasionally acerbic expression. She
helped bolster my confidence to drive education reform in the face
of vested interest opposition, especially when I was being criticised
by the teacher unions – a frequent occurrence. She was as little
impressed by them as I was and equally deplored their habit of
personalising disagreements.

On one occasion she willingly helped me 'protect' Ulster school
children from exposure to some pretty sexually explicit material
about the dangers of AIDS which had come from central government. This might have been of some use in England but it would
not have been well received by the socially and sexually more
conservative families of Northern Ireland. My officials had insisted
this information had to be distributed 'because it was government
policy'. Indeed they took delight in deploying this argument against
me. Sister Genevieve and other teachers stopped that proposal dead
in its tracks when I organised a select 'public consultation' on the
documents, having first held a private consultation with Genevieve.

Friendship with nuns has not been part of my normal life experience but Sister Genevieve was one of a kind. She carried out
her stressful job with vigour, large streaks of common sense and
compassion, a no-nonsense approach and a twinkle in her eye.

A lot of my early skirmishes with civil servants stemmed from
a more serious problem. My governmental brief was clear. It was
to implement our national policy to renew, reform and improve
schooling in the UK for the benefit of the children. However,
education reform, which focused on school governance, curriculum
improvement and better examination outcomes, had lain dormant
prior to my arrival. Nick Scott, never a leading Thatcherite, or even
a Thatcherite, did not initiate much educational policy change in
Northern Ireland, despite its early start in England. His officials,
now my officials, had successfully argued against it. I was expected
to begin the process. Tom King made clear that he would be

supportive, especially if the going became tough, but would leave the policy and handling to me.

Officials thought the education delivered to the Province's children, under their guidance, was pretty good. At most they believed existing arrangements only needed to be tweaked. They certainly did not need reform. Maybe reform was necessary in my constituency, they said, but it was not needed in my home town.

'Do you not know, minister,' they would say, 'Northern Ireland schools produce the best A level results in the United Kingdom? So why change?'

It was true (and still is) that NI's grammar schools were always at or near the top of the UK schools' results league. It was also true, however, that some NI schools – too many of them Catholic maintained schools – delivered some of the poorest results in the UK. Whatever, my change agenda was not welcomed. And this dispute did not foster a spirit of mutual trust. It was their role as civil servants to advise and, as they saw it, I was setting aside that advice almost as a matter of principle.

All in all the department and I made a stuttering start. It was not 'love at first sight'.

Any new minister is faced with the task of reading numerous files. These set out all existing policies together with their pros and cons. A new minister has to master these briefs quickly for several reasons, not least so that he or she can promote public confidence in government policy. And, of course, unless he understands those policies and their implications he cannot judge whether they are working as they should or decide if, when and how they need to be changed. In my experience it proved impossible to induce public confidence in the teacher unions. Their political ideology and sense of self-satisfaction created too high barriers. They knew better than government. Thankfully, individual teachers were a different matter, less belligerent and less know-all. But I acknowledge the unions were a pain not least because the Province's media too often took its anti-government lead from them.

Talking of individual teachers I developed a pitch to them which often helped to break down suspicion. After all, overwhelmingly, they did not know me, they just knew about me, relying on media reports and trade union prejudice.

Most weeks in the Province I would visit at least one school. I tried whenever possible to be there about lunchtime so I could meet teachers informally in their lunch break. When given the floor I never started by trying to persuade them on any idea or policy. Instead I started by apologising – to their surprise. I would say 'Remember last week when you were all in here saying to each other "If only that b****** Mawhinney was here I'd really like to tell him"; well, I apologise for not being able to be here then. But I am here now, so please tell me.' Invariably there was mildly embarrassed laughter, then they embarked on a relaxed conversation.

From day one, files began appearing. Each one had to be read and assimilated. The papers were well written – apart from the jargon – so the task was not unduly complicated – it just consumed hours of time and countless brain cells. Naturally there were issues in the files I did not understand and about which I had no background information so I wrote questions in the margins seeking clarification.

After a few weeks in the job John Parkes appeared in my office without prior warning. He set the tone by dispensing with social pleasantries and insisted on standing. 'Minister,' he said, 'my colleagues and I are most distressed that you do not find our advice satisfactory.'

'What are you talking about, John?' I asked.

'On virtually every policy paper submitted you have written probing questions. Everyone knows that ministers' questions are their polite way of indicating dissent,' he replied.

I was genuinely surprised. No one had told me of this ministerial convention, if indeed it was a convention.

'John,' I said, with forced restraint, 'I am a scientist. I learn by asking questions. It is hardly surprising that there are aspects of these papers which make sense to you but which I do not understand. So I asked questions in order to learn and understand.'

Somewhat grudgingly, I thought, he accepted the logic of my point and also my assurance that no criticism was intended. The truth is, however, that I was irritated by his attitude and approach. A friendly enquiry over a cup of coffee, rather than a formal stand-up meeting, would have been a better way to help a new minister learn. So I added, perhaps ungraciously, that if I did have criticism he would not need to deduce it.

That skirmish became part of the folklore of my learning process. Obviously effective departmental working requires cooperation between minister and officials. The tone of this meeting did nothing to foster such cooperation nor, probably, did my reply.

†

On reflection my first few months, though difficult at times, were important and mainly enjoyable. Becoming a good minister involves on-the-job training. You have to learn from mistakes and misjudgements as well as from success. And you have to learn to listen. The art of knowing when to bite your tongue – and when not to – is also part of the political art of leading. Like much else in life the theory cannot be taught effectively; you have to work an apprenticeship and I worked mine with Department of Education officials.

The long process of education reform made little initial progress. My 'top of the office' team included the Permanent Secretary, the Chief Inspector of Schools, the Finance Officer and about four of the most senior officials. Some were enthusiastic but most took their lead from the Permanent Secretary, which from their point of view was sensible for he was their line manager and they expected him to outlast me. As this was my 'show', they made clear they expected me to identify the failures to be addressed, propose the new ideas, explain the necessary changes and lead the discussion. After all I was the one who was dissatisfied with the status quo. There was no initial sense that this was to be a cooperative venture, though all of them were scrupulously polite.

After many hours, during which we achieved little, even though everyone was superficially supportive, I was extremely frustrated. We were just not getting anywhere. One day, in semi-desperation, I floated a bizarre idea. I suggested we did a little playacting. At the beginning of each session, I said, 'Let us all figuratively "take our hats off". Let us forget about job titles and hierarchy and just be experienced, knowledgeable adults seeking together to plan a new venture. Courtesy would prevail but deference and seniority would not. If I am wrong then you must tell me so and argue your corner. If you believe I am right, or moving in the right direction, please say so. For my part I will retain no "memory" of the arguments and disagreements but will remember the bright ideas. Hopefully by the end of each meeting we will have reached some conclusions. At that point we should all put our "hats" back on, you will offer the newly developed advice and I will make the appropriate decisions. We will keep no account of how we reached them.' The Permanent Secretary indicated he was content. But they all looked at me in amazement.

After a tentative start this simple ruse quickly unblocked whatever it was that was inhibiting them. Hierarchy became less important. Conversations and arguments prospered between them as well as with me. Ideas emerged. Advice sharpened. Progress was made. And courtesy was maintained throughout.

The only official record of our meetings was the formal 'hats on' conclusions at the end of each session. Thus education reform was born and nurtured. And in the process good working relationships were established and friendships kindled. Taking our 'hats off' became part of the departmental storyline. It made possible significant, beneficial educational change in the Province and a lot of the credit goes to John Parkes and his colleagues. They made a huge and valuable contribution to the educational, social and mindset changes which subsequently occurred.

Northern Ireland is a very conservative place. Frequently change is unwelcome and fiercely resisted. 'Ulster says No' is not just a political slogan, it is often a social mantra. So I got most of the 'blame' for insisting on changing the comfortable educational status quo – and rightly. That is what ministers are for. Given that this was Northern Ireland there was little positive credit available to a British minister at that time, or any other. Nevertheless the educational improvement was progressive – as was the improvement in relationships between children brought up in different traditions who, until then, had been separated by school systems.

The educational change we established included:

- New curriculum and examination oversight bodies to improve the integrity and professionalism of the educational experience and its delivery, and new subject curricula.
- A new council with responsibility to improve educational standards in Catholic maintained schools – run in cooperation with the Catholic Bishops. Standards in Catholic maintained schools soon began to rise.
- New arrangements to help all children learn with and about other children in Northern Ireland who did not share their presuppositions.
- Protection of and an enhanced role for the Irish language.
- A third state-funded schooling option – integrated schools – where the ethos and aspirations of both political traditions were valued equally.

When I decided to legislate the last option – against the unwavering advice of civil servants, churches (Protestant and Catholic), Education and Library Boards and NI political parties, all of whom argued for the status quo – Northern Ireland had only one integrated school. Today, over twenty-five years later, there are more than sixty and the number is rising. Integrated education has prospered and with it a slowly growing political message.

All those integrated schools started because parents wanted the best for their children and that 'best' included mutual respect between the historic traditions, no matter what they themselves had been taught. Lagan College and Hazelwood School, the original two, have been kind enough to say consistently that, without my help, it is possible they would not have survived and prospered.

Certainly my decision to legislate a third option was crucial to the spread of the integrated school movement and is still so recognised, even though it was friendless at the time.

Looking back on my more than eleven years as a government minister, this particular educational change is the single most satisfying thing I accomplished on behalf of Her Majesty and her subjects.

But what to do about the majority of pupils who attended state and Catholic schools and who did not rub shoulders with pupils from the 'other' tradition? We built into the overall curriculum two new courses – education for mutual understanding and cultural heritage. These helped explain each tradition to the other, much more in relationship terms than was common in more traditional teaching. They encouraged neighbouring schools to expand their thinking and learn to do things together in cross-community settings. In this way we moved at least some of the integrated schools' philosophy into 'mainstream' education. And we integrated these new courses into core curriculum subjects so that 'dissenting' teachers could not ignore them or easily refuse to teach them.

It was my unexpected privilege to play a significant part in reducing educational apartheid in Northern Ireland. Back in 1975 in the book *Conflict and Christianity in Northern Ireland* (co-authored with Ron Wells) I wrote: 'How bright the prospects for peaceful co-existence in Ulster can be while children are educated separately is a matter of considerable doubt'.

As Education Minister I inherited that problem or, to put it another way, I was given the opportunity to do something about it – and did. In one sense those two propositions always go together. It is commendable to have the insight to spot and analyse a problem, it is a privilege to be afforded the chance to solve it.

†

I said earlier that 'hats off' became part of the department's storyline. An official once used it on me in a different setting.

When the amounts of taxpayer money to be distributed to schools, colleges or libraries each month rose significantly above budget, for whatever reason, I was supposed to authorise the payments. This did not always happen despite regular reminders to officials.

One morning, over breakfast, I read a local newspaper report that the department had given an extra few million pounds to colleges of further education, about which I knew nothing. On arriving at the office I asked my private secretary to let me see the officials' request for the grants to be distributed, with my signed agreement attached (I knew no such document existed). Then I waited, with new-found patience. She made enquiries and confirmed that no such authorisation had been sought or given.

Sometime later that day a senior member of the finance department arrived in my office. He was an excellent civil servant and a fine Christian with whom I worked easily. After pleasantries and a period of silence David Woods said, 'Minister, may we take our hats off?'

'Of course,' I replied.

'We made a mistake. We know we are required to have you authorise new, additional expenditure and suspect you think we are deliberately going behind your back by making the decisions ourselves. We are not. Before you came Nick Scott left all these decisions to us. Making them became commonplace. But we are trying to change our mindset and our systems. I apologise for not getting your agreement for this payment. It will not happen again' (and it never did).

Without the freedom to talk to each other 'normally', his telling me what had happened while simultaneously defending the integrity of civil servants would have been difficult. 'Hats off' smoothed the way.

'David,' I said, 'why don't we put our hats on again? Thank you for stopping by. I always enjoy talking to you. Now, as we both have much to do I suggest we get back to work.' There was no need to mention payments.

My tenure as education minister lasted nearly five years. Unfortunately, after a few years, John Parkes decided to retire early. I regretted his decision and said so. Perhaps our occasionally strained relationship contributed to his decision, only he knows, but I do know from others that it was not the primary reason. That remains private to John. However, if the strain between us was a factor, I am sorry.

I first offered John a large departmental reception to mark his years of service. He declined. He similarly refused a smaller more select reception. So I indicated that I would take him to dinner to say thank you. He also resisted that but I insisted.

Our meal at the Old Inn, Crawfordsburn was excellent, unlike the evening. John, in his very civilised way, told me what he thought of me and the way the department was run. Suffice to say, John had not enjoyed, at all, being caught up in the considerable controversy that implementing the new government education policy had engendered both in the conservative Northern Ireland public and in the educational establishment. I did not respond, much less in kind. This was John's evening.

His words, however subjective, made uncomfortable listening. No minister sets out deliberately to antagonise his civil servants. But it can happen. Sometimes fault lies with the minister, sometimes with the civil servants, often both. Personality and policy clashes take place in every arena where people work together, particularly in hierarchical systems. Given how he felt it was best for John to move on.

While neither our temperaments nor our ways of working were easily compatible, I held John in higher regard than, clearly, I was able to convey at the time. It is good to be able to set the record straight.

Fortunately the majority of senior officials in the department did not share John's views. When the time came for me to leave Education and take on new responsibilities in the NIO, comments from these colleagues were reassuringly and, at times, almost embarrassingly appreciative. Two, in particular, from the education reform team, told me how much they had enjoyed working with me – 'the best minister' they had served. One told me that 'hats off' had been the key decision of my tenure because it had facilitated all that had been achieved. And I treasure the many letters they wrote, especially the one from the Chief Inspector of Schools.

Education was not all hard work and public criticism. There were many positive initiatives which generated good feeling and raised morale. Because I believe that society all too infrequently says 'well done' and 'thank you' I decided to invite pupils with the highest A level mark in each subject in the Province each year to a reception at Stormont to celebrate their achievement (though extracting the 'winners' from among the A grades caused another serious battle with officials). Each pupil was accompanied by his or her parents and headteacher and I presented each with a memento commemorating the subject achievement. We sent pictures of the presentations to appropriate local newspapers so family, friends, neighbours, and school friends could add their congratulations to the pupils. Each evening ended with a buffet supper.

Pupils were pleased, if occasionally suffering teenage embarrassment. Parents were proud as punch. Head teachers felt valued personally and on behalf of their colleagues.

The minister felt he had done something affirming and constructive which people would remember and value.

In case you are wondering if so much focus on educational reform meant that other aspects of my portfolio were neglected: the Province had a new library built in each of my years, arts funding per head of population attained its highest ever level and rugby and football did particularly well.

†

My ministerial apprenticeship obviously extended beyond the confines of departmental policy and personalities. Three other lessons remain etched in my memory. They each shed light on how government works – and on my naivety.

In my six-plus years in Northern Ireland I undertook 903 ministerial flights. In those days security was a serious problem so, initially, we flew with the RAF – until they priced themselves out of business – after which we flew in privately owned jets which were leased on a daily basis, until commercial flights became a 'safe' option.

Each time we flew out of RAF Northolt we were escorted to our plane by an RAF officer who snapped to attention and saluted as our plane moved off. The senior minister on board was supposed to acknowledge the salute through the cabin window.

I was never comfortable with this arrangement, especially when I was the only minister flying. Saluting the Secretary of State was fine but I was the lowest of the low on the ministerial ladder; I did not feel worthy of such recognition.

So after many weeks had passed, I made a well-intentioned but serious misjudgement. I asked my private secretary to put a minute into the NIO system saying that, in future, I would be content if saluting me were to be discontinued. What I should have done was have a private word with an appropriate senior official for guidance.

A sharp rejoinder arrived from the NIO Permanent Secretary – copied to senior officials and my ministerial colleagues. So much for privacy! Did I not understand, he enquired icily, that one of the foundations of the armed forces was that officers salute more senior ranks? As I held a post equivalent to the rank of brigadier of course they should salute me and they would continue to do so. The Permanent Secretary would take no action and considered the matter closed. He made clear his disappointment with my attitude. I was embarrassed by my ignorance. I had no idea I 'was' a brigadier.

My second abiding memory of my early ministerial days was prompted by curiosity – a perfectly natural trait in a scientist. About ten days after I was appointed a minister I was given my first pay slip. I read it with some surprise. Knowing the published rate of pay for a Parliamentary Under Secretary and my appointment date, I calculated that I was due to receive more.

This anomaly bugged me. The money was not the important issue, the apparent 'discrepancy' was. I wanted to understand how the system worked or if, hard to believe, a mistake had been made.

Finally my frustration reached breaking point. I explained the anomaly, as I saw it, to my new private secretary and asked him if, discreetly, he would seek an explanation. But, I stressed, he must do it discreetly. I was delighted to be a minister. The pay was important to us but not so important that I wanted to make any waves, or create the impression that I was complaining, or seeking to make trouble, or being difficult so soon after my appointment.

The explanation turned out to be both straightforward and believable although news to me. Although I was announced as a minister on a Wednesday, Her Majesty's commitments and busy diary had meant that my appointment papers had not been placed in front of her until some time later – perfectly understandable and appropriate. Clearly such normal delays did not prevent a new minister from carrying out his or her responsibilities.

Commonly speaking I was thought of as one of Mrs Thatcher's ministers. In reality I was a member of Her Majesty's government and my appointment commenced only when she said so, by signing the appropriate paper. My payment commenced from the time I was approved in the Palace, not in No. 10. I learned something fundamental about our constitution.

My third memory relates to an event that happened later in my time in the NIO but which bumped me up against a reality which I have never forgotten. In addition to being responsible for education some of my time was spent as minister for political development. In that role one of the things I did was host dinners at Stormont in an effort to enhance cross-community dialogue. These occasions brought together people who in the everyday course of their lives would otherwise never have met.

One evening a Catholic priest arrived so late that dinner had already started. He looked dishevelled and agitated. He sat beside me staring at his food and saying nothing. His hands shook. This particular dinner was taking place shortly after two British soldiers had been battered to death, literally, in west Belfast.

'If you want to remain quiet,' I told him after a while, 'no problem. If you want to tell me, no problem. If it is confidential and you cannot tell me, no problem. Whatever you choose, you are welcome and I am glad you came.'

Slowly he told me that some young men had painted a mural in his parish glorifying the soldiers' deaths, which had occurred nearby. He had painted out the mural. The next day the mural was reinstated and again he had removed it.

The previous night the mural had reappeared yet again. When he had gone to remove it a few hours earlier he had been confronted by local 'hard men' who were IRA sympathisers and/or members.

Apparently the conversation went as follows:

What the f*** do you think you are doing, Father? Leave that f****** mural alone.

I will not have such sentiments projected in my parish. People might think they reflect local opinion. The church will not countenance them. They have to go.

Leave the f****** mural alone, Father. If you paint over it again we'll kill you.

If you kill me, so be it. I will not have that mural in my parish.

He proceeded to paint over it. He had come straight from that confrontation to my dinner. No wonder he was agitated.

It was salutary for an education minister to be reminded that learning is not just theory and classrooms. It is also about what works, and happens, in everyday life.

One person the IRA did kill was Marie Wilson. She, her father Gordon and others were gathered around the Enniskillen War Memorial on Remembrance Day 1987 when the terrorist bomb exploded. Gordon's strong Christian faith shone through nationally when he forgave those who had injured him and killed his daughter. That Jesus-based faith was equally real in his living room when I later visited him and his wife.

It became my job to come up with a fitting permanent memorial to those killed and injured in this outrage. John McConnell, Michael Murphy (chief executive of the local Education and Library Board) and Gerry Burns (chief executive of Fermanagh District Council) helped me. We considered all the 'normal' memorial initiatives – ranging from a plaque (no soul) to a community/sports hall or fountain (too costly for local people to maintain over the years).

I thought a lot about Gordon's spirit of forgiveness and reconciliation, and then had an idea, designed to reflect it. With the strong support of John, Michael and Gerry I set up a trust to enable young people from the two traditions to go out *together* to areas of the world where discord prevailed so they could learn lessons from other people's attempts at reconciliation. They were then to bring those lessons back to Northern Ireland and promote them, two by two – Unionist and nationalist, Protestant and Catholic together.

The Enniskillen Bursary Scheme was born. Today, twenty-five years later, hundreds of Northern Ireland's best young people have travelled the world learning together, with those who have had a different upbringing, how to value and promote reconciliation. They and the Province are better for their experience.

I remain proud of that particular inspiration and am sorry only that, living in England, I could not play a more hands-on role in its development and outreach.

My time at education in Northern Ireland introduced me to a truth regularly underscored during my twenty-six years in the House of Commons and subsequently in football administration. It is great to be liked but it is crucial to be respected. Without respect it is almost impossible to achieve anything worthwhile.

This fundamental difference is often not easy to achieve. We all want to be 'one of the boys' or 'girls' – to be embraced by others. Perhaps warning against this was what St Paul had in mind when he told the Church at Rome not to 'let the world squeeze you into its mould'.

Finally, as I reflect on my whole ministerial career, the three policy issues which gave me most personal satisfaction were integrated education, the Enniskillen Bursary Scheme and being the minister who started the political journey to the Good Friday Agreement. Perhaps this list is not too surprising for an Ulsterman.

7

Persuading American Opinion

O ur children are dual citizens, British and American, so the major
geographic influences in their lives have been transatlantic. As
well as spending time with their grandparents in Michigan, David
took his primary degree at the University of Texas and his MBA at
Harvard University. Stephen was born in Iowa City and Alison did
a voluntary gap year at Buckhead Community Church in Atlanta.

Betty, from a suburb of Detroit, has spent nearly all her adult life
in England. I, an Ulsterman, studied in Michigan, taught in Iowa,
served on the board of an Indianapolis-based company, have been a
trustee of Boston University and am the UK special adviser to the
(American) National Football League.

During my time as a minister, while I visited a number of
European countries, plus Japan, Korea, Mexico and Australia, my
main international exposure was in the USA. Partly because of
my knowledge of the country, Tom King gave me the challenging task of trying to persuade North Americans of Irish descent to
withhold their support and dollars from the IRA. Both Margaret
Thatcher and American Presidents, starting with Ronald Reagan,
were committed to shutting off this support for the IRA.

A number of senior American politicians also lent their political
weight to that process. Understandably they always differentiated
between Irish Americans supporting violence (against) and Irish
nationalism (for). Also they made clear that they were not endors-
ing the so-called British 'presence' in the North of Ireland. They all
favoured an Ireland united by democratic means but had no idea

how that might happen in practice. None of them had any effective or alternative response to the British policy of abiding by the democratically expressed will of the majority.

Our view in government, and in the Northern Ireland Office in particular, was that more persuasion could and should be tried at a grass-roots political level – which is where I came in. The theory, even in the mid-1980s, was that if Irish-American opinion could be shifted away from implicit – and sometimes explicit – support for the IRA, then it ought to become easier for the US government, working with the British and Irish governments, to persuade people in Northern Ireland, and indeed the whole of Ireland, to move towards a normality that rejected the use of Semtex and the Armalite rifle as a supposed determinant within our democracy. Indeed some would interpret President Clinton's involvement in the events leading up to the Good Friday Agreement as an indication that this long-term policy objective had some success, though it is easy to exaggerate Clinton's importance.

My brief was to go to America at about eight-month intervals to do what I could to persuade Irish-Americans not to support terrorism. This meant meeting influential leaders, both in politics at the national and State levels and in the media. It also meant taking every opportunity to do radio work and newspaper interviews. These were all designed to try to convince opinion formers and the wider public of two main facts. First, that the IRA were neither freedom fighters nor some form of outlandish, aggressive social workers. And, secondly, that British and Irish citizens in both jurisdictions, in the island of Ireland, had all the same legal rights that Americans correctly proclaimed were the bedrock of democratic societies. Too many Americans did not appreciate that fundamental reality.

I remember a visit to Boston, as a backbench MP, which well illustrates this point. Our excellent deputy consul, Barbara Eachus, arranged for me to be interviewed on several radio shows. I spent hours taking callers' questions. The level of pro-Irish, anti-British sentiment, ignorance and sheer prejudice in these self-selected contributions was amazing and depressing. The callers would never let facts get in the way of their mythology. To most of them history had stopped during the time of Cromwell, the Irish potato famine or the early twentieth century and Irish independence.

The radio stations seemed to think that these essentially local programmes helped their ratings. On one occasion, having been invited to do a thirty-minute slot, I was twice asked on air if I would extend my stay because the level of listener interest was so high. I wound up answering questions for two hours – and turned down a request to stay longer. It was glaringly obvious why Boston is called the capital of Irish America.

Speaking of Barbara Eachus, she always made good use of my ministerial visits. On one memorable day she managed to get me a 'ten-minute' meeting with the leader of the Massachusetts Senate, Billy Bulger. Billy was one of the most influential and controversial political figures in the Commonwealth of Massachusetts at that time and Barbara's initiative was seen in both the consulate and the State House as an amazing coup.

Billy, a visceral Irish-American, and I immediately clicked. He told me about his job and his progress up through Boston's political ranks. He ordered coffee. I explained what I was doing in town, being careful to stress the democratic basis of my message. The ten minutes expanded effortlessly.

About forty-five minutes into my visit Billy briefly broke off to welcome a family of constituents who had come, by appointment, to have their photograph taken with the Senate leader in his office, but he would not let me leave.

These days it is hard to convey how unusual and significant was the visit of a British minister to the Massachusetts State House at that time. Understandably, like their constituents, local politicians were very pro-Irish and sometimes anti-British. Obviously this was a stance that attracted constituents' votes. The fact that Billy Bulger – the most Irish of them all – was willing to spend time with me sent a buzz of quizzical amazement around the building.

After about an hour and a half Billy asked if I had previously been in the State House. When I answered no he immediately insisted on showing me around. His staff's jaws dropped as did the jaws of those accompanying me from the consulate. This was unheard of.

When we had viewed the Senate Chamber, Billy knocked on a large door and, without waiting, entered. A surprised lady told him 'he' was in and, without fanfare, we walked through a second door. In front of us, in his shirt sleeves and fancy braces, sat the Governor of Massachusetts, Ed King. He too was surprised to see us (we were not in his diary) and even more surprised when Billy introduced me. We exchanged pleasantries and I explained the purpose of my visit. At that time it felt like I might have been the only British parliamentarian Governor King had ever met.

Billy enquired where I was off to next. When told that I was meeting the editorial board of the *Boston Globe*, he made an uncomplimentary remark about the newspaper (I gathered it frequently criticised him politically) and arranged for his car and driver to take me and Barbara to our destination.

After a grilling by the board, Barbara told me that Boston's Mayor White wanted me to call on him too. Originally he had point-blank refused to receive me, 'a British minister', but when he had learned that I had spent a long time with Billy and had met the Governor, I guess he changed his mind. He may not have understood why a Brit was being feted in the State House but, for reasons of domestic Boston politics, he was worried about being wrong-footed by the other two politicians. Hence the invitation. So back we went to the centre of Boston. Much to Barbara's chagrin we kept the Mayor waiting while I ate a hamburger. I was so hungry I had a severe headache.

Mayor White's reputation for being pro-Irish was more hard-line than most. Barbara warned me that the 'interview' would be difficult. In the event, this senior 'republican' (in Irish terms) talked with warmth of his meeting with Queen Elizabeth II on the Royal Yacht *Britannia* during her visit for the American bicentennial in 1976. He was almost drooling. Amazing. I explained why I was in Boston, encouraged him to keep his distance from the IRA and left.

So ended one of the more fascinating days of my life. A day, to that point, without parallel in dismantling barriers between the British and the Irish-Americans in Boston, at the highest political levels.

Much later Billy Bulger got into serious political difficulty when his brother became a high-profile fugitive from justice. I know nothing significant of the matter. Speaking only on the basis of how you find people, Billy and I got on fine. I liked him, not least because he obviously cared about the welfare of his constituents, and we maintained a friendship for some years after our first memorable meeting.

Each 'political' ministerial trip to the USA consisted of visits to Boston and Washington, DC plus one other city. These included Chicago, Philadelphia, New York, San José and San Francisco. Wearing my education hat I also visited the Shenandoah Valley twice. Boston, as the 'capital' of Irish America, provided a special opportunity to influence those who were important leaders of Irish opinion nationwide. And visiting Cardinal Law was a fixed part of each visit to the city.

John McConnell, who always travelled with me, knew Monsignor Murphy, who ran the Cardinal's office. As you might expect, the Cardinal was pro-Irish unity, but only by peaceful, political means. He was against the political use of violence, IRA style. These issues were part of our regular agenda and I used to brief him, confidentially, on political developments. When he spoke publically on Irish-related matters in Boston I wanted him to do so as one who was well informed and therefore authoritative. He was always supportive of our efforts to normalise relationships in the Province, and discreet. Sometimes, helpfully, he pointed me in the right direction locally.

Incidentally it took moral courage to speak out against the IRA in Boston. That organisation had a lot of support in the city. Some applauded its violent anti-British agenda. Others misguidedly saw these users of the Armalite as little more than a sort of persecuted social workers looking out for the poor and downtrodden minority. There was one pub in downtown Boston which the consulate warned me never to enter. It was so violently pro-IRA, I was told, that if they ever discovered who I was, while there, I might not survive the experience – literally.

Long after our meetings ceased Cardinal Law became the focus of serious attention and controversy around the issue of paedophile priests in the Boston diocese. Again I know nothing substantive about the issue and will not comment. But, as before, speaking only as I found, Cardinal Law played an influential part in help-ing to shape the wider circumstances in which the Good Friday Agreement could become a possibility.

However politically well intentioned Cardinal Law was, he was first, foremost and always a spiritual leader. Despite our back-ground and ecclesiastical differences, we often chatted easily about our shared faith. On one occasion, as he was escorting me to his front door, he pointed to his private chapel at the end of the corri-dor. To his evident surprise I asked if I could see it. It was a large room transformed into a sanctuary with an altar and prayer rail at one end.

We went in. Our officials remained clustered around the door. I asked why we should not pray given that we were both followers of Jesus Christ. He responded positively and we knelt together. It was hard to gauge which set of officials was the more surprised.

Influencing Irish-American opinion was never an easy option. On my first ministerial visit to Boston our consul invited vari-ous local opinion formers to dinner to meet the new minister. As they were introduced to me some said they had come only out of respect for our well-liked consul. Some made clear that they had no time for the British. Others ostentatiously and with loud protests refused to shake my hand. They said boldly that they saw me as the oppressor of the Irish in the North. Later, some of these protestors became good friends with whom I worked closely, setting up, for example, the tripartite Boston, Derry, Galway economic regen-eration venture. Betty and I even entertained one of these initially antagonistic leaders, and his family, in our home in Barnet.

Progress was made. I became the first British minister commended in a *Boston Globe* editorial for policy initiatives in Northern Ireland and also the first to attend and address the prestigious annual Irish-American Fund Raising Dinner in Boston. The Irish were represented only at ambassadorial level.

Like any visitor in a foreign city I needed help to meet significant local people. In addition to our consuls general, who never tired of offering assistance, one such helper became a valued friend. When we met initially Jim Howell was chief economist of the Bank of Boston. Later he set up his own economic consultancy and I persuaded him to do some work for the NIO. For thirty years Jim, and his wife Linda, have helped smooth my path and given me sound advice, as well as wonderful friendship.

Jim also paved the way for my election to the board of trustees of Boston University (BU) after I had left government. The university was looking to appoint one or more 'overseas' trustees who would be active in enhancing and spreading the university's interests. My university background, knowledge of the USA in general and Boston in particular, and my record in government got me the job – together with Jim's recommendation. He was one of the most influential trustees, having served for about twenty years.

The next few years were both stimulating and frustrating. I met many influential local people as well as successful fellow trustees drawn from the ranks of Boston University graduates across the country. My time in government and my knighthood intrigued them and created opportunities for me to chat about Britain and Ireland and the peace process. Regrettably, and too often, the conversations were fairly superficial. Trustee parochialism was impressive!

The university greatly valued its traditions and rightly so. Questioning these, in the name either of good governance or of modernisation, was at best tricky. At times it was seen as something akin to disloyalty to the institution. Jim and I both challenged prevailing orthodoxy in areas where we thought challenge was appropriate, particularly in and around the work of the committee which was charged with rewriting the university's governance rules. Once these new, and better, rules were adopted both of us were fired. Clearly we were no longer thought traditionally sound, though the new governance regulations were some reminder of our usefulness and, if you will forgive me saying so, our common sense. Personally I was of little importance to either BU or the wider Boston community but Jim's treatment was a disgrace. From my point of view it was sad that the university failed to accept or even understand that it did not know how to derive significant benefit from international trustees.

With few exceptions, most of my fellow trustees knew as little about UK–Irish relations, and 'the troubles' in the North, as did most Bostonians. Equally, they were not easily persuaded of the need to remedy that deficiency. Having said that, BU was, and remains, an impressive and excellent university and exemplar of sound learning. I am proud to have been associated with it.

My BU trusteeship led to one of my more interesting political encounters. For some time BU cultivated an exceedingly wealthy and influential Middle Eastern businessman who, it hoped, would make a multi-million-dollar donation to the university. One day, in the Commons, I received a call from the BU President's office. This businessman was planning to give a high-level dinner in London in a few days' time. The President had been invited, but did not want to travel. Would I represent the university? Apparently the businessman had indicated that a trustee who was a senior British politician and a knight would be an acceptable substitute.

On the evening I knew no one and for a long time was ignored by all. Then a member of the 'home team' introduced me to a very well-dressed and -spoken young man with a shaved head, before such a sight became commonplace.

'I am Saif Gaddafi,' he said. From our chat I learned that he was doing a PhD at the London School of Economics and was enjoying experiencing our country. He asked what I did. I told him. In which government departments had I been a minister? Northern Ireland? That must have been a challenge. At this point I decided our conversation needed a reality check. I agreed that being a minister in the Province had indeed been a challenge and added that that challenge was increased because the IRA was trying to kill me and my colleagues 'with weapons you had sent them'.

Perhaps not surprisingly, the conversation terminated abruptly and was never resumed – which I regretted. I would have enjoyed debating the morality and politics of Mr Gaddafi's father's killer trade, especially on behalf of those who had been killed and injured.

I am happy to record that I never spotted in Saif Gaddafi the promise of the New Libya which Tony Blair and Peter Mandelson apparently found so persuasive. For me terrorism sympathies cannot be erased with expensive aftershave.

In Washington, DC I visited Congressman Tom Foley regularly, then the Speaker of the House of Representatives and an impressive figure. He was very supportive of what our government was trying to do and enabled me to meet leading members of the strong congressional 'Irish' lobby, usually over a meal.

Individually most of them would not have given me the time of day. However, spending time with a British minister on Northern Ireland issues was, to them, a small price to pay to stay on the right side of Speaker Foley. And, of course, conversation during the meals gave me the opportunity to arrange personal follow-up meetings.

Interestingly the British Embassy in Washington could not or would not even try to arrange my meetings with the Speaker. They thought I was too junior a minister to be bothering his diary. And, explicitly, they did not want to irritate the Irish Embassy. Instead these meetings with the Speaker, which were very important to my mission, were organised through a former Congressman and friend of John McConnell's – and later of mine – Charlie Dougherty of Philadelphia. It tells you something about Foreign Office systems that at least one of the then junior civil servants who proved so unhelpful to this aspect of government policy (actually complaining to me when he heard I was to meet the Speaker, and about that time reprimanded for publicly speaking against a pillar of the government's Northern Ireland policy) went on to a knighthood and a distinguished Foreign Office career. Just another example of that department's marching to its own drumbeat, I guess.

No visit to Washington, DC was complete without a meeting with Representative Joe Kennedy – a Congressman from
Massachusetts and part of the famous Kennedy family. He and I
had a strange love–hate relationship; perhaps a respect–disrespect
relationship would be a more accurate way to describe it.

One story about Joe illustrates the complexities of this aspect
of my work. Tom King, as Secretary of State for Northern Ireland,
once addressed senators and Congressional representatives in
Washington, DC. In the question-and-answer session which
followed Joe was aggressively anti-British in his remarks, to the
point of shock – not just to the British delegation present – and
maybe even offence. Reports of the row, which spread beyond
American shores, alleged that in addition he had been personally
discourteous to Tom.

Joe was as nationalistically Irish as his family antecedents might
suggest. He appeared to have little or no time for the British and
certainly none for the British in Ireland. He could be as charming
as his uncles Teddy and John (the former President) but was not,
or perhaps sometimes chose not to be, as diplomatically skilled
as they.

He and I locked horns a few weeks after that incident in
Washington. Joe was visiting Belfast, supposedly on a fact-finding
trip. Some of us thought that his visit might owe more to the fact that,
as Congressmen have to be elected every two years, a demonstration
of anti-Britishness in Belfast might be worth votes in Boston. Joe
might have denied this suggested motive for his trip, if not the truth
of the observation. Anyway, in front of the media, some of which
I seem to remember he brought with him, Joe berated an ordinary
police constable on the street for the way he was doing his job. Joe
chose to allege that police officers in Northern Ireland were oppress-
ing nationalists in the way they carried out their responsibilities. He
had no basis for doing so and certainly not with this ordinary, hard-
working policeman just serving his community. His actual words
are no longer important, but their effect was to create a storm in
Belfast, whatever their effect in Boston. Incidentally, police officers

in Northern Ireland overwhelmingly behaved professionally and were even-handed.

That very evening I was to host a dinner in Stormont for Joe and his entourage, along with local worthies. It was our first meeting. Northern Ireland ministers and civil servants, not to mention local people, were outraged by Joe's behaviour, which had been screened on our evening television news as well as in Boston. The common thought was that Congressman Kennedy was wrong in what he said, wrong to pick this fight, especially for political propaganda purposes, and wrong to pick on a policeman who could not answer back. (He might have denied this propaganda charge but no one in Northern Ireland would have believed him.)

Those travelling with Joe sensed the tension and distaste in Stormont and tried to calm the situation – to little avail. 'Sometimes we have to let politicians do what they want to do and not get too worked up about it' was their message. Their 'spin' convinced no one. They did not seem to understand the depth of the anger which had been caused and which, at least in the dining room, was being suppressed only by British good manners. Not that they much cared for they had achieved their preferred good Boston coverage. To be fair, I sensed some embarrassment behind their defence of their boss. Even to them the whole incident with the policeman was transparently a set-up job.

Conversation during dinner was not a great success. It did not flow. I was courteous and civil towards Joe but neither warm nor welcoming. I was righteously angry at the injustice of his remarks. Joe was quiet but in no way apologetic.

In an attempt to rescue the evening from the increasingly sullen wake which was developing, a senior civil servant suggested to the assembled company that, as the minister present, I might like to explain British policy in Northern Ireland and towards the Irish Republic for the benefit of Congressman Kennedy and his party. He had not 'cleared' this suggestion with me, though I accepted that it was designed to be helpful.

I stood up, welcomed Joe perfunctorily, with as much grace as I thought the occasion required, and then said bluntly that I had no intention of explaining our policy. Perhaps with some deficit of grace, I added that I had better things to do with my time. I told the diners that the Secretary of State had set out British policy a few weeks earlier in Washington and had been treated with what, allegedly, amounted to abuse and disdain by our guest, who had refused to accept what Tom said. His behaviour in Belfast earlier in the day made it clear that he had learned little and was not disposed to change this.

I sat down abruptly. Kennedy said nothing. The Northern Ireland guests tried not to look too pleased. The atmosphere was charged. Quickly Joe's officials and mine took us into a separate room and left the other guests to mingle and disperse.

Joe was not amused by what I had said. After robust exchanges, in both directions, he finally understood that our righteous anger outdid any emotions he felt. He left early to continue his fact-finding visit, which produced no further incident.

The evening generated one benefit. It started Joe and me on a relationship of friendship marked by candour if not diplomacy. Every time I visited Washington, DC thereafter I visited Joe in his office and looked forward to doing so. Joe always stood to welcome me. Frequently his hair was tousled as if he had been running his fingers through it as he sat at his desk. And although our exchanges were tough, they were never outright discourteous. Sometimes his toothy, typical Kennedy grin suggested that in some sense he was enjoying himself. And he always escorted me back to his outer office when we had finished.

Each visit proceeded along similar lines, almost as if orchestrated. Joe spoke, uninterrupted, for about ten minutes, regaling me with unsubstantiated stories of how British ministers, like me, and our forces, badly treated the nationalist community and deliberately discriminated against them. He could well understand why some in that community would take up arms and fight, even though he, of course, did not encourage them to do so. In truth it was all pretty unpleasant stuff. Perhaps its main redeeming feature in my eyes was that, overwhelmingly, what he said was not true.

I then spoke for a similar time telling him that he did not know what he was talking about, that he was wrong and that as time went by it was disappointing to note his knowledge and understanding did not seem to be improving. I would explain what was really happening in the Province and tell him that, as a democrat, he had a responsibility to condemn violence unequivocally. If he would work with us on that, the combined message would be more effective. For his part, he replied, he could see little advantage in any American or Irish person working together with us. We always parted with mutual expressions of respect.

The sheer repetitive nature of our meetings meant that I failed to persuade Joe of the facts of life in Northern Ireland and of our goodwill. Maybe, however, a sense of being held 'accountable' through our meetings may have tempered some of Joe's public utterances.

Notwithstanding all of the above, Joe could be charming and friendly when he chose. Congress was the poorer for his decision not to seek re-election.

Obviously I talked to many hundreds of influential people in Boston, Washington, DC and Chicago. Only a few are mentioned here. Similarly I talked to many influential New Yorkers, particularly in the national media and business communities, but I will relay only one New York conversation both because of its unexpected twist and because of its effect on me personally.

The New York Catholic diocese was then led by Cardinal O'Connor. Our consul had made arrangements for me and John McConnell to have breakfast with the Cardinal and his aides in his residence. The reason for the meeting, in addition to influencing Irish-American opinion, was to brief him about our education reform programme in Northern Ireland and how we were establishing higher standards of teaching and governance in our schools as well as breaking down religious and sectarian barriers. I told him there would be a new body, Church related, to oversee the running of Catholic schools (at the request of his brother bishops) with direct access to me, programmes in education for mutual understanding and cultural heritage as well as new curricula and statutorily based integrated schools. He was deeply interested and appreciative of all our ideas (unlike Cardinal Law he appeared not to be aware of the Irish bishops' views on integrated schools).

After a long conversation in which he probed my reasons for making such radical changes, he leaned forward and, to my amazement and John's amusement, asked me if I would be willing to become the director of education for the Catholic diocese of New York. He created a clear impression in my mind, and in John's, that his enquiry was meant to be taken seriously. He offered me the job. Director of Catholic schools in New York. Me. Amazing.

I thanked him for the compliment and his confidence and reminded him that, whatever my present government position, I was just a simple (Protestant) Belfast boy. 'Cardinal,' I said with a smile, 'thank you but no thank you – and that answer will keep us both out of trouble; me back home and you with Rome.' With a warm smile and seeming regret he agreed.

We then went on to have a deeply theological and profoundly practical discussion about the Christian virtue of hope. He stressed that to him, not least in his dealings with people, this had to be one of the major foundations of what we Christians believed. After all, it was at the heart of Jesus' teaching. If we were genuinely to practise our faith in the public arena, for the common good, then our policies needed to give and reflect hope. Without hope people had no motivation to change for the better and little reason to plough through life's difficulties. This in turn meant they faced too much temptation to ignore 'the rules' and do their own thing. Upholding human dignity required hope. He repeatedly prayed in aid Jesus' teaching on the subject.

I have never forgotten that conversation. It helped shape and focus the rest of my public service and I will always be grateful to the late Cardinal.

†

Obviously, being asked to influence the presuppositions and views of the 20 per cent of American citizens who took pride in their

Irish roots was an overwhelming assignment. I understood I could achieve only a minuscule amount but any positive change was worth the effort.

In life any of us can be asked to do things which seem on the face of it impossible. I try to be realistic, which means neither suffering despair or delusions of grandeur about the task I have been asked to tackle. Any positive difference made, no matter how small, is worthwhile. Good people will give you credit for trying. Detractors may deride you for not achieving very much. My personal policy has been largely to ignore them. And I remind myself of the old, but true, saying – no one erects monuments to critics. As the Chinese proverb says, a journey of a thousand miles begins with a single step.

During my last years as an MP a popular song, much played on the radio, had a repetitive chorus line which reflects my philosophy – both political and Christian. The words are: 'When you have the choice to sit it out or dance, I hope you dance.'

So what did I learn on these trips of persuasion? I learned that I did not have to like people in order to work or seek common ground with them. And I learned not to be too dismissive of the fact that, in some circumstances, others were indeed ignorant. That I was better informed than they were did not necessarily mean that I was smarter. Perhaps for the first time in my life I realised that they saw me in much the same terms as I saw them.

I also learned that you do not always have to accept the solutions to problems that others offer you. Sometimes, by thinking laterally and focusing on what is really important, you can break down other people's prejudices. Acting sensitively is also important. There is seldom any point in winning the argument if in doing so you lose the relationship you want or need to foster. As the Good Book tells us, be helpless as doves, wise as serpents, industrious as ants and turn the other cheek.

Let me finish with the most fundamentally personal lesson Cardinals Law, O'Connor and Daly and Sister Genevieve taught this Ulster Protestant.

I grew up in a Christian home embedded in Northern Ireland's

Protestant tradition. I had no pre-university knowledge of or exposure to Catholic peers. The tribal barriers were too high. I was led to believe that Catholics and Protestants had different faith systems. In fact these fine Catholic Christians taught me that we have a common faith in Jesus Christ. The differences, for there are differences, are theologically secondary not primary. As a consequence, in my political career, I have sought to lower Christian ecclesiastical barriers by emphasising what we have in common – theologically – instead of concentrating on the differences. For a Belfast boy, that change in thinking has been fundamental and may reflect the single biggest lesson I learned.

8

A Policeman's Lot

Half my ministerial service was in the Northern Ireland Office. From my appointment, in January 1986, to my becoming Health Minister in Whitehall in May 1992, over 500 people were killed in terrorist activity in the Province. Thousands were injured.

Government ministers were constantly at risk. In my early years we were not even allowed to fly to and from Belfast on commercial services. When, later, that restriction was lifted for junior ministers we flew under assumed names, which changed regularly.

We were constantly accompanied by Special Branch officers. They were wonderful – professional, relaxed but alert, sensitive (they knew when to chat and when to be quiet) and often dryly funny. They were never pretentious and regularly put themselves in the firing line for the common good of ministers and the local community.

This chapter, illustrating events in which RUC officers played a significant role, is meant to be a tribute to those gallant men and women to whose commitment to protection and service I owe my life.

While paying tribute to Royal Ulster Constabulary officers (now known as the Police Service of Northern Ireland) I must include Cambridgeshire Constabulary's Special Branch officers. They were equally professional even though the terrorism pressure on them was less. A number became personal friends. Indeed, for years after their service with me had ended, we would meet annually in the Bombay Brasserie restaurant in Peterborough to enjoy each other's company and reminisce.

As Northern Ireland's Security Minister I was also 'covered' by the Metropolitan Police. For years they kept an eye on our home (and quickly answered alarm calls when one of the children 'accidentally' pushed a panic button) and for eighteen months gave me close protection. They shared all the admirable characteristics of their colleagues, although in London a sense of humour was not as advanced as it was in Belfast and Peterborough.

To all three groups of serving officers – thank you. I am in your debt.

The leader

For a significant part of my time in the Province Sir Jack Hermon was the Chief Constable. His force was full of brave police officers who handled situations of great risk – and gave their lives – to thwart the efforts of people who behaved with murderous intent.

Predominantly, ministers and senior RUC officers related to each other only through work. It was in no one's interest to create a public impression that we formed some sort of social fraternity. We did not.

I had only two serious personal interactions with this Chief Constable. The first was very early in my ministerial career, in fact on my first weekend duty. When my plane landed on that Friday afternoon I was whisked directly to Stormont. An Orangemen's march was planned for the following Monday – a holiday – and the police wanted ministerial approval to close a road and reroute the march for reasons of public order and safety.

Those who know the Province's history will know how emotively committed marchers are to their traditional routes – on both sides of the community. Changing parade routes was always a major ask; so big, indeed, that the police could not make reroute decisions, ministers had to do so. When a march was rerouted many police – sometimes with army support – were often required to see that the law was observed.

At Stormont I was ushered into a large meeting of civil servants and senior RUC officers in civvies. This was just a preliminary discussion to help me, the new minister, grasp what I could and could not do within the law. The decision-making meeting would come later.

Sir Jack was a forthright man. He commanded great respect and attention not least because he exuded authority and gave the impression that he was comfortable with his responsibilities. He explained the issues, highlighting the threat to security and the potential for public disorder, and gave reasons why he would be asking me to exercise my legal authority. Other officers and civil servants supplemented what he had said and my questions were answered clearly. We agreed to meet formally the next morning.

When I arrived the next day I found Sir Jack and his colleagues in full uniform. The Chief Constable made a thorough case in a formal manner. The previous day's briefing helped me to understand the issues. Questions posed by me, formally, were answered formally. Only our titles were used as we addressed each other.

When the process of request and explanation was complete, silence descended. Everyone looked at me expectantly. I adjourned the meeting and left the room to consider the Chief Constable's request. Everyone looked stunned. Sir Kenneth Bloomfield followed me.

Ken was an outstanding civil servant. He was intellectually impressive, understood his role and had good personal sensitivities. Given his long experience, he was easily the most knowledgeable and subtle civil servant in the NIO. He was also a good friend (and remains so) and wise adviser.

Was I all right? Did I have a problem with the Chief Constable's presentation? Did I need help?

I told him I was fine but given the seriousness of the request and the likelihood of ensuing public disorder – whatever I decided – a short reflection before deciding seemed appropriate. An instant decision subsequently might be used, legally, to imply that I had not given the issue sufficient consideration.

Ken smiled and agreed with me. Apparently Friday's pre-meeting was supposed to have given me the time to think through the

issues (which I had) and secretaries of state usually gave an immediate response in meetings like this, which explained why everyone
had seemed so surprised. Ken said he thought it admirable that I had
sent a more considered message to police and officials alike.

As Ken and I discussed the issue I said I was minded to agree
to the request. I cannot now remember whether Ken or I suggested
that, before any announcement, it might be a good idea to brief
the Secretary of State. This made persuasive sense and I rang
Tom King.

After hearing my report Tom sounded understandably disturbed,
as such decisions were normally taken by him. It was only the vagary
of weekend duty that had caused this one to fall to the most junior
member of the ministerial team, not yet three months into the job
and with virtually no security experience.

He asked if I wanted him to come over. No, I said, I believe I
have acted appropriately and reached the correct decision.

Had anyone checked that I had the legal right to make the decision? Yes. My position was based on lawyers' advice.

Who was advising me? I listed the senior officials and added that
Ken was with me.

'Put him on.'

Ken was generous about my behaviour, the process adopted and
my willingness to listen to and analyse advice. He told the Secretary
of State his presence was not necessary, which, I suspect, did not
wholly please Tom.

We reconvened the meeting and, formally, I told the Chief
Constable his request was agreed. I signed a paper to make the decision legally binding. Tom came over on the morning of the march,
sat in his office, unneeded, for several hours and then returned
to England.

The march was rerouted. Some public disorder did occur, coupled
with some verbal posturing, but nothing serious.

My second major interaction with Sir Jack was altogether different. He was a great rugby fan. In those days most people who
migrated to the top of the various strands of professional activity in

the Province leaned towards rugby, rather than soccer, because most of them had emerged from grammar schools where rugby was the dominant sport.

By way of example, I was no exception. INST (the Royal Belfast Academical Institution), the grammar school where I was educated, was a boys-only school with one of the best rugby records in Northern Ireland, and no soccer team.

As Minister for Sport I tried to go to Lansdowne Road, Dublin whenever possible to watch Ireland play their rugby internationals. These day visits were not arranged just to indulge a personal love of sport. It was government policy that ministers should use all reasonable opportunities officially to visit the Republic in order to strengthen bonds of mutual interest. In those days rugby provided one of only a few naturally occurring opportunities.

For security reasons I was not allowed to drive to Dublin. Instead we flew by small jet to a base near the city. I was then driven with a Gardaí (Irish police) escort to the home of the British Ambassador to lunch with his other guests. In this way I got to meet many influential Irish people. After lunch we were off to the match and then back to the plane and Belfast.

Jack normally drove to the games where he was the guest of his opposite number in Dublin – both for lunch and the match.

On one such weekend there was serious and public tension between the two police forces (and indeed between the two governments) over a hard-to-resolve security issue. (The issue itself is not important here.) Rather foolishly, the head of the Gardaí decided to express his displeasure over the inter-governmental impasse by not inviting Jack to the international game – and by letting it be known that the absence of an invitation was deliberate. It had the effect, as he must have known it would, of increasing tension on both sides of the border.

As was probably intended the media reported the 'snub'. I read about it in a newspaper story early in the week leading up to the Saturday international and rang the Chief Constable personally. After pleasantries I invited him to join me as my guest at the match. He said he was very touched by my thoughtfulness but, in the circumstances, thought it would be better if he did not go. He said it was preferable for the dispute to be confined to the two police forces rather than be escalated to governmental level (though we both knew that it already existed there politically). While he spoke nobly he sounded like a man who was putting duty before his instinct as a rugby fan.

I told him I would really appreciate his company. His 'no' seemed overlaid with hesitancy. So I told him that as minister I wanted him to go. His presence as my guest would underline to all in Dublin that our government not only held him in continuing high esteem but also that we agreed with the stand he was taking.

'Events might transpire on the ground which could cause you embarrassment,' he replied. He did not want to take that risk.

'Chief Constable,' I responded, 'I am asking you formally to be my guest. I do so conscious of all the possibilities, including political and public order ones. I am assuming responsibility – and I am not easily embarrassed.'

We flew down and spent the time getting to know each other. Our Ambassador went out of his way to give Sir Jack a warm welcome. His other guests were delighted to see the Chief Constable. When we arrived at the rugby ground both of us were a little tense. We were about to find out if I had precipitated an international diplomatic incident. As we got out of the car Irish rugby fans around us started to applaud. Sir Jack smiled and the applause strengthened.

Then something genuinely surprising happened. The Gardaí officers who had been assigned to protect us lined up to shake Jack's hand. Other officers appeared and joined in the generous welcome. It was all a pretty clear indication that rank-and-file Irish officers did not wish to be associated with their boss's action. The police brotherhood easily crossed the international border. This message preceded us into the lounge.

In the receptions, both pre- and post-game, we mingled with the great and good who were the Irish Rugby Football Union's guests. I sought out every Irish minister, former rugby international, Irish business leader and newspaper editor I could find and introduced them to our Chief Constable. Those in the room from Northern Ireland needed no encouragement to approach and welcome him. Jack charmed them all.

The message we delivered could not have been clearer. British ministers and the RUC were close. We were of one mind. My political objective had been achieved and Jack had a great day. Unfortunately I cannot remember any details of the game.

On the flight home Sir Jack was strangely quiet, almost withdrawn. Eventually he said quietly, 'Thank you. You did not need to do that. You took a risk for me. I am very grateful.' After another long period of silence he asked what plans I had for the evening. 'None,' I answered. I was on my own as Betty was not in the Province that weekend.

'Would you be kind enough to join me for dinner?' he asked.

We ate at 'his' table at the Ballyholme Yacht Club. During the meal he paid me a compliment I have cherished ever since. 'During my years as Chief Constable,' he said, 'I have believed that professional proprieties could best be preserved if I kept my distance socially from ministers. We have formal meetings and attend formal functions together but otherwise I have had no contact with ministers in private or on what might be described as a friendship basis. This is the first informal meal I have ever eaten with a minister by himself. It is a pleasure to do so with the only Ulster-born minister we have had. This is my way of saying "thank you" for today. It is also my way of saying "thank you" for the way you treated me on your first Easter weekend. It would have been improper for me to have said so then but no minister has ever treated me with greater respect.'

I still treasure that remark.

From that night on, Sir Jack returned to his policy of keeping a proper distance from ministers, including me. Following a number of years in retirement Jack died after a long period of ill health. I am pleased to put on record my appreciation of a tough cop and a fine man.

Eternal vigilance

One day I fused three of my ministerial responsibilities during a visit to Londonderry. (Historically the city was called Londonderry. If you came from the Unionist tradition you used that name. If you were nationalist Irish then the city was called Derry – as was its local authority and football club. For convenience, only, I will call it Derry and hope that this will not adversely affect anyone's political blood pressure.) As Public Information Minister I visited the local newspaper in the morning and in the evening hosted a dinner for local business figures and politicians – wearing my political development hat.

Sandwiched between these, as Education Minister, I visited Magee College, part of the University of Ulster. The visit went well. The senior staff were friendly and, while showing me round, acceptably argued their case for more resources and told me of their plans. For the most part students seemed uninterested in my presence, which was normal. A few Sinn Féin supporters gave me lip, otherwise the visit was unexceptional but useful from my point of view.

While walking across the campus with senior academics my armoured car suddenly drove across the grass and stopped beside us. My Special Branch minders said, 'Get in, minister. No, you cannot say goodbyes. Get in. Now.'

We sped away immediately. No one said anything. The driver concentrated on driving at speed while the other officer told his colleagues, by radio, that we were exiting the premises.

When we were well away from Magee I asked the obvious question. Apparently my vigilant police team had found a bomb some yards ahead at the side of the path on which we had been walking. It was definitely time to get out of there. Others dealt with the lethal device with the same professionalism that had been displayed in finding it. Without those officers I might well not be writing this.

Bill Addley has been my friend since school days, the nearest I have had to a brother and the best man at our wedding. He and his wife Ruth, also a good friend from school days, were then living in Derry where Bill was a local Presbyterian minister. My programme that day included a teatime break at their house. In the circumstances, when we got there, we noted that local security had been obviously and suddenly enhanced, to the curiosity of their neighbours.

Bill and I were drinking tea and watching the TV news when my picture suddenly appeared on the screen.

'The IRA have just announced', the newsreader said, 'that they decided not to assassinate the Education Minister, Brian Mawhinney, during his visit to Magee College today in case innocent passers-by would be injured!' The idea that the IRA were concerned about innocent bystanders was a novel concept for most Ulster people.

In my six-and-a-half years as a Northern Ireland minister I had a number of 'difficult' security experiences. This may be the closest I came to being killed.

That TV newsflash posed a difficult personal decision, one which I really resented having to make. Should I judge this to be just a local story with no broader significance? If so, I would not need to ring Betty and tell her. There was no point in upsetting her unnecessarily.

Or was this likely to become a national story? If so I had to tell her immediately that I was fine so that she could reassure the children before they heard the story through the media.

I decided the second option was the more likely, which turned out to be a good call. The news item figured prominently on the national evening news. Friends were deeply shocked, which simply underlined how little they understood about my job.

This story has a postscript. About fifteen years later I was a Parliamentary Fellow at St Antony's College, Oxford University. At their request I organised an evening seminar on Northern Ireland for their series on reconciliation. Alongside me, as speakers, I invited Peter Robinson and Martin McGuinness. The popular perception was that, when I was an NIO minister, Martin controlled the IRA in and around Derry. I have neither knowledge nor information about the bomb uncovered during my visit but I have always found it hard to believe that its placement would have come as a surprise to Martin.

When I was inviting Peter to speak at Oxford I told him Martin too had been invited. 'No problem,' he replied, 'but I will not shake his hand.'

Would I?

Each of us would have different ways of deciding how to answer that question. I chose to reflect on 'forgive us our trespasses as we forgive those who trespass against us' – and did.

When Martin arrived I went out to meet him – for the first time. He gave me a warm smile of greeting which, sadly, did not reach his eyes.

High risk

One day John McConnell rang to tell me that Father X would be in touch (his name is not important to the story). 'As a kindness to me, minister, would you please see him?' he said. But I was warned. Although he was not 'involved' (shorthand for saying that he had no active IRA connections) he was not a 'friend'.

Perhaps I should digress briefly to clarify and commend the practice of church ministry in the Province. The Roman Catholic Church had priests who, overwhelmingly, led worship and tended to their parishioners' pastoral and spiritual needs conscientiously and in harmony with their holy vows. The same was true of Protestant church ministers. Again, the huge majority solely and impressively involved themselves in ecclesiastical ministry. Sadly, in both Catholic and Protestant churches, there was a (small) minority of clergy who got too close to the men of violence.

A day or two later my hard-working and very reliable private secretary, Ros Earnshaw, told me that Father X had rung and wanted a private meeting with no civil servants present. 'I assume you will not want to see him,' she said sensibly. But I made an exception and asked her to set up a meeting here in the department, but not in my office. I did not want him to know where it was located in the building.

'Friendly' would not characterise his demeanour when we met. 'Gritted teeth' comes more readily to mind.

'I do not want to be here,' he immediately started. 'I do not support you or your colleagues. You Brits have no right even to be in my country.' (Bizarre, I thought – it was my country too!) 'But I have to be realistic. You are here. I need help and John McConnell tells me you are an honourable Christian man who will listen fairly to what I have to say. It goes against all my instincts but I am willing to take his word for it, though that does not mean I believe him. But I am angry to find myself in this demeaning position.'

He waited for my response. I made no reply other than inviting him to proceed, which appeared to surprise him.

'I run a church in Y,' he told me. 'You know it is a very poor, working-class area of Belfast. Young people have literally nowhere to do anything except on the streets or in my church hall. Without that hall all of them would gravitate to the IRA, instead of the many that do so now. My problem is simple. The parochial hall is falling down. We have no money to repair it; nor does the diocese. I need a quarter of a million pounds. Can you find some grant? Will you give it to me?'

After a short discussion about what activities he organised for local people I gave him the standard ministerial response. I would consider carefully his request and be in touch.

His expression said it all. He knew this would be a wasted effort. Why had he bothered denying his beliefs by coming to see this typically uncaring British minister? He left in a marked manner.

Back in my office officials arrived to satisfy their curiosity. I told them what he wanted and instructed them to find £250,000. For once the phrase 'there is no alternative' (which is seldom true in politics) seemed apposite because I had believed his analysis.

A couple of days later I rang the priest personally and told him he could have the grant. He was pleased for his young people. For himself and his church, he said, he wished he had not had to ask.

I concluded with a single question. Would he like me to come and present the cheque personally, as it were 'on the record,' or would he prefer it to be forwarded quietly in the mail? The first option would record the government's appreciation of the work he did. On the other hand he had made it abundantly clear why he might not want that appreciation. Either way neither I nor the government were looking for praise, it was he who deserved the recognition. It was his call.

'You won't come here,' he replied. 'And even if you wanted to your guards wouldn't let you. Too dangerous to meet the people who live around here.' I told him those were my issues, not his. All he had to decide was how to receive the money.

'It would be all right if you came.'

'Good,' I told him, 'I will be in touch.' Then the trouble started. My Special Branch officers, with my best interests at heart, flatly refused to take me to where the church was located. 'It is too dangerous,' they said. 'It is in the heart of IRA territory.'

'That is why we will go,' I maintained. 'I have given my word so please make the necessary arrangements.' A battle of wills followed. My minders got support from their superiors in the RUC. 'Too dangerous' was the decision. 'We would have to redeploy 100 police officers, 300 army personnel and an army helicopter to hover overhead in order to ensure your safety. No go, minister.'

Eventually I became exasperated with the police for the only time in my Northern Ireland service. 'Tell your superiors that I appreciate their professional and real concern. Invite them to meet me in the Secretary of State's office. We will let him decide if he finds it acceptable to have "no go" areas in the United Kingdom, areas where government ministers cannot venture.' (I was taking a risk for, unknown to them, I had not spoken to the Secretary of State). I did not underestimate their concerns and did appreciate that they were in my best interests but this had to be a ministerial decision.

In the last resort, all agreed that I could go. A very large number of security personnel were redeployed to keep me safe. Indeed it must have been a genuinely dangerous trip because two unique (to me) precautions took place.

An armoured car would not be sufficient protection, I was told. People can see who is in it as it passes. So we will transport you in an unmarked armoured van with windowless sides. In that way your identity will be protected until we actually arrive at the hall.

Secondly, you must be out of the hall and back in the van in no more than ten minutes. If you stay beyond that limit we will literally pick you up and carry you out. The priest has been warned.

When we arrived at the hall in a normal-looking working-class street, we were met by the priest, a few parishioners and a photographer from the *Belfast Evening Telegraph*.

The priest did not want flowery speeches so I shook hands with all present, thanked them for their community service, handed the priest a cheque for £250,000 and had the event recorded by the newspaper. I was back in the van eight minutes after leaving it.

When we got back to relative safety in the centre of Belfast I could contain my curiosity no longer. Why the threat to carry me out, I enquired?

'When a minister is spotted in an IRA stronghold,' my minder said, 'a sympathiser will try to find some young person with an easily impressionable personality and low IQ. He will be told to go to a nearby house, ask for the gun which is in a specified hiding place, then return and shoot the man who will be identified by his IRA handler. Our intelligence suggests that in these circumstances a minister can be under threat of assassination after fifteen minutes. So we set a ten-minute limit for safety purposes.' No minister has ever been assassinated in this way but to me the implication was clear. An earlier attempt had been foiled, or so I believed.

My admiration for the work of the priest in such an environment increased. The fact that he did not like British ministers was irrelevant. To the best of my memory he did not ring even John McConnell to say thank you.

I have often reflected on that morning. Was I right to put myself at such risk? Was I right to add huge risk to the already risky lives of RUC officers and army personnel? Was I right to overrule official security advice?

And was I right to do all of the above to help nameless people

I did not know and who neither liked nor believed in me – all in the name of upholding some idea like universal democratic government?

Sometimes the moral high ground is important, and not just to Christians. Of course I recognised the danger both to me and to the RUC officers in that street – potential assassination targets themselves. It would have been easier to have put the cheque in the post, but I did what I thought was right. In this I followed Mark Twain's prescription, so admired by former US President Harry Truman. 'Always do right! This will gratify some people and astonish the rest.'

Thank God (literally) that it all went off peacefully. And thank you RUC. I am sorry I put you into such a difficult situation.

The Cardinal

Cardinal Cahal Daly was a godly man and greatly concerned to implement what was good for his people. He knew violence was not defensible, and said so repeatedly, giving outstanding leadership in the process. He and I became good Christian friends who met regularly and talked freely. His Christmas cards were easily the most spiritually focused of the thousands we have received. I mourned his recent death.

Cardinal Daly was rightly proud of his Catholic heritage. He enthused as he showed me around his cathedral in Armagh and pointed out the cardinals' hats of his predecessors hanging from the high ceiling. And he cared deeply about 'his' Catholic schools and worked hard with me to improve them physically and in terms of their quality of education. Our only significant difference was over my intention to put the option of government-funded integrated schools on the statute book. He worried that this legal right would undermine the Church's message about the importance of Catholic education.

I am told that, within the Church, he was held in high regard for his leadership, his intellect and his spirituality. A few thought him occasionally too political, but he handled the issue of republican violence with courage and skill as well as with clarity both in the Church and in the community. And in the hours we spent privately discussing these difficult life-and-death issues he was always firm in his resolve and clear in the limits of his ability to exert influence. In that sense he was politically astute.

However, this story, like the others, is about the police. Some years after I had left the Northern Ireland Office (while I was Party Chairman) a serious difference arose between the Cardinal and the then Secretary of State, Sir Patrick (Paddy) Mayhew QC, MP (now Lord Mayhew).

Those organising an Orangemen's march wanted to parade down their traditional route, which took them through a largely Catholic area. The local Catholics, understandably, did not want them walking past their homes. Eventually the parade was given permission to use the traditional route over the protests of many, including the Cardinal.

I learned that communications between the Secretary of State's office and the Cardinal's had broken down. Each believed the other had given certain undertakings which had not been honoured. Whatever went wrong (I do not know – historians can determine) each man felt he had been 'let down' (a euphemistic phrase) by the other. Trust became strained, made worse by street unrest.

In Northern Ireland political progress is possible only on the basis of persuasion. If there is no trust there is no progress. Any cardinal, or indeed any other senior churchman, by behaviour and word influences the atmosphere in which persuasion can thrive or die. Equally, secretaries of state have the legal and physical might to insist, but doing so may sometimes also stunt the power of persuasion. So resolving this impasse was important.

Some weeks after the fateful march I had a private phone call from John McConnell. Although still a civil servant, John was more widely connected and trusted politically by all sides than anyone else in the Province. He rang to convey a personal message from the Cardinal. For understandable reasons, neither John nor the Cardinal wanted the Northern Ireland Office to know of his 'unofficial' call.

The message was simple. Would I be willing to go to Armagh to meet with the Cardinal privately? I was the only British minister he trusted or would talk to – which was a sad state of affairs and politically unhelpful to government. I told John I would get back to him.

Two things struck me. The only British minister the Irish Cardinal would talk to was a Belfast-born Protestant. In human terms this was ironic. In fact it demonstrated that a shared Christian faith can transcend social, religious and political differences. My second reaction was more pragmatic. The Cardinal's request could create political difficulty inside the government. I might be Northern Ireland born but I was no longer Northern Ireland responsible. Clearly it would not be sensible for me to go without the Prime Minister's approval. And how would Paddy Mayhew react? If he dug his toes in, John Major would be unlikely to force the issue. Doing so was not his style, sometimes regrettably, even for an important issue like this.

Being Party Chairman, I had no difficulty getting to see the Prime Minister. I explained the background and the phone call (leaving out John McConnell's name). John Major sanctioned my going but told me to 'clear it' with Paddy. Paddy, when I approached him, said that if I wanted to go it was fine with him. He supposed it was good that the Cardinal wanted to talk to some British minister.

Two things needed to be done before I left on the trip. I asked the Prime Minister to hand-write a personal letter to the Cardinal, for me to deliver. He readily agreed and handed me a sealed envelope.

Secondly, I had to alert the security forces of my impending visit. Their response was that the security situation around Armagh was too dangerous for them to mount an operation to get a Cabinet minister in and out of town safely, so the visit would have to be postponed, perhaps for some considerable time. No detailed reasons were given, not even on the secure telephone line from No. 10 which I used. I wondered if they had a sense that their Secretary of State might think I was interfering, even though I had told them the visit had been cleared by Paddy.

I did not accept their analysis, pointed out that my visit was urgent and requested that appropriate security arrangements be made for a visit to take place a few days later.

A second refusal followed.

My tone the third time was sharper. I made it clear that my trip stemmed from a decision at the top of government and that, if they had a problem, they were to ring No. 10, from which I was calling. In the event they gave the go-ahead.

When I flew in I was met by two of my former minders in an ordinary car: no armour plating, no escort, nothing. As we approached Armagh there was still no sign of security so I asked what arrangements were in place. 'Local commanders', I was told, had decided that the security situation was too dangerous for them to provide cover for my visit. And, anyway, they were short of manpower. And I was no longer an NIO minister. So, as I had insisted on ignoring their advice and had come, I could proceed at my own risk and in a low-profile way which, they hoped, would not attract the IRA's attention. Someone appeared to have decided that this non-NIO minister was 'expendable' if the worst came to the worst. The lives of the Special Branch officers with me, who were their colleagues, did not seem to have figured in their calculations.

It was an appalling decision, and one of the most serious blots on the RUC's reputation in my time. To this day those who made it should be ashamed of themselves not least for ignoring, with malice, a direct instruction from their Prime Minister – without even having the guts to tell him.

I never was briefed if this was genuinely a local 'rogue' security decision or one sanctioned at NIO level. I would find either explanation unacceptable. Maybe an element of politics had crept in. Maybe Cahal's behaviour or initiative was resented. Maybe my official reappearance in the Province was resented. Who knows? I would be amazed if Paddy Mayhew knew – he is an honourable man.

Needless to say I did not tell the Cardinal, the Prime Minister or Paddy. I still think the decision disgraceful, not least because it exposed two fine RUC officers to officially determined exceptional risk – as if they did not matter to their bosses. They mattered to me and I thank them; so should the government and the NIO. They played a significant part in getting relations between the Cardinal and the British government back on to a constructive track. The officers must remain anonymous but they know who they are. I am in your debt.

Minister missing

This last story turned out to be less serious – indeed humorous. It was also unique. That fact in itself is a form of praise for the police service.

While a minister in the Province I ruptured my Achilles tendon playing in a fun cricket match one evening. I was in plaster for fourteen weeks after which physiotherapy was conducted at St Thomas' Hospital in London, Dundonald Hospital near Belfast and the District Hospital in Peterborough. Medically this was not a good long-term arrangement as my permanently swollen and stiff ankle still testifies.

Even at the time it was obvious my injury was serious. My minders on the boundary heard the crack of the tendon snapping and saw me fall in noisy pain. They raced to the wicket and pinned me to the ground while searching for the bullet hole. Eventually they understood the problem. In case you are wondering, cynically, if I was feigning some of the agony, two weeks later both my arms still bore the fingerprint bruises made by my minders, so hard did they have to press to keep me still.

Weeks after the accident I was on weekend duty. Betty, and John and Judi Broadhead were with me. On the Saturday morning we went into Belfast to shop, going our separate ways and agreeing to meet later. Betty and I were driven down Royal Avenue to the main indoor shopping complex in the city centre, accompanied, of course, by two minders. Betty wanted to buy a skirt so we went into the large department store. My ankle was very sore and I was hobbling along with the aid of a stick.

The police officers gave us some personal space. They followed, but not too closely, which was fine because no one was expecting us to be there. Surprise is a good defence against potential terrorism or murder.

Betty picked some skirts to try on and headed towards the changing rooms. When we turned the corner towards them I could see a chair behind the half-pulled curtain in the cubicle right by the door. This was a no-brainer. My leg was really hurting. I went in with Betty, pulled the curtain and sat down. Bliss.

When she had made her selection we emerged to pay. I looked around. No minders. We walked around looking for them. No minders.

Eventually we bumped into a man who introduced himself as the store's security manager. My minders had been looking for me, he said. No, he did not know where they were. Would we like him to escort us to the exit?

I said yes, thinking he meant the exit of the shopping complex. In fact he meant only to the exit of his store. This was just another example of what I learned over the years was a relatively common reaction. Of course people did not want me to die at the hands of terrorists. But what they *really* did not want was for me to die on their patch.

Betty and I agreed that we should start walking back to the meeting point, a good half mile away (my poor leg). I was confident that my minders would reappear any moment. In any event, if they did not, I would approach the first police officers or soldiers we met on the street and ask them to escort us. Out we went into the crowd.

'Hi Brian' ... 'Oh look, there's that minister' ... 'How are you, minister?' ... 'Who's the bird?' ... 'There's that f***** Mawhinney.'

The comments kept coming as we struggled through the crowd on the footpath. Most were friendly, some were not. It was a tense walk rather than a threatening one.

The problem, of course, was that some IRA sympathisers would recognise us, especially as we were passing the end of the 'nationalist' Falls Road. If that happened a report of us walking alone through the city could be transmitted to IRA headquarters, from which some IRA gunman could be sent to dispatch us.

You've guessed it. Not a police officer in sight. No soldiers patrolling in our area. We made our way up Royal Avenue, the focus of stares and varied comments. Fortunately for our safety and my leg we experienced nothing worse than a little jostling.

Just short of our meeting point we met my officers coming towards us. They had returned to the car in case we had gone there. Before they could say a word I said, 'We are fine. There is no harm done. And there is no need to report this – as far as I am concerned.' They told me that 'minister missing' had already been reported. 'Calm everyone down,' I said, 'and let us all forget about it. I certainly will not pursue the matter.'

This incident too passed into ministerial 'folklore'.

In the six-and-a-half years I was an NIO minister my Special Branch minders were outstanding: professional, friendly, and competent beyond belief. I probably spent about 900 days in the Province. The fact that there was only one such story in all that time (and I was significantly to blame) highlights how excellent they were – only one 'incident' among thousands and thousands of possibilities. Thank you, guys. I am and always will be grateful and impressed.

9

I Said, No Surprises

Throughout my more than thirty years in politics I have repeated the same three-pronged mantra. No surprises. No 'bounce'. I *do* want to know. Everyone got the same message.

Of course surprises happen but I do not like being surprised, particularly at a late stage and especially by information which has been known for some time and which could have been useful when I was having to make choices. Nor do I appreciate having to make decisions when timing excludes all options bar one. Knowing what is happening means having the ability to exert influence. So I like to be kept informed.

That was my philosophy and those who worked with me both in politics and in football humoured me. They made my life easier and for that I thank them.

Reflecting on the limitations of this mantra I remembered some of the genuine surprises that happened to me.

Ted Heath

My introductory surprise happened when I was first trying to become an MP.

As the Conservative candidate I was contesting the Stockton & Billingham constituency during the October 1974 general election. Eight days before polling, my agent told me the party leader would be coming to Stockton on the Saturday.

I was told to meet Ted Heath in a city centre pub, and have a pint and a sandwich for the benefit of the press photographers and TV cameras. The media photograph Conservative Central Office really wanted was of us walking through the street market in Stockton, after which we would drive to Middlesbrough, though separately of course. On the Saturday afternoon Ted would make his set-piece speech for the benefit of the Sunday newspapers.

The day was a nightmare for me. While politicians – even pretend ones like I was then – seek the limelight, I was uncomfortable, both in the pub and with the transparent falseness of the arrangements, and lacked self-confidence. Strange as it may seem, all I wanted was for my first taste of national politics to be over as quickly as possible.

Ted was thirty minutes late. He and I may have been the only Conservatives in the pub and the locals did not hide their annoyance at this political and media invasion. Nor can I blame them. This was my first experience of how inconsiderate and pushy national press photographers can be in pursuit of a picture. Everyone in the overcrowded bar was inconvenienced.

Ted did not chat to me nor respond to my initiatives. We just stared at our pints, or at each other, like a couple of grumpy old men who wished they were elsewhere. The walk through the market went better, but as we made progress past the market stalls there was a last-minute change of plan. Some Central Office guru decided Ted should take this ready-made opportunity to speak to the crowd. A flat-bed truck was found from which he could make an informal speech. No one would introduce him. He would simply address the crowd and move on. Good old-fashioned politicking. As the local candidate I could stand behind him on the truck bed – silent.

The two of us climbed up and hundreds of people gathered around. Ted tapped the microphone to make sure it was on and this tapping quietened the crowd, increasing their sense of excitement. I did not anticipate the surprise that was coming.

In the silence, with the microphone live and in front of about 400 Stockton voters, Ted turned to me and said, 'What did you say your name is?' Local people got the message – their candidate was a nobody. He had not managed to register, even with his leader. Did

Stockton & Billingham really want a nobody MP? The embarrassment and surprise were almost literally painful.

I was less surprised that Ted *never* mentioned the incident to me,
then or later.

Cyprus

Most of my overseas ministerial visits were to the USA or the
European Commission, although I did visit a number of other
countries. One visit, to speak at a two-day health conference in
Cyprus, provided one of the bigger surprises of my career. I was
representing the UK because Virginia Bottomley MP, the Health
Secretary, declined to go. She said she did not enjoy such trips.

The President of Cyprus opened the conference and I was one
of the first morning speakers. This meant that, for the rest of the
conference, I was free both to listen and to 'network'.

At lunch on that first day our Ambassador enquired if I had plans
for that afternoon. No, other than attending the conference, I said.

Would I like to see something of Cyprus?

Yes I would, I replied, having learned previously that it was
usually sensible to accept such Ambassadorial offers. So off we went
in his official Bentley, the Union Jack flying on the bonnet.

We approached the demarcation zone, manned by troops with
guns. This separated Greek-controlled Cyprus, where we were,
from the rest of the island, which was controlled by Turkey. To my
surprise our car slowed but did not stop. The troops acknowledged
us but made no attempt to prevent us entering the demarcation
zone. We were given free passage. Although the UK had no
diplomatic relations with Turkish-controlled Cyprus, we spent the
next two-and-a-half hours touring that part of the island (having
removed the flag from the car bonnet). We saw beautiful scenery,
unspoiled and underdeveloped. Local people were neither friendly
nor unfriendly – more curious than anything else.

The next morning the Ambassador asked if I had any plans for
lunch. When I said 'no' he offered to take me out to eat. At the
end of the conference's morning session he and the car picked me

up and, as on the previous day, the health civil servants accompanying me were not included. Again, he did not say where we were going.

As we headed into the demarcation zone, without hindrance, the Ambassador explained that the former ambassadorial residence was situated in the zone. We still owned and maintained it, even made occasional use of its facilities, which was why the Greek Cypriot guards did not question our driving into the zone. They assumed we were going to the former residence. Clearly, no one on the Turkish side told them about our excursions into their territory. One surprise was explained. A bigger one awaited.

The residence, where we were going for lunch, was a large house set in spacious, well-maintained grounds. In front of the house was a large turning circle/parking area. On it were set out trestle tables covered with fine white tablecloths and many dishes of food. Gathered around the tables was a large group of men. Clearly most were Cypriots, dressed in jackets, trousers and open-neck shirts – before 'tie-less' became trendy. Some were embassy staff.

The Ambassador told me, in a matter-of-fact voice, that these men were the Turkish Cypriot Cabinet – the governing body of that part of the island with which we British had no formal relations, and that they were my guests for lunch.

Yes, I was surprised. I was way out of my comfort zone but the Ambassador gave me the impression that for him this was only mildly unusual, if at all.

I told him I was no expert on Britain/Greece/Turkey/Cyprus relations, antagonisms and sensitivities so a briefing would have been helpful. His answer was very smooth. 'Do not worry, minister, just rely on your political skill and judgement. If we did not have confidence in you we would not have arranged this.' It was only at this point that I realised that the previous day had been some sort of 'test', which apparently I had passed.

The Turkish Cypriots were charming and dignified guests. They were friendly in a reserved sort of way and seemed somewhat over-awed by the occasion. They also appeared to hold a British minister in higher regard than did most Brits! I tried not to show my surprise as all this developed.

No one asked any unduly awkward questions nor did they lobby me to persuade the British government to treat them as it treated the Greek Cypriots. We simply enjoyed the buffet and the unusual social occasion. I made sure I spoke to each man.

If this was not unusual enough, twenty minutes later I had the 'big' surprise. A car entered the grounds, stopped in front of the house and out of it stepped Rauf Denktash – President of the Turkish Republic of North Cyprus.

We were introduced by the Ambassador, whom he greeted as an old friend, and spent the next twenty minutes chatting over our buffet lunch. Clearly, Mr Denktash was pleased that I was there. He said so. He was instantly friendly if a little cautious, which was understandable. As with his Cabinet colleagues we avoided high-level policy discussion, though he did brief me on his Cyprus perspective.

When it came time for him to leave he did so with a genuinely appreciative goodbye. For obvious reasons there had been no speeches. His departure was the signal for the rest of us also to leave. Before we did I shook hands again with each member of the Cabinet. The Ambassador and I exchanged only pleasantries on the drive back until we were approaching my hotel, by which time my curiosity was no longer containable.

'Does the Foreign Office know what we are doing?' I enquired, having visions of my receiving serious earache from the Foreign Secretary or Prime Minister on my return home.

'You do not need to worry, minister,' was his non-reply. He said that he hoped I had enjoyed my visit, and let me know it was in our country's best interests to have friendly relations with those with whom we cannot have diplomatic relations. Then he added, as an aside, that I was to attend a reception that evening with the President of Cyprus. 'It might be a good idea not to tell him where we have spent the afternoon.' Even in my somewhat bemused and very surprised state, that sounded like common sense.

So much for the idea of ministers being in charge.

Other than my wife and Judi, I told no one of my diplomatic adventure, certainly not any civil servants. No full report was made to the Health Department. Indeed no one in it showed any interest in what the Ambassador and I had been doing. Or maybe they did know and decided that it would be better if the Secretary of State did not.

To this day I do not know if the Foreign Secretary approved, or even knew of, my visit to Turkish Cyprus and my meeting with its President and Cabinet. He never said and I never asked. On reflection this may have been an example of what many suspected – that the British Foreign Service appeared sometimes to have its own separate agenda which, put nicely, at times ran parallel with British government policy – though seldom behind it.

Rauf Denktash impressed me. And continued to surprise me. For the remaining years that I was a government minister he sent Betty and me a personal Christmas card each year.

John Major

Sometimes the biggest surprises in politics come from colleagues you think you know and with whom you have worked closely. Between 1995 and 1997 I spent a lot of time with John Major, occasionally surprised by the attitudes he adopted. But he kept one of the biggest surprises until we were both opposition backbenchers in the 1997–2001 parliament.

One day he rang me and asked if I would come to his office. Now. Arabella, his PA, greeted me coolly. Ever since she had created an unnecessary and, by me, unappreciated tension during the 1997 general election campaign she and I had sought to avoid each other whenever possible. John led the social pleasantries while Arabella produced the coffee.

After she had left us he asked me if I knew that James Goldsmith, the leader of the Referendum Party during the 1997 election, was to publish his memoirs the next day. The question reminded both of us that a significant number of Tory voters – mainly those of a right-of-centre, Eurosceptic persuasion who had become alienated

from us in government – had cast their votes for the Referendum
Party rather than us.

No, I replied. I had had no personal dealings with Goldsmith,
though as Party Chairman I had been aware of his pretty ruth-
less reaction when his party's candidate, Peter de Savary, standing
against Seb Coe in the 1997 election, had wanted to withdraw in
Seb's favour during that election.

John became hesitant. Then he dropped his bombshell. 'Did I tell
you that, during the run-up to election day, I talked to James about
whether there might be a basis on which our parties could work
together?'

I was amazed, which, for me, is a stage beyond surprised. I had
thought that in the period running up to the election John and
I had been pretty open with each other. We had certainly had a
number of very politically sensitive conversations both about policies – especially Europe – and Cabinet colleagues which, clearly, he
had trusted me not to leak. They have still not leaked.

'No, *Prime Minister*,' I replied. 'That was something else you
forgot to tell the Party Chairman.'

'Do you think he'll reveal this in his book?' John asked, ignoring
my sarcasm.

'I have no idea; I do not know the man. Nor do I know what
undertakings you gave each other before you embarked on your
conversation. On the other hand it would be a significant political
memory, by any standard, and it would certainly shine new light
on that piece of electoral history. For that reason, if for no other, I
would not be surprised if he did.'

'What do you think I should say to the media, if the story is
included?'

'I don't know. Presumably you could explain what you were trying
to achieve.'

'After the media finishes with me they will go to you. What will
you say?'

'I will think of something not too unhelpful,' I replied, 'but only
after I have got my surprise under control.'

John never told me details of the conversation, what if anything had been offered or why it had been rejected on both sides. Nor did I ask. On reflection I do not think John told any other senior colleagues of the contact. It was not just me who was cut out of the loop. Michael Heseltine would probably have told me had he known for he would not have been pleased. John would not have dreamed of telling Ken Clarke, who would have exploded, again. Nor, given my knowledge of Malcolm Rifkind (the Foreign Secretary), do I think he would have risked sharing the news with him.

On the whole it is a good job that the Prime Minister's initiative (he led me to believe, though his words were not specific, that he rather than Goldsmith had made the first move) was not successful. Any sort of pact would possibly have split our party, ensured ministerial resignations and caused, probably, a greater election defeat. Some wavering Conservative voters might have been attracted to remain loyal but many others would have decided that this was not an appropriate way for a great party to behave.

In any event such a pact would have made no difference to the overall electoral outcome. John must have known this, which is why his initiative was so surprising. He and I, in private, had examined in detail our European policies and their associated political personalities on a number of occasions. We had discussed changes in both, but each time he decided he did not feel comfortable nor was he so convinced that sufficient political or national benefit would follow to initiate any change. I came to the conclusion weeks before the election was even called that, having explored all possible permutations, our policies were set, as were the personalities to whom they would be entrusted. In fact John and I only had one more in-depth re-examination of our policies, which happened during the election campaign. No amount of internal Cabinet or party dissent (of which there was too much on both sides of the argument) was going to change John's position, nor were any late opinion polls. I had prepared for the election on that basis.

A paint job

The word 'surprise' is neutral. It covers both pleasant and unpleasant experiences. One of the less enjoyable ones occurred to my wife and me directly outside the Houses of Parliament.

In 1996, on what was clearly going to be the last State Opening of that parliament and my last one as a minister (given the opinion polls), Betty decided to come with me to the ceremony. Afterwards we met, as agreed.

Did she want to walk over to College Green with me and watch while I did a BBC interview on the Queen's Speech with John Prescott for Labour? Or did she want to wait in the family room until I returned when, whichever she decided, we would go for lunch, which had always been our plan?

I still remember how she hesitated for a few moments before deciding to accompany me. A fateful choice.

On a pleasant autumn day we crossed the road outside Parliament and started to make our way down the path which bisects College Green towards the temporary BBC studio. Suddenly there was shouting behind us. Several plastic bags of paint sailed past us and exploded on the pavement. Other bags followed, a number of which hit us. For a short time it rained paint – but only on Betty and me. Clearly I was the primary target but my wife got hit too. As the bags landed on and around us they disintegrated and we were both covered in paint – from head to toe.

Neither of us ran nor did we look round to see who was attacking us. We just kept walking.

Betty was magnificent. She never flinched. The look of quiet determination and disdain on her face said it all. Anyone who underestimates my wife makes a big mistake. She is quiet, loving and caring. She would do anything for people, especially the family, and is a great source of help and encouragement to many, including me. But she is tough and not easily intimidated.

For the record, a man and two women were arrested, charged and found guilty. They had decided to attack any recognisable member of the Cabinet who happened to be passing, claiming to be upset by the government's immigration policy. (To us, at the time, what they were shouting did not register. Neither of us had any idea what their problem was.)

I need to pause for a moment and say 'thank you' again to Alan Duncan MP, who was then my PPS and is now an impressive government minister. Alan had happened to be walking nearby, had seen the attack, noticed that there were no police present and decided to effect a citizen's arrest. Even more outstanding, he had had to hold the attackers for over twenty minutes, without physical restraints, until the police arrived due to an appalling miscommunication within the Metropolitan Police network. Without Alan's initiative and courage, no one would have been brought to justice. He was hailed for his 'going beyond the call of duty' action – and deservedly so. He was and still is a good friend.

Many subsequently commented on the fact that neither of us ran nor sought to confront. Perhaps our years in Northern Ireland had taught us to try to remain calm. But it would be fair to say that we were very 'surprised'. Because the attack was unexpected initially we had had some concern. However, this soon passed as it became obvious that there was no real physical threat.

Throughout it all we tried to exercise some outward Christian control. Betty in particular was widely praised for her restraint. She deserved every compliment she received. Being willing to be pelted with paint, without complaint, is a seldom-invoked test of the marriage vows.

Our clothes were ruined. I had taken so many hits that the paint had seeped through the suit fabric to my shirt which, literally, stuck to my back. Betty's clothes were covered in paint blotches made worse when I put my arm round her shoulder. But it was the huge number of paint spots on her hair that stand out in my memory along with the hour it took me to remove them with a turpentine-soaked cloth. Paint and turps – not the best hair spray!

As we approached the temporary BBC studio I took off my jacket. Those working there thrust paper towels at me to wipe some of the paint off my face and hair. John Prescott gave me his clean, carefully folded, pocket handkerchief. A thoughtful gesture.

The BBC team were obviously more concerned that I get miked up for the interview after the 1 p.m. news than they were about my condition. Poor Betty was left to fend for herself.

John Prescott's primary concern was neither my health nor peace of mind but that I would blame Labour supporters for the attack, the consequences of which were visible for all the TV viewers to see. I made the not unreasonable response that I did not know if the attackers were Labour Party members but I was sure they were not Conservatives.

The interview was a mixture of the Queen's Speech and the paint attack. Afterwards I gathered up my paint-sodden jacket and returned his handkerchief to John – still neatly folded and unused. His response reflected a return to normality when dealing with me. 'I don't want to read any newspaper stories about me offering you my handkerchief to clean up,' he said. If he was sorry about our ordeal he forgot to say so.

I thought about going into the Chamber in my painted state to sit on the government front bench while John Major opened the debate on the Queen's Speech for the government. While I was perceived as a tough and partisan chairman of the party, I was pretty sure that in the Chamber some sympathy and camarade-rie would outweigh any 'serves him right' feelings; though the latter would certainly exist. Of course there were then, and always will be, many who enjoy the sight of an MP covered in paint.

However, we went home. We needed to bathe and change our clothes. Also I wanted to make sure that Betty was not too upset by what had been a very unpleasant episode.

Eventually we collected something over £700 of the £1,000 deemed appropriate compensation by the magistrate. Regrettably, but in keeping with the experience of too many of my constituents, neither the police nor the court did anything to ensure that the justice which had been decreed would be fully enforced. That was not a surprise.

Honours even

In politics, as in other walks of life, money and power can be a combustible combination. Fair or not, one of the Blair government's legacies will be the so-called 'cash for honours' episode. Mr Blair protested that there was no causal link between giving money to the Labour Party and the receiving of honours. Many were sceptical. No police charges were brought, but, as is often the case in politics, some of the public still believed that there was no smoke without fire.

Rich people have always been among those elevated to the House of Lords or given knighthoods. Many have added valuable experience and wisdom to our legislature and given millions of pounds to good causes.

Some rich people – along with many others – donate money to the political party of their choice. This has always been the case and in a free society they should be allowed to do so. History is full of generous benefactors, of people doing good. As a result tens of millions have benefited. Such giving is part of the civic and social cement which holds society together. In a democracy, giving money to a political party in furtherance of the democratic process is definitely one way of doing good.

The law, however, draws a distinction between doing good and buying influence. It is illegal for political parties to sell honours. Laws, however, do not stop individuals from hoping that an exception may occur in their case. Nor do they make people good; they simply mitigate bad or dubious behaviour.

I know some will say that it is easy for me, with both a knighthood and a peerage, to be cool about the importance of honours. I was genuinely surprised when John Major broached the issue of a knighthood. Yet there are many for whom these aspirations are hugely important. Incidentally, if ever their wish were granted, they would soon be disappointed by how little difference a title makes to their daily lives.

Even those with a scrupulous eye on the law and propriety relating to honours can quickly become aware of the grey areas caused by raised exceptions. These can often be generated either by the politicians or the potential financial donors while both carefully shy away from explicit promises.

As Party Chairman I inherited and applied a strict policy on party donations and did not hesitate to repeat it to anyone I thought needed to hear it. And I did so in a way which dispelled any idea that part or all of the policy was negotiable.

We did not accept money from:

- Donors who attached strings to the donation
- Anonymous donors
- Foreign donors
- Criminal donors

Over the intervening years the law has changed as has the public mood. Today there are more restrictions on giving and more openness about who gives – including how much they give – which primarily derive from strongly held media-driven perceptions rather than much established wrongdoing. I inherited a policy of confidentiality – which implied trustworthiness – and was told to work within it. I did so, honourably. I was never asked by John Major to be a financially reforming chairman (such an idea was not on his agenda) – just to raise money. I was then, and remain to this day, sceptical that any individual's donation can buy, in policy terms, anything seriously worth having.

Since my day the issue of political donations has become more akin to a blood sport. Political correctness has led to a nasty habit that tends towards reputation trashing. Causal links between established wrongdoing and inappropriate influence, on the one hand, and political donations or benefits in kind, on the other, seem to me pretty shallow, for the most part, when examined objectively.

That having been said, personally I would have preferred more openness even in my time. Transparency makes it much harder for dubious political instincts to prosper in both giver and receiver. It also makes it harder for political opponents and the media to generate smears and unfounded allegations.

The best political defence to charges of buying influence or honours remains openness, coupled with an appropriate, independent watchdog organisation. I wish we had been the government which started the process of greater statutory transparency. Left to myself, and without the pressure of having to gear up the party to fight a general election, I would have done so.

Despite the law and our tough rules, I have no doubt some of those who dreamed of honours may have hoped that they were important enough to influence the process. Such dreams were not purchasable in my time though one person's 'dream' created one of the biggest surprises in the whole of my parliamentary career.

Most of our donor contact was handled by the party's joint treasurers – the late Lord Hambro and Lord Harris of Peckham. They deserve most of the credit for the huge sums of money raised. Their personal integrity and persuasiveness helped to convince people to give, while their characters protected the party from unfounded accusations. Subsequently Phil and Pauline Harris became our personal friends. They are models of outstanding philanthropic generosity.

One day Charles Hambro rang to tell me that a very well-known businessman wanted to meet me privately. I told him to go ahead and make the necessary arrangements. To have refused such a well-known man would have caused unnecessary offence. The two of us met for breakfast in Charles's London flat, which he had made available, because it was private – as the man had requested.

While we ate the man told me at length, almost lyrically, how much he appreciated our country and its institutions, particularly the House of Lords. In glowing terms he reflected on its wisdom and constitutional importance. He thought it must be wonderful to be a member, to be able to contribute to the governance and greatness of our country.

I listened with care. He did not specifically ask me to arrange a peerage for him so that his 'dream' could be fulfilled. But his message was crystal clear even though he spoke on the right side of propriety. Fortunately he was in full flow and not expecting me to say anything. So I just listened.

He then changed the subject, telling me of his long-term support of the Conservative Party (of which I knew of no supporting evidence), of his admiration for John Major and that he would like to do something tangible to help us, for he did not want a Labour government – Old or New. He clearly understood that any gesture, if it were seriously to improve our chances of re-election, would need to be spectacular. So he had decided to buy a national newspaper and direct its editorial policy to be supportive of the Conservatives for however many months remained before the general election. Did I have a newspaper preference?

It would be no exaggeration to say that I was genuinely surprised but I kept a straight face throughout his pitch. No one previously had offered me a national newspaper, with or without strings attached. I thanked him for his generous instincts, professed myself ignorant of which newspaper proprietors might be willing to sell quickly and said that he should probably give his idea further careful analysis. I had no suggestions.

As for the House of Lords, I reminded him, hopefully with a light touch, that individuals became members through processes for appointment which were both well established and policed. I did not promise or even hint at the possibility of further contact, much less a further meeting to pursue either issue. Indeed I made absolutely sure he received no encouragement for his implied linkage.

We parted amicably. My chances of an editorial chair vanished without trace as his car turned the corner! From that day to this he and I have not spoken. No national newspaper was purchased. No peerage, or any other honour, was offered, much less bestowed, by the government or the Conservative Party. To the best of my knowledge the party did not receive a subsequent donation.

He may have continued to dream, but dreaming is neither illegal nor unethical. If it were all of us would be in trouble. As Jesus once said, the one who has never sinned should cast the first stone.

In due course this gentleman was honoured by New Labour. I would have enjoyed being a fly on the wall during any discussions held prior to that announcement.

It is a good idea, minister

One Transport 'surprise' was the nearest I came to having to consider resigning as a minister. It arose around a major policy mistake I made while in that department. Subsequent governments would disagree that it was a mistake. Secretaries of state, in both parties, have expanded the policy at enormous cost and little useful purpose, in my judgement.

While secretaries of state have to approve all policy decisions they often delegate to junior ministers the responsibility for carrying forward the legislative detail. There is simply too much work for one person to do.

In my day legislation governing motorway speed limits was inflexible. Limits were imposed by parliamentary regulation and could be changed only by regulation. There was no such thing as variable speed limits. They were 'invented' during my time.

Responsibility for initiating this new policy lay with one of my ministers. The plan in essence was to erect gantries across parts of the M25 on which variable speed limits – 20 to 60 mph – could be posted and changed in light of prevailing travelling conditions.

I was initially sceptical. Officials were righteously insistent. I should have maintained my scepticism but instead allowed myself to be worn down. On congested roads drivers drive more slowly, especially if the weather or traffic conditions are poor. External restrictions are unnecessary and often irrelevant. I know this is obvious but I missed it.

I should have rigorously questioned officials' insistence that external variable speed restrictions were needed before agreeing the proposal but did not. I could argue that I was too busy on other ministerial matters and, anyway, it was right to trust the judgement of my ministerial colleagues. But the fact remains; I approved the proposal without sufficiently rigorous scrutiny. So the control room was established, signs were erected, money was spent. We were ready to unveil our newest idea.

The department thought the initiative so important that the Secretary of State should do the motorway launch. A date was fixed. A draft press release was written. On the morning before the launch, my private secretary came into my office. One look at her and I knew I was in for a big unpleasant surprise.

'There is a major problem, Secretary of State,' she said. 'Our lawyers have just told me that no legal cover exists for the introduction of variable speed limits on the M25. Parliament needs to approve this scheme but no regulations have ever been submitted for its consideration. If you decide to proceed before legislative cover is obtained, the government would be vulnerable. Speed limit reductions would have no legal validity. The police could not enforce them nor prosecute those who broke them. In those circumstances no one knows what might be the effect on vehicle insurance. Your personal position could become very difficult.

'How do you wish to proceed, Secretary of State?'

She and I talked about how we had got into this pickle. The preparatory work was the responsibility of the Highways Agency. No Transport Department official knew whether they had taken legal advice or, if not, why not. And if they had taken advice, why they had not shared it with the department.

Unwittingly I was on the verge of acting illegally – big time. My excuses would have cut no ice with the Prime Minister, my colleagues, the media or the public. I could be accused of being negligent – certainly incompetent. No politician has a rosy future in those circumstances.

If I called off the launch there could still be significant political embarrassment through the press. Fortunately for me my private secretary, with typical sound judgement, had put the press release on hold.

The full and very frank conversation I had with the chastened chief executive of the Highways Agency and his legal director which followed need not detain us. The bottom line was that no legal advice existed, no legislative cover had been sought and no way would I trust either of them in future. I think they understood that.

After officials had left my office my private secretary, Una O'Brien, and I quickly agreed that the launch had to be postponed.

I would not knowingly act illegally. Nor did I need senior departmental officials to tell me what was right. I believed they should have tested the legality of the proposal with the agency long before it came to me. Clearly they had not. In those circumstances I decided they were disqualified from offering opinions on what should happen next.

As at that time I trusted only my private secretary, who alone had undertaken proper due diligence, together we drafted a new press release which said, simply, that the launch had been postponed for technical reasons. The phrase 'technical reasons' is often used by government. Never, in my experience, was it used more accurately or did it cover so much trouble.

I was very fortunate. No journalist queried the change in plan. Neither departmental officials nor the Highways Agency thought it was in their interests to leak what had happened.

When the crisis had passed, I signalled to the departmental Permanent Secretary that I wanted to review the running of the agency. However, before we had a chance to do so, John Major resigned as Conservative Party leader and I was moved from Transport to become Party Chairman.

Parliament later approved variable speed limits. In my view governments since my time have wasted millions of pounds of taxpayers' money. The number of variable speed limits has grown enormously to no discernibly useful purpose. The decision I made in good faith was the wrong one. It was wrong because the limits are ineffective and unnecessary, as I often remind myself when crawling along a motorway at 15 mph when the sign says the limit is 60 or driving myself on an open road without another car in sight when the sign says there is a 40 mph limit. Millions of pounds of taxpayers' money had been diverted from better use. I apologise. Hindsight is always 20–20; and always comes too late.

His Holiness

A few years after my appointment to the Northern Ireland Office, the Archbishop of Armagh, Cardinal O'Fiaich died, in 1990. At an appropriate time following his funeral people started speculating about who the Church would choose as his successor. One morning at 'prayers' (our regular meeting of NIO ministers and senior officials) we were informed that the Papal Nuncio had been in touch with the department. It was his job to take soundings throughout Ireland, both within the Roman Catholic Church and outside it, before offering advice to Rome on who the new Archbishop should be. He had expressed interest in learning any views the British government, in the shape of the NIO, might have. This sparked a long discussion.

Should the government have a view on this Church matter and, if so, should we share it with the Nuncio? If we were willing to share it, should he meet ministers or officials or just receive a letter? Was his request too politically sensitive for ministerial involvement? Should it all be handled by the Permanent Secretary or another senior civil servant, like John McConnell? What if news leaked of government's involvement; would there be unhelpful political or possibly violent repercussions? And if news did leak would our involvement, even only as a consultee, be thought to undermine the spiritual strength of the new appointee?

We talked for a long time and kept coming back to the question of whether it was the job of government to have a view on who the new Archbishop should be.

Finally, and to my surprise, the Secretary of State and officials all agreed that we should respond positively and that the task of briefing the Nuncio should be entrusted to me. For the avoidance of doubt, I had not volunteered. They decided I was the minister with the most knowledge of Irish church matters so I should talk him through the various options. But who should I recommend? Whoever I decided would be the government's judgement, I was told. But be careful, the Secretary of State added. And be discreet. This is highly politically sensitive. News must not leak. The implication I took from these warnings, whether intended or not, was that if there were a public row any discussion with the Nuncio would be explained away in terms of my having taken a personal initiative.

I could just see the spokesman saying: 'Well, you know how it is with Mawhinney and religion...' though I was certain Peter Brooke would not have joined in the spin operation.

John McConnell handled the arrangements once he and I had agreed them. The Nuncio, Archbishop Gerada, whose brother, it transpired, was my constituent, was invited to be my guest for lunch at Hillsborough. I also invited six or eight other Catholics who were prominent in the Province's business or public life. The Papal Nuncio happened to be in Northern Ireland on Church business, they were told – which was true. As was the normal courtesy in such circumstances, the government was hosting a lunch for him, which was also true.

Unknown to these guests, who were invited for a 1.00 p.m. lunch, Archbishop Gerada was invited for 11.30 a.m. It was a beautiful sunny day and, after coffee, the two of us walked alone in the magnificent solitude of Hillsborough's grounds. We talked of bishops and significant Catholic laity. I offered my clear opinion, for which he thanked me, saying others had spoken similarly.

I was delighted, but not surprised, when the Pope appointed Bishop Cahal Daly to Armagh. He and I never spoke about my peripheral role in his appointment process. No doubt he would have been as surprised as I was. This was not what a simple (Protestant) Belfast boy expected to be doing or probably was expected to do, particularly as a government minister.

It is wonderful and surprising what doors a shared Christian faith can open.

10

Drugs, OK?

Politics is a strange mixture of words, the will to do and action. Action and will are particularly important. The failure to deliver a promise or commitment at a level that satisfies public expectation can be very damaging to a government – as all Prime Ministers discover.

But words are important too. Some of the most effective politicians are those who can inspire or restrain others just by the words they use. Churchill during the Second World War comes to mind. Barack Obama winning his first presidential campaign is a fine contemporary example.

And the will to govern – to identify an issue that needs to be addressed, to develop a policy, to apply that policy appropriately and then to defend it against the facts of life – figures crucially in all aspects of politics.

Perhaps the single biggest failure of government policy throughout my years of political activity under Thatcher, Major, Blair, Brown and Cameron has been the failure effectively to combat illegal drugs. The use of such drugs has increased over the years, with only an occasional dip, despite robust ministerial words, lots of activity and good intentions and the spending of hundreds of millions of pounds.

As Health Minister, for two years I was responsible for handling the health aspects of the government's drug strategy. The way we, as a government, handled the issue was not always impressive; sad given the serious and at times dangerous health consequences of illegal drug taking. Even more sadly, our record reflects the standard outcome of little significant change over the past twenty-five years.

Personally I do not approve of and have never been attracted by the use of illegal drugs, whether they are mind bending, mood changing, performance enhancing or euphoria inducing. Their widespread use reflects the drift of our society away from personal accountability, respect for the law and some element of rationally based decision making and towards one which is dominated by the supremacy of 'feelings'. During my years as an MP our society moved from having a reasonably well-developed sense of right and wrong towards a 'tolerant pragmatism' which derides such absolutes and lauds 'how you feel' and 'doing your own thing' as long as these do not 'hurt' anyone else. Drugs, of course, do hurt the user and other innocent people but that reality has not registered overly much in the general consciousness. It is hard for government to develop a sense of community if individualism is rampant. 'I know what is best for me' can clash with the idea of the common good.

Incidentally, for those interested in Christian perspectives, both these trends, drifting away from right and wrong and elevating what is good for me over the common good, are contrary to what God intended of government. He ordained the institution to have two main, practical functions. Firstly, to define right and wrong and then to promote the former and oppose the latter. Secondly, to raise taxes to be spent for the common good (Romans 13).

Emotion is very important in national, community and personal life but it cannot be allowed to become the only or even the overwhelming factor which determines, explains, defines and/or excuses all human behaviour. In case you think I exaggerate, consider our media, which is a good mirror of our society. Interviews based on 'who, where, when and why?' have been largely replaced by 'how do you feel?'

I realise that to social liberals, trendy pragmatists and the so-called modern young I am old fashioned and out of touch. So be it; but that does not necessarily mean I am wrong. Unlike too many of them I believe illegal drugs can and do damage physical, mental and psychological health; and the more drugs are used the more damage is likely to be caused. That damage may be immediate or become apparent later. The fact that no immediate downside seems to occur after drug taking has never been to me a persuasive argument for indulging. Cigarettes are a good, and parallel, example. The feelings induced do not last. Some feelings are bad as are some of the consequences of smoking.

As a radiation biologist I know that small doses of ionising radiation, hardly discernible, may not cause immediate, observable damage in humans or animals. In the long term, however, cumulative damage – including cancer – becomes apparent and may be permanent and lethal.

As a Christian I have been taught, and always believed, that human beings are more whole when they retain an unimpaired faculty to make rational decisions and moral judgements. Drug taking distorts and undermines those functions. I do not believe that when God created men and women in His image His ideal was that they should exist in an emotionally driven mental miasma.

My purpose in these reflections, however, is not primarily to persuade you to my view on drugs. Rather I hope to help you understand drug-related issues in public policy terms, so that you can form a judgement about how government works or does not work.

Governments' official view of drugs during my thirty-plus years in Parliament is easy to summarise. The use of 'illegal' drugs is wrong. Not all drugs are equally damaging. People caught breaking the law should be punished. Levels of punishment should vary depending on the allegedly damaging nature of the drugs used. (Sadly New Labour undermined this one.) The suppliers of drugs should be treated more harshly than the users. I believe all these statements and have defended them in public.

In reality, however, government hypocrisy on this subject is never too far below the surface. Take, for example, the fact that an increasing number of people now caught using drugs are being cautioned by the police rather than punished by the courts for their law breaking. The reasons for this are not complicated but are worth exploring because they are hugely indicative of the reality of our national drugs policy.

More and more people, and in particular more and more middle-class people, take drugs. By doing so they effectively signal their unwillingness to be subject to the law of the land. In other words they are refusing to give their consent to be governed in this area of their lives. The greater the number of people taking this view the harder it is for government to insist on a rigorous application of what Parliament has decided should happen. And the danger is that these people, once they realise that there is no serious penalty for withholding consent, will be tempted to withhold their consent to be governed in other aspects of their lives.

Additionally, were the laws to be applied righteously, government expenditure would have to soar. A significant number of extra police, judges, court officials and prison officers would have to be hired; the latter because more jails would need to be built. Citizens would complain bitterly about the extra expenditure and tax. In the process many of them would be signalling their contempt for the underlying policy as well as complaining about the raid on their pockets. So governments continue to talk tough but act less so. That discontinuity is what I labelled hypocrisy.

This analysis may be dismissed by some as old fashioned and hard line. In fact it simply plays out the logic of our legislation and practice. In my view the reality is that government cannot overlay appropriate action on its rhetoric because the public would simply not stand for it. The rebellion would be both economic and social. The level of taxes needed to pay for a coherent and effective drugs policy would cause considerable upset. And that upset would be enhanced by the disruption that fines and jail sentences would cause in the lives of hundreds of thousands of people, maybe millions; not to mention the criminal records that so many otherwise upstanding members of society would incur and the turmoil those records would bring into their otherwise respectable lives.

The truth is that many feel comforted when they hear harsh words about the perils of drugs – as long as no one, especially government, takes those words to their logical conclusion. If governments were to speak in line with how they act the public would charge that ministers had gone soft on drugs. The perception that such an allegation would be politically damaging is widespread in government. Even those who take illegal drugs do not seem to mind the tough rhetoric – it is tough action they resist.

The signs that many do not really want government policy, as enacted by Parliament, to be rigorously implemented are all around us. For example, as I said earlier, increasingly the instinct of the police, encouraged by government, is to caution offenders rather than prosecute them. This is defended by political and police rhetoric which tries to persuade the public that cautioning is a legally serious matter and a significant deterrent to future law breaking. The public does not believe this for a minute, maybe because it is not so and the number of drug takers keeps rising.

Another social phenomenon is increasingly evident. Drugs used to be a 'problem' associated primarily with the working class and those who were poorly educated. Their drug use was explained, or excused, as some form of escapism from relatively hopeless lives. That rationalisation never impressed me. The number of 'poor' people who live good, productive lives, who become first-class parents and role models, who are moral and ethical leaders in their communities, who set standards and values for their neighbours and who become financially successful in their own businesses or in the nation's business, is too high, in terms of both quality and quantity, to justify sweeping generalisations which allegedly explain away drug taking by the poor. The dream of personal betterment and determination to live upright lives has never been the sole prerogative of the middle classes, however much some would like to think so.

When the middle classes and professional people started to take drugs in increasing numbers, these so-called working-class explanations became embarrassing to those who made them. They were no longer persuasive. So spin took over. Social liberals linked up with elements of the media and so-called 'recreational' drugs were born. 'Recreational' was a great spin. It sounded legal. It sounded healthy. It sounded fun. It clothed the middle classes' behaviour with a cloak of justification and virtue. After all, recreation is widely perceived to be good.

But the taking of such drugs is still illegal.

Thereafter political and social rhetoric started to drift away from what the law still requires. The implication of the new definition was that recreational drug taking was new, acceptable and not really what the law had in mind. Social drug taking in small amounts could do no harm – surely? And anyway celebrities did it, as in some cases was publicly obvious, so it must be OK. We all knew that it was not, but no one insisted that the emperor wore no clothes. The very size of this new recreational phenomenon made the thought of tackling it politically unattractive. Too many self-important people would be upset.

Government drug policy has always included prevention and helping people get off drugs as well as being about deterrence and punishment. Ministerial rhetoric regularly proclaims this. Unfortunately the applications of the law and statements of policy are often out of sync.

Deterrence is impossible to measure accurately because we have no way of knowing what really goes on in the minds and hearts of millions of individuals. But the rising number of users over the years suggests that government policy has failed this objective.

Some are punished but possibly only a minority, which itself induces public cynicism. Indeed it could be argued that the number of users might even imply some element of public approval for drug taking. The numbers may also be interpreted as indicating that, for many people, the risk of drug taking leading to legal punishment is so small that it is a risk worth taking. After all few people willingly and knowingly volunteer to acquire a criminal record.

If this analysis is even approximately correct then it raises a fundamental question. Should government action not proceed more closely in line with legislation? Or indeed is the legislation deliverable?

As for the important goals of prevention and helping people off drugs, the issue is whether the will exists to deliver them. Let me give you two illustrations. During my year as shadow Home Secretary, following the election of the Labour government in 1997, I decided I needed to learn more about our prison system. Years as an MP and minister had broadened my understanding of security and police work. But, apart from visiting the notorious Maze Prison in Northern Ireland, my knowledge of prisons and the prison service was limited. Incidentally, for a short time, I was Northern Ireland's Prisons Minister. I soon clashed with officials and prison staff on the realities of who was actually dictating policy and why there was, to my mind, a large divergence between rhetoric and reality – but that is another story.

So, to educate myself, over a period of months I visited about ten prisons all over the country, including the high-security Whitemoor and major prisons in Liverpool and Durham as well as open and women's prisons.

Prison governors and officers welcomed me courteously. Drug smuggling and use were recurring topics of conversation. Their common view was that a significant proportion of the drugs in prison were brought there by those who visited the prisoners. Neither keeping visitors and inmates apart nor searching visitors seemed to be an effective barrier to drug movement. Some drugs were thrown in over the prison walls, after pre-arrangement.

'Do you use trained sniffer dogs to detect drugs during the visiting periods?' I asked.

'No,' was the reply. Neither prisoners nor their visitors would like that. The procedures would be too intrusive. Morale would suffer. I understood the argument. I simply did not agree with it, if the prevention of drug taking was to be a priority.

Politicians' rhetoric about tough anti-drug regimes in prisons does not bear serious scrutiny. And the officers' statements were probably true. What society and Parliament need to decide is whose views should prevail. If the decision is taken to get tough, we would all have to brace ourselves against the possibility of a bout – maybe a prolonged bout – of prison unrest. The public's determination and patience would need to be tested – maybe severely – before some prisoners and officers would accept that the days of drugs in prisons were to be over or at least definitely on their way out. But think also how prisoners would benefit if that were to happen.

I remember tabling some parliamentary questions in the first New Labour parliament about combating drug use in prisons. The answers indicated that the whole prison service had only a very few trained drug sniffer dogs. In other words even if the service had wanted to move its practice closer to ministers' tough rhetoric, it could not have done so. The reality is that neither ministers nor the prison service seriously want the severe disruption in prisons which a robust anti-drug policy would create. The smooth running of our prisons requires an element of accommodation between officers and inmates. A tough drugs policy would destroy that accommodation though, probably, only in the short term. 'Out of sight, out of mind' might be an understandable practical political policy, but it does nothing to respect human dignity or health.

Estimates vary but, to choose a conservative one, let us say 50 per cent of all prison inmates have had a relationship with drugs. Some were caught manufacturing or distributing drugs. A number were caught in possession. Prisoners committed crimes to generate the money needed to feed their habits: theft, burglary, assault, fraud, murder. Sometimes the drug problem took the form of violence on the streets or against personal partners. Given these facts any sensible policy should accord high priority to using prison time to make a serious effort to break prisoners' drug habits. This would be good for the offenders, would create social benefit and would reduce violence in communities up and down the land. And crime levels would fall alongside demand for prison places.

Sadly, it is simply not a political or prison service priority to make genuine, hard-edged efforts to get prisoners off drugs. If doing so was a priority then the flow of drugs into prisons would stop or at least slow to a trickle. Another aspect of a rigorous anti-drug policy might be to link freedom from drugs, scientifically established, to early prisoner parole. Presently such an idea is unthinkable.

Let me digress for a moment to add a further depressing and related observation. In my prison visits I regularly talked to prisoners with mental health problems and enquired how these were being handled and whether drug use had played a part in the genesis of these problems. Did they receive treatment intended to improve their underlying health condition or was any treatment simply focused on short-term control of their behaviour to make it socially more acceptable? The replies suggested that the latter prevailed and, in many cases, illegal drug use was indeed associated with the incidence of mental illness.

Through the good offices of one of my former medical students who remains a friend, I visited a large prison medical unit. While talking to an enormous man, bulging with muscle, I became conscious that prison officers and doctors had formed a close ring around me. Later I was told that this man's mental illness caused him to attack strangers with no advance warning. His behaviour was being 'controlled', I was assured.

After visiting a number of prison medical units I decided that the effectiveness of our policy on treating mental health problems in prison was about on a par with the effectiveness of our policy on dealing with illegal drug use. Very depressing. I should add that the medical staff are not to blame. Some of our most dedicated medical practitioners and nurses work in prisons.

My visit to the women's prison was particularly disturbing. Many inmates appeared resigned and hopeless, more so than was the case in men's prisons. So that I could develop a better understanding, the governor arranged for the two of us to have lunch in the prisoners' dining room with six women. They each told me why they were there and that they were well treated. I am sure this was true but given the presence of the governor it was unlikely they would have said anything else.

The part of the conversation that particularly sticks in my mind was about their futures. When asked if they thought they would be back in prison after completing their sentences two of the six immediately said 'yes'. The governor estimated privately that four or five of the six would return.

The reasons were salutary. None of the six had educational achievements or work-related skills. They believed they had no one to help them into decent jobs. Regrettably they were not learning anything in prison which would significantly help their employ-ment prospects – even supposing potential employers would prefer ex-cons over other job applicants.

So these women planned to return to the 'care' and 'protection' of the men with whom they were living when they were arrested. Most of these men were involved in the drugs trade, the governor told me. So the women's prospects were poor and drug related. But what struck me most forcefully was that no one really seemed to care.

The women themselves were resigned and hopeless in the most fundamental meaning of those words. The state seemed not to care. The women's communities and partners seemed not to care. And by its absence in any meaningful sense, most of the Christian church seemed not to care, which was important to me if not to everyone.

There is nothing like visiting prisons and learning what really happens there to make you want to re-examine society's strong preference to lock up people. We do that more than any other European country. Maybe we should. But surely when we do we should make much more strenuous efforts to ensure that, once released, the prospect of people returning to prison is greatly reduced. Given the present high reoffending rates, that would be a considerable challenge and a goal to cherish.

Some prisoners are evil. Some are without any discernible moral framework and have no respect for others – their rights, their well-being or their property. But many struck me as just helpless to help themselves. If the collective 'we' do not help them, they will remain helpless. It would be in our own interest, even our own selfish inter-est, to help them. Strongly linking eligibility for parole to attaining higher educational standards or achieving greater vocational skills would be a good place to start, as would addressing the use of drugs.

'Tough on crime, tough on the causes of crime' was a great sound bite. Everyone liked the first part (and many now feel let down by New Labour's failure to deliver). The second part was equally important but by and large it was ignored, to the detriment of us all.

Government rhetoric about helping drug takers to kick their habit, whether in the community or in prison, is impressive. The problem is that any real will is hard to find.

For years, prevailing government policy has been based on 'harm reduction'; not abstinence, not stopping drug use, not 'just say no'. These latter were dropped by so-called experts as ineffective. Harm reduction was a safer strategy, not least because it was harder to assess its effectiveness. Now that is cynical. In reality harm reduction may help a minority off drugs eventually, but the majority are simply helped to pursue their habit more safely. This was the common policy under all governments.

Harm reduction should, of course, be an important component of any drug policy; syringe replacement, for example, can literally save lives. But at its heart lies continuing drug use.

A harm reduction policy, which gives only a nod to stopping drug use, is a policy which does not rise to the magnitude of the challenge which drugs pose. Maybe it does not even appreciate the magnitude of that challenge.

In case you think I exaggerate let me tell you of a visit I paid to Liverpool as the Health Minister responsible for drugs policy. I went to one of the main NHS centres which served local drug users. The staff greeted me warmly and were pleased that I was visiting them rather than just concentrating on the city's hospitals.

They started by stressing that they were not judgemental towards those who were using drugs. Although drug taking was illegal, they would never contemplate referring any case to the police. They then briefed me on their work, for about twenty-five minutes, during which I listened carefully and said nothing. They told me about the services they offered, the harm reduction advice they gave, their work in the community and how they tried to stabilise some people's habits when they were in danger of getting out of control. They offered a good and professional service.

The staff impressed me as well intentioned, good hearted, socially aware people who were dedicated to helping their 'clients'. Clearly they worked hard to make their clients' lives more tolerable – and I am sure they did.

When it was my turn to speak I warmly commended and thanked them for their efforts. Later I asked how many people they had succeeded in getting off drugs in the previous twelve months. The mood of the meeting changed. They made clear they were outraged both by the question and by my nerve in asking it. They were not in the business of 'getting people off' drugs. Having that as a target would be judgemental. Clients should decide for themselves if they wanted to kick their drug habits. It was not the centre's job to intervene or seek to direct. They were there simply to help people protect themselves.

My second enquiry unintentionally, but interestingly, added petrol to the growing flames. 'You told me', I said, 'that you focus on treating the whole person. That is important and I welcome that. The churches in Liverpool, with their two archbishops usually acting as one in public policy terms, are experts in dealing with the spiritual needs of people and in supporting them socially. Their areas of expertise complement those things that the NHS does well. Bearing in mind this excellent focus on helping the whole person, what relationships exist with the churches and what do they contribute to implementing this focus that you are pursuing?'

Their reaction was not just negative, it bordered on the vitriolic. Only the chairman of the NHS Mersey Region, who was accompanying me, appeared to understand the point I was making. The NHS drug team definitely would not.

In reality, there was no focus on the whole person. And, I was told, asking for the spiritual and socially supportive help of the Churches was out of the question. They might have different priorities! Clearly obliterating drug habits was not that important to this dedicated group of NHS employees.

In the time it took me to get back to the department an official complaint had been lodged about the inappropriateness of my questions. How dare I, a mere minister, 'attack' these 'experts'. This depressing response to my visit simply underlined the failure of our policy. Their reaction to the sort of questions most members of the public would have asked illustrated just how far apart government rhetoric and action had drifted. We told the public we were on their side in the battle against drugs – but in practice too often we were not.

My civil servants' reactions to the Liverpool team's complaints were interesting. Some defended their minister. Others seemed sympathetic to the views of the Liverpudlian team. Most lacked the energy, nerve or integrity to say anything much.

Corroborative evidence existed to sustain my suspicion. In my time – and I have no reason to think that any major change has taken place since within Richmond House (DoH headquarters) – there was a strong antipathy to examining, with an open mind, alternative drug treatments, most of which were designed to free people from their drug habit.

The late Dr Meg Patterson, a Christian doctor friend, had successfully used electrical stimuli procedures to help people break drug habits. She and her husband George also provided Christian counselling. The results were impressive in the relatively small number of patients treated. I had to instruct the department to examine her work to determine if it could or should become an additional anti-drugs weapon in our NHS armoury. Their scepticism was instinctive not scientific, and their examination ceased when I left the department.

Another small Christian residential programme had better results in freeing people from their addictions than did the NHS. I invited them in to meet officials, whose reactions were similar to those towards Dr Patterson. Again the examination of the process stopped when I left the department.

This divergence between words and actions did not apply only in the drug treatment arena. There was a parallel divergence within government itself. Michael Howard, then Home Secretary, took a robust view towards those who acted illegally with drugs. He wanted tough penalties applied not just to the importers and sellers but also to the users, especially those who used the more dangerous drugs. A lot of people shared his thesis that 'prison works'.

At least in one respect it absolutely did. Prison's primary success lay in taking some drug sellers and users off the streets. In that sense it was an effective harm reduction policy for society at large and important for that reason.

Virginia Bottomley, then Secretary of State for Health, took a somewhat different view to Michael. To her drugs were more of a health/social problem which required an added emphasis on treatment rather than just on punishment. Of course she supported prison sentences, particularly for sellers, but users needed more sensitive handling.

With Michael and Virginia not seeing eye to eye, government drug policy became stalled because no agreement could be reached at Cabinet Committee level. The more the two secretaries of state dug in, the less prospect there was for agreement on an effective policy. One day, during a vote, the Leader of the House, Tony Newton, asked me to drop into his Commons office for a chat. Although at that time he was senior to me, he and I got on well. I said I would. No civil servants would be present. It was to be a political chat, and private. Please do not tell the department, he said, so I did not.

Tony told me that the Prime Minister was unhappy with the state of the government's drug policy. He wanted issues between ministers resolved so that we had a coherent strategy under clear leadership. In short, he wanted Tony to become the drugs policy minister and to be its public face. What did I think and, more importantly, how did I think Virginia would react? We talked about the issue for quite a long time, including the personalities of the two secretaries of state. The problem was that their positions were hard to reconcile. I told him I thought it unlikely that either Michael or Virginia would easily give up their departmental responsibility in his favour. And their sometimes strained chemistry made working together more difficult.

As we bounced ideas around, I suggested a different approach. Why did the Prime Minister not set up a new oversight committee on drugs policy which he, Tony, could chair? Clearly the Home Office and the Health Department would need to be represented on it. He could invite me and my opposite number at the Home Office, David Maclean, to be the two departmental ministers and deputy chairmen, I suggested. All three of us got on well and respected and liked each other. And if deals had to be done, which meant that both departments had to 'give' a little, then why not let the ministers of state take the strain? As Cabinet ministers, Michael and Virginia could always talk to Tony outside the more formal structures of the committee's work and at the same time maintain their departmental responsibilities. They could also be briefed by their ministers, in whom each had confidence.

Tony thought this was a good idea. He said he would talk to David and consult his Cabinet colleagues and the Prime Minister. Soon this new format was in operation. It gave us a more coherent government policy in public but the gap between rhetoric and action did not close noticeably. As predicted, the oversight committee seldom met, while Tony got on with the job.

This problem got worse after we lost the general election in 1997. Tony Blair appointed a retired senior police officer to be his drugs 'tsar'. This was less effective than our arrangement because, unlike Tony Newton, he did not have the political strength which came from Cabinet membership. I said at the time of the appointment that this experiment would not work and that the failure would be the fault of the system and not of the individual. It did not work.

Labour's record was further eroded by a Home Secretary decision: to reclassify certain health-damaging illegal drugs as less dangerous than in reality they were. This meant that possession and use of them became less serious offences and police cautions became the normal response to users. Previously they had been subject to more severe penalties. I fear these decisions owed more to ministerial unwillingness to provide necessary additional prison places and finance than it did to enlightened (in their eyes) social policy.

Eventually New Labour set about dismantling its new system of drug classification. The health dangers of some drugs – dismissed as scaremongering earlier – were rediscovered.

As I reflect on the ineffectiveness of drugs policy over the last twenty years the lack of effective focus does not stem primarily from government incompetence or hardness of heart. The problem is much deeper. It appears to be two-fold. First, there was the difficulty of persuading public opinion. A democracy can only operate by consent. Without public consent to be governed – which means being willing to accept restrictions and penalties in our everyday lives which, left to ourselves, we would not impose – effective government breaks down and with it the rule of law.

Two examples of consent withdrawn come to mind. Miners withdrew their consent to be governed by the Heath government. Whether the government's policies were right or wrong, many citizens refused to consent to live under them.

The second more recent withholding of consent in my political lifetime occurred over the Thatcher government's imposition of the community charge or 'poll tax'. People complained bitterly and some rioted. A significant number of people refused to pay this 'unfair' tax and chose to go to prison instead.

What has consent to be governed got to do with drugs policy, you ask? I believe the use of illegal drugs is now so widespread in our society that any attempt to pursue a 'hard line' policy of punishment or prohibition, at least quickly, would be so divisive that public consent for the new policies would not be forthcoming.

The use of illegal drugs has become what I referred to earlier as an 'emperor's clothes' issue. Reversing the reality of widespread use could be so difficult as to be well-nigh impossible in the short term. Everyone recognises that it is easier to dream up draconian laws than it is to implement them. And everyone knows that the Treasury could not afford to fund draconian drug-busting aspirations even if they were thought sensible. Taxpayers would likely rebel and withdraw their consent from the levels of taxation which would be needed to fund such a fight.

Finally, most people share the common thought that it is neither judicious nor polite to say what I have just said. Which is why this is an emperor's clothes issue. I will be accused by many of being either 'soft' (not a word as often applied to me in my political career as I would have wished) or defeatist. I think I am realistic. And without realism there is little hope of a coherent or effective anti-drugs policy emerging.

I said there were two reasons underlying the relative failure of all governments' drugs policies. The second reason is embedded in that British oft-talked-about issue of 'class'. Illegal drug taking has spread throughout every level of our society. Drugs are purchasable on the streets and in many clubs and pubs. All you need is cash, a casual enquiry and a willingness to break the law. And if you don't have enough cash there is always the plastic card or mugging, burglary and robbery.

Drugs are rife in universities and have been for a long time, as some 'respectable' middle-aged professional and political people boastfully testify. The words 'celebrity' and 'drugs' are too often used in the same sentences; though many celebrities do not indulge, and would be outraged and rightly inclined to sue at the very sugges-tion, if it were made personal. And some say that, at least, they did not inhale. When the police are provoked to the point where celebrity behaviour – whether sports, movie, television or business related – leaves them no alternative but to bring legal charges, the public believes the courts give celebrities lighter sentences than 'ordinary' people get.

Drug use is no longer solely a working-class phenomenon, if it ever was. It is rife throughout society. So how is it that those in prison on drug-related charges seem to come mainly from the working class? The answer is probably not encouraging. If the police were vigorously to pursue middle-class and/or professional people who are drug takers and the users of so-called recreational drugs then the consent to be governed could quickly evaporate. The prospect of millions of middle-class and professional people and celebrities with drug-related criminal records – with all the social and economic consequences which flow from such records – is not a 'real' scenario to most people. Indeed to some it is almost literally inconceivable. So blind eyes are turned and double standards prevail. It seems to be 'acceptable' to jail working-class people in proportions which would be deemed unacceptable if applied to the middle class. That distinction damages our democracy.

There is little evidence that any government can win the battle against illegal drugs in present circumstances and under present policies. For success to occur, the British people will have to agree to a range of tougher policies and greater expense. Or many drugs will have to be decriminalised with new, associated health-related governance. Or we will just have to agree to put up with the huge difference which exists – the hypocrisy. We, the public, may complain but government knows that there is a limit beyond which we are not willing to push those complaints for reasons of self-interest.

†

One final personal reflection. In Peterborough there is a large house in which a charity provides beds and meals for men who literally have nothing. Many have hopeless, chaotic lifestyles. Some are just 'down on their luck'. Many people try to help them change, which is hard work.

At one point the Conservative-run Peterborough council wanted to withdraw its grant and close the home because it was widely believed that drugs were used on the premises. As the MP I took a contrary view. For some human beings the benefits of food, clothing, heat and shelter can outweigh all, or at least most, other considerations.

I told the charity that I would visit the house to offer them support against my colleagues' intentions, and bring the local newspaper with me. I spent a long time drinking tea and talking to those who used and ran the home. Eventually everyone relaxed sufficiently to accept the genuineness of my interest. The subject of drugs came up.

LEFT A young Coral and Brian.

RIGHT The first Mawhinney graduate, with an honours degree in physics from Queen's University Belfast. Forty-five years later, Queen's gave me an honorary doctorate in Laws to recognise the fact that I was its only graduate in the preceding century to achieve a British Cabinet post.

Following our wedding in Michigan we had a second reception in Belfast for Northern Ireland friends. Betty and my sister Coral got dressed up. My grandmother Wilkinson was also present.

LEFT With the family in the grounds of Thorpe Hall, Peterborough, at the start of the 1979 general election.

BELOW The freshly elected Members of Parliament for neighbouring constituencies of Huntingdon and Peterborough, in 1979.

Contemplating heading for the office.

LEFT Visiting Peterborough's Asian Cultural Centre where I had many friends, with the Home Secretary, the Rt Hon. David Waddington MP.

RIGHT Many senior Tories offered me their support by visiting my constituency. Geoffrey Howe and I set up a game of snooker in the local Conservative Club.

LEFT Jim Prior was a good friend and politician whom I much admired. When he became Secretary of State for Northern Ireland, he was persuaded, against Margaret Thatcher's initial instincts, to change our policy in the Province to 'rolling devolution' which I had proposed a year earlier, thus laying the foundations on which today's Northern Ireland Assembly is constructed.

RIGHT The helping hands of many friends assisted my re-election to the House of Commons in 1983. After boundary changes I had been told no Tory could win the new Peterborough. My majority doubled.

ABOVE With Cliff Richard, whose songs I enjoyed and whose Christian faith I admired.

LEFT Being Education Minister was not all hard work. Sometimes it was just fun.

LEFT As Northern Ireland's Security Minister, I visited many sites of IRA atrocities. This bombing took place just a few days before 25 December. My ironic summary for the media, 'Happy Christmas from the IRA', seemed to catch the mood of the moment, for it was transmitted around the world.

RIGHT With John McConnell. Among the previous generation he was Northern Ireland's most effective and trusted political operator and a valued friend.

General Lesson.

CHRISTIANS should endeavour, as the Apostle Paul commands them, to live peaceably with all men (Romans, c. 12, v. 18), even with those of a different religious persuasion.

Our SAVIOUR, CHRIST, commanded his Disciples to love one another. He taught them to love even their enemies, to bless those that cursed them, and to pray for those who persecuted them. He himself prayed for his murderers.

Many Men hold erroneous doctrines; but we ought not to hate or persecute them. We ought to hold fast what we are convinced is the truth; but not to treat harshly those who are in error. JESUS CHRIST did not intend his Religion to be forced on men by violent means. He would not allow his Disciples to fight for him.

If any persons treat us unkindly, we must not do the same to them: for Christ and His Apostles have taught us not to return evil for evil. If we would obey CHRIST, we must do to others, not as they do to us, but as we would wish them to do to us.

Quarrelling with our neighbours and abusing them, is not the way to convince them that we are in the right, and they in the wrong. It is more likely to convince them that we have not a Christian spirit.

We ought, by behaving gently and kindly to every one, to show ourselves followers of CHRIST, who, when he was reviled, reviled not again. (1 Peter, c. 2, v. 23.)

Issued,

November, 1863.

I distributed this lesson in Christian reconciliation (initially given to all schools by an earlier education minister in 1863) to every school in the Province to emphasise the integrated and cross-cultural importance of the new curriculum.

With the two Archbishops of Armagh – Robin (now Lord) Eames and Cardinal Cahal Daly. I worked constructively with them both and benefited from their wisdom.

Sometimes you wait ages to meet a Prime Minister and then, like buses, two come along at once!

In 1995–97 it was my privilege to work the political jungle with a good friend, the impressive Deputy Prime Minister Michael Heseltine. We even devised Party posters together – much to Ted Heath's disgust.

At Norma Major's invitation, I umpired a number of charity cricket games in aid of Mencap. In this particular year I benefited from the expert advice of Brian Close, England's former Test captain, and the legendary umpire Dickie Bird – who was graciously tolerant of my efforts.

I was England's Football World Cup bid deputy chairman – seldom a happy or enhancing experience.

With Betty and our friend Delia Smith, about to watch Norwich City beat Peterborough United – again!

Celebrating twenty-five years as an MP with family and friends in Peterborough. Joan Reeve, whose initiative and confidence set me on the parliamentary path, is highlighted.

Being introduced into the House of Lords as Baron Mawhinney, of Peterborough. Grandson Noah 'represented' his dad.

A seventieth birthday party in 2010 in Northern Ireland. A wife, two sons and a daughter, their three spouses, and ten grandchildren. What a blessing.

Did the residents use them? Some did. Were the staff involved in their provision? Definitely not. So how were they accessed?

The resident I was talking to looked at me with a mixture of surprise and disdain. Were all MPs so naive? 'Give me a fiver, thirty minutes and a promise you won't have me followed,' he said, 'and I'll get you some heroin.' I did not give him the money but I believed him. Others confirmed his promise. Too often and to too many in our country this is the real world.

So, as the local MP, what about *my* rhetoric and action? I supported the home, which remains open. It still meets fundamental needs. And no doubt drugs are sometimes taken there (though not with official approval). Should the home remain open or be closed? And if the answer is the former what are the implications for the local anti-drug policy? 'Peterborough police crackdown on drugs', the local newspaper reports, but it is a losing battle. This MP always supported the police in their action. I also took the initiative (prodded by John Harper-Tee of the *Peterborough Evening Telegraph*) to set up Peterborough's first anti-drug organisation for those who wanted to kick the habit – no questions asked.

So my rhetoric and action were never totally aligned. My rhetoric was 'harder' than what was achievable. In reality there never was an opportunity to support government actions that were in line with my political rhetoric. Had such actions occurred I would have supported them. Having done so I am not sure that consent towards me locally would not have been withdrawn, no matter how good an MP my constituents thought I was. In short there are no easy policy or moral answers to the dilemma we collectively face. What is needed is a genuine public debate. If sincere, it will not be comfortable.

My initial contribution would be to examine the criteria by which prisoners qualify for parole.

A postscript

As a teenager I was very interested in becoming a prison officer – not for reasons of imposing discipline but because, as a young and idealist Christian, I wanted to help prisoners reform their lives. In today's somewhat disdainful parlance, I wanted to be a do-gooder.

The weight of university education coupled with a better understanding of how the world actually works sank that aspiration, in practice, which to me carries a measure of regret. But the feeling lingered on, which may explain why a rather heavy policy issue found its way into my book.

11

Her Majesty's Treasury

Apart from 10 Downing Street, with its associated Cabinet Office, Her Majesty's Treasury (HMT) is the most influential department in government because it raises the 'government's' money (actually our money – the taxpayers' money) and controls its expenditure. It also tends to micro-manage departmental budgets unless their ministers are vigilant. So the Chancellor of the Exchequer is always a senior and significant politician in any government. Getting him on side is second only to persuading the Prime Minister when a Cabinet minister wants to introduce a new policy.

This was certainly true for the governments in which I served. In Tony Blair's government, Gordon Brown, the Chancellor, was even more important and influential because he insisted on doing more micro-managing than was usual or indeed good. His interference made departmental secretaries of state weaker. As a consequence Gordon became more responsible for the ensuing failures in both social and economic policy. His famous claim to have abolished 'boom and bust' will live long in the memory, probably longer than the austerity necessitated by his last 'bust'.

I know from experience that disputes between Cabinet colleagues can be properly resolved only if the Prime Minister is politically strong enough to impose his or her will, and is willing to do so. The former was a Blair issue, the latter an occasional Major one. Blair allowed Brown and HMT to impose their views by being intrusive and demanding and by creating internal tension. It must have felt akin to being bullied. As my friend Lord Levy says in his book *A Question of Honour*, 'Tony [Blair] delayed ... because of a familiar tendency – increasingly damaging to all concerned, including Tony himself – to avoid personal confrontation with his Cabinet ministers at almost any cost'.

While Gordon Brown drove domestic policy, Tony Blair 'did' the world: Europe, the USA, war and political schmoozing. For a long time he did them effectively both nationally and internationally. Eventually, however, people came to realise that political activity alone is never enough.

The Chancellor followed the broad tradition of his Labour predecessors but with more political skill. He was an awesome tax-and-spend Chancellor – big time – while avoiding much of the criticism that this approach had hung around the necks of previous Labour Chancellors. The recession and financial crisis highlighted his lack of prudence in not putting anything aside for a rainy day, as my granny used to urge me to do. And his legacy is an eye-watering debt mountain, of immoral proportions, which will burden our grandchildren for years to come, though less so if the Cameron government succeeds. Short-term pain will lead to medium-term gain, as long as today's senior ministers can maintain public confidence in their competence and political savvy. Unquestionably coalition leaders would be assisted in doing this if they sorted out their differences in private before they presented a policy to the electorate. If the coalition wants to be accepted as government it needs to act like government bound together by collective responsibility, not as two parties thrown together, struggling for internal supremacy.

In my twenty-six years in the Commons, Tory governments operated with more traditional, though still powerful, Chancellors. One became Prime Minister. Others changed twentieth-century history. All would claim, with justification, that they behaved honourably and in the national interest.

My direct dealings with HMT started after my promotion to Minister of State in the Northern Ireland Office. For some months

I was the Province's 'Finance Minister'. Enormously aided by able officials, I assisted and monitored the budgets of my NIO colleagues and supported the Secretary of State in arguing with HMT over how much money the Province should receive. On the whole we were treated fairly.

In Northern Ireland partly, but only partly, because of the economic effects of (primarily) IRA violence, the public sector proportion of the overall economy was, and remains, far too high. Sustainable prosperity needs a blossoming private sector and less dependence on public expenditure. Ulster's disproportionate addiction to public spending is counterproductive if any serious attempt to increase individuals' disposable income is to succeed.

More than twenty years after I was Northern Ireland's finance minister, public expenditure in the Province is still in the 65 to 70 per cent range – as it was then. This may ensure a less uncomfortable lifestyle for many Ulster people in the short term (and I acknowledge that for most people life is stressed at the moment) but it makes a much more comfortable lifestyle in the medium term less likely.

Initially HMT's attitude to reimbursing the NIO, following major bombing and arson attacks by the IRA, perplexed me. Government did not carry insurance and private insurance did not cover terrorist risk so when schools, medical centres, housing estates, police stations, roads or retail premises were destroyed the taxpayer paid. I sometimes thought HMT required too much justification for what appeared to be obvious reimbursement claims. Maybe they wondered if we were guilty of padding them.

We had a policy of never publicly discussing the cost of an atrocity – in case the IRA would be encouraged to believe that cost might be able to undermine the government's commitment to this part of the UK. It never did. A single night's terrorism could be very expensive, costing the taxpayer literally tens of millions of pounds. Clearly this could not and should not fall solely on Ulster taxpayers. Payment was the responsibility of taxpayers in the whole UK. And we paid without complaint, though no one liked it.

When I moved to the Department of Health my exposure to government finance and HMT increased considerably. For her own never fully revealed reasons my 'boss', Virginia Bottomley MP, insisted that I be included in all discussions about the department's budget. (I think she may have received guidance from John Major to include me but I never asked either of them directly.) She did once mention that my involvement was sensible because I had handled finance in Northern Ireland but I felt she was never wholly confident in her dealing with HMT. While this unexpected development increased my workload, I did not mind. It enhanced my influence; handling money always does in any organisation.

Given this opportunity, I vigorously argued my corner. In my adult life I have seldom seen much point in attending meetings without trying to influence their outcome. As a child I grew up in an environment where 'children should be seen and not heard'. But, as the Bible mentions in a somewhat different context, 'when I became a man I put away childish things'. Of course Virginia and I sometimes disagreed, though not as often as some might have supposed, but we always reached a common position.

I was genuinely surprised, however, that she refused to see the Chancellor or Chief Secretary unless I accompanied her. This was so unusual that even officials who understood that I had no 'power' to make her include me told me privately that they too were surprised. They thought her insistence on my presence weakened the department's dealings with the Treasury. But she never wavered in this even when the Treasury protested. My standing in the department and in the broader political world increased as this 'policy' became more widely known.

Conversations with HMT followed what I was to learn was a standard pattern. Initially we would be told, usually by the Chief Secretary, the Cabinet minister who oversaw departmental spending, that we were asking for too much money. We had to be more restrained. Meetings with the Chancellor usually occurred only after a departmental Cabinet minister had refused to reduce his or her demands to a level the Chief Secretary thought acceptable.

Like others we would be sent away from meetings to pare back our demands, with a reminder of the government's political commitment to control public expenditure ringing in our ears.

The Department of Health was also responsible for government submissions to the independent bodies who recommended pay rises for health workers. Every proposed increase for doctors, nurses and others was greeted with howls of protest. Even those submissions for which I had responsibility had to be 'cleared' by HMT because it had overall responsibility for public sector pay, which was a large part of public expenditure, and they never trusted spending departments to be sufficiently austere.

And, of course, we had to argue for our own departmental budget – money to run the central departmental service as well as provide public services. Each year HMT required us to make efficiency savings, their euphemism for reducing expenditure. Nevertheless the discipline of efficiency savings was a good one, and one which usefully could be applied with vigour to many other public organisations, including local government. Despite trenchant efforts I failed to persuade John Major to include a mandatory local authority efficiency commitment in our 1997 manifesto.

Our only meeting with Chancellor Norman Lamont MP that I remember was on the perennial problem of prescription charges. These could not be cash limited because government had no control over how many prescriptions doctors would write. HMT hated this open-ended expenditure line. They wanted budget certainty and proposed many ingenious ideas to persuade us to agree to limitations. We never would. We were not going to be the health ministers who rationed prescriptions, who would have to tell doctors to amend their treatment decisions. Nor would we contemplate standing in front of TV cameras in February or March trying to explain to the British public why their government would not allow any new prescriptions to be written before the start of the next financial year in April. The argument that there was 'no money' would not have persuaded anybody.

Also we all knew that if the issue had to be taken to the Prime

Minister or Cabinet we would win hands down. Controlling public expenditure was important but not that important!

On the other hand, the pharmaceutical industry constantly complained that the government was not spending enough on drugs. We were regularly threatened with the prospect of the industry moving overseas if we did not treat them more generously. Pharmaceutical companies never showed much appreciation for our efforts to keep drug budgets 'unlimited'. On that issue they clearly saw Virginia as the 'goodie' and me as the 'baddie'.

In our time I never believed this threat to move country, not least because the industry did well out of the public purse. On the one occasion I was responsible for negotiating our national deal on pharmaceutical pricing, I insisted on a tight outcome – tighter than officials recommended and much tighter than the industry wanted. As the saying goes, I was not flavour of the month, except perhaps in the Treasury. Notwithstanding the range of pressures we had to handle from both the industry and the Treasury, necessary drugs remained available to patients at reasonable cost to the public purse – no mean feat.

Kenneth Clarke MP became Chancellor while I was at Health. Ken, a former Health Secretary, had a well-established antipathy to excessive public expenditure, including in health, so our negotiations with HMT continued in a robust form, often about what 'excessive' meant. At least he understood the importance of year-round availability of prescription drugs.

My exposure to the Treasury increased enormously when I became Secretary of State for Transport. During those eleven months my private office and senior officials were in almost daily contact with officials at both HMT and No. 10. The start at Transport could hardly have been more difficult. I was appointed in about the fourth week of a national railway strike, trains were running spasmodically or not at all and millions of people inconvenienced.

Initially there were silly media stories speculating that a new Secretary of State heralded a serious chance to resolve the dispute – as if, somehow, the transport breakdown was the personal responsibility of my predecessor. Even more bizarre, those writing such stories wanted to be taken seriously as expert political and transport journalists!

My single early 'toe in the water' public observation was that at some point people would have to talk to each other if the dispute was to be resolved. This statement of the obvious elicited some fierce media criticism suggesting that I was a 'softie' who was out of his depth. Best ignored. I judged fairly quickly that this dispute had to run its course to the point where the rail unions were ready to negotiate seriously. Attempts to do this before 'the time was right' would be counterproductive. So I sat tight, kept my own counsel, was deemed intransigent and listened for the nuances in other people's utterances.

Thus developed an unnecessarily long, traditional nationalised industry dispute. Rail unions cared little for their customers as they demanded extra taxpayers' money to 'solve' the problem on their terms, i.e. higher wages. Other equally strident voices demanded that rail workers be 'punished' for inconveniencing the public and damaging the economy. For our part we persuaded the public to see the dispute as one between employers and employees – which, of course, in one sense it was.

I kept in contact with the British Rail chairman, Sir Bob Reid, and his senior executives mainly through my officials but occasionally on a personal basis. I do not think that either the chairman or I found in the other a new best friend but our relationship was genuinely courteous and correct. We both knew that eventually British Rail would need government approval to spend outside its agreed budget. I had no extra money to offer but made it clear that if and when the British Rail board made a formal application for a budget increase, set within an approved revised business plan, then I would seriously consider their request. In reality if British Rail wanted more money I would have to persuade HMT to 'give' it to me. They, in turn, would need to be convinced that the extra finance would enhance the public good.

No. 10 and HMT were briefed regularly – often daily. Given that the dispute ran for fourteen weeks you can see how inter-related the three departments were and how much added work was involved. The public shared our disinclination just to 'give' the union leadership more money. Indeed the public mood hardened against the 'strikers' as time passed. This was largely because the travelling public made alternative arrangements to get to work or to work from home so the level of inconvenience was better accommodated.

In the department the end result we wanted was improved rail services and the industry made more efficient so we started thinking about how much taxpayers' money might be needed to accomplish these twin objectives. Settling the dispute through a general pay increase was never a possibility.

In addition to departmental activity, I regularly attended a special Cabinet committee set up to oversee the handling of the dispute. Initially the committee's attitude was hard line. This probably derived, in part, from the fact that I was a new Secretary of State and as such was not seen as 'battle hardened'. Relatively quickly, however, my colleagues decided I was 'tough' enough (Ken Clarke took longer to be persuaded). We worked through the summer recess examining the terms of a possible settlement. Having colleagues' political assessment of my officials' technical work was very helpful.

By being hard to convince, Ken gave the impression he was not prepared to agree anything until the unions threw in the towel, even though he was too smart to believe this would happen. He was no great admirer of this nationalised industry nor its management. Sometimes this disapproval made the work we had to do, in anticipation of a time for settlement, more difficult.

Eventually the unions signalled their willingness to move towards a negotiated settlement. The first thing we did, on getting those signals through British Rail, was check them independently. If they were real – good. If, however, they were simply wishful thinking, woolly aspirations or indeed a BR ploy to get us to make more money available to them, we needed to know. Eventually the Cabinet committee was persuaded that the unions seemed willing to focus on improving work practices, as a basis for settling the dispute, rather than just demanding a pay rise. Public pressure and government firmness had worked.

Then we encountered a bizarre problem. Ken Clarke went on holiday. Without a word to us or his colleagues, he went bird watching (as I recall) in a distant part of the world where his mobile phone 'did not work'. He arranged to contact his office maybe two or three times a week but only in 'touching base' mode. Treasury officials told us any resolution of the dispute would have to await his return.

The Cabinet committee continued its work. Eventually a properly costed strategy was developed based on changing work practices. In this way government provided a suitable basis on which British Rail could negotiate. It was accepted by the BR board, who, of course, had been involved in the discussions, offering advice to the committee through my officials.

Having reached internal agreement we found ourselves snookered. The economic package needed to fund our proposals had to be cleared by the Chancellor. No argument. But he could not be contacted, so the strike continued. I was not amused, the more so because my wife and I had cancelled our summer holiday so I could always be available to handle the dispute! The Chief Secretary refused to intervene.

Days later the Chancellor rang his office. Afterwards we were told contact had been made but that, in a short conversation, the rail dispute had not been mentioned. Treasury officials said they were sorry. The strike continued – unnecessarily.

A day or two later I was summoned to No. 10 to brief the Prime Minister. He wanted to understand the details of the package we were seeking to establish as government policy, reassurance that BR could handle the negotiations and to examine the politics of settling the dispute. How did I plan to ensure that it was 'our' policy and 'our' costings that would prevail?

He appeared well satisfied with the briefing and was complimentary about our work. When would negotiations begin? 'I do not know,' I replied, making an instant decision to tell him about our problems contacting Ken for his approval. Not only could we not get his agreement, I said, we could not even talk to him. HMT claimed not to know precisely where he was.

John made clear he had not been told that his Chancellor was allegedly incommunicado. This was not acceptable and he would look into it. A few hours later, Ken was on the phone! He gave me some earache about going to the Prime Minister, and defended his right to have a holiday, after which we discussed the proposed package. Being Ken, he expressed doubts. Being me, I slowly became exasperated. I told him his officials, in whom he appeared to have more trust than he did his Cabinet colleagues, were content that the package met all his requirements. I suggested he obtain comfort from them and then tell me whether the government could proceed. There was no need to make further mention of the Prime Minister. I was confident that No. 10 officials, on the Prime Minister's orders, would be pushing HMT in the same direction we were.

Eventually the package was cleared (by a call from the Treasury not from an international bird-watching hide) and I set about 'selling' it to the BR board. Naturally, and constructively, the BR chairman explored alternative ideas and raised questions about our costings. We agreed the costings were 'tight'. In fact, without telling BR, I had reduced the amount of extra money we would add to their budget to conclude a deal with the unions, below the sum made available by the Treasury. In this way I would have room for manoeuvre in case the negotiations reached stalemate. I knew there would be little advantage in going back to colleagues seeking more than we had agreed, especially after my problem with the Chancellor. Of course it could be argued that if I had given BR all the Treasury money the chances of stalemate would have been reduced. It was a political call and my risk to take. And it remained a closely guarded secret known only to a few of my most senior and trusted officials.

My Cabinet colleagues were in a 'not a penny more' mood so getting extra funds would have been difficult though probably not impossible. Having to return to them, however, would have undermined their sense of my political competence and therefore my ability to do my job.

There was another factor. I had long believed the unions would settle for less extra money than my colleagues believed. Perhaps, at that early stage of my Cabinet career, I had not learned the skill of accurately conveying my thoughts to colleagues when we had been discussing how much extra to set aside. They were all clear, however, that I was the one in the firing line.

BR's board agreed the objectives to be achieved and accepted that the additional resources offered were sufficient to deliver them, with one exception. They had reservations about one objective. I made it clear that I was not minded to remove this condition and eventually the chairman accepted it without enthusiasm.

The employee–employer negotiations started. Many hours of prior 'discussion' had narrowed the issues and the outline of an agreement had emerged before the formal negotiating began. Now a work-related, financial solution had to be agreed.

Hours passed.

About 9 p.m. my private secretary and I walked to a nearby restaurant for a meal. About midnight (as I recall) the BR chairman came into my office to report that they had a deal.

Congratulations were quickly followed by questions about the details of the agreement, while the unions remained in another room awaiting my reaction.

I spotted 'an oversight'. There was no mention of the objective about which the chairman and I had disagreed earlier.

We did not raise it, I was told. BR was not keen on it and we knew the unions would object so we thought it better to get a deal – and we did. It is within your parameters, Secretary of State, so we hope you will find it acceptable without this extra condition.

A quick decision was needed. The unions were waiting. There was no need to consult officials. This was a purely political decision.

My Cabinet colleagues and I had agreed a settlement mandate. Together we had collective responsibility for the agreed parameters. If I told them I had agreed a deal which delivered most of what we wanted but had not even tried to secure one aspect of the mandate I would be in an exposed position. And the deal would be less than might have been brokered for the public good.

On the other hand, I could announce an immediate end to the longest rail strike in recent history, on good terms and at much less cost to the public purse than people expected. If I insisted on this extra aspect being agreed with the unions they might decide that it was the 'straw that broke the camel's back' and walk away. No deal. Strike to continue. Blame the Secretary of State. I could see and hear the headlines. I was in no doubt that everyone would brief the media against me – probably including some in the department and certainly in BR.

However, we were so near a deal that even if the unions walked away it would probably not be long before everyone got around the table again.

I looked at the BR chairman. He smiled. 'There is no deal,' I said. 'I am afraid I am going to insist on this final objective being agreed. You will have to return to the table. Now.'

He was not happy and said so. 'They will not agree this addition, Secretary of State. They believe they have a deal. They will react badly. Almost certainly they will walk out and blame you. They will certainly want more money.'

I lowered my voice to lower the temperature. 'Go back and agree this last objective, please. Make clear this is the only issue outstanding. After agreement on it there is a deal. And', I added, 'agreement should not be bought. The completed deal should be within the financial package already agreed by the unions.' My room cleared except for my private secretary. Una O'Brien gave me a long look and told me I was being 'courageous'.

In the early hours of the morning we put out a press statement telling the country that the strike was over. I reported this formally to the next Cabinet meeting and added that I had used only about two-thirds of the extra resources which the Chancellor had made available to me. Cabinet was pleased. The Prime Minister was complimentary. The Chancellor was surprised.

Any improved relations between the Department of Transport and the Treasury did not last long. They really hit the buffers a few months later as we addressed the annual issue of the departmental budget for the following twelve months. Each year each department submitted its proposed budget to HMT. On its receipt HMT would (figuratively) laugh and send it back telling each Secretary of State to get real. 'Did we think the Treasury was full of money?' they would ask – or words to that effect.

Eventually each department and HMT agreed a paper for the Cabinet committee set up to resolve differences between the Chancellor and his spending colleagues to consider. It contained what expenditure had been agreed and the variations which were not agreed. The Chancellor chaired the committee (which is an indication of the realpolitik of the situation). I would have preferred to have had the Deputy Prime Minister, Michael Heseltine, in the chair – but no one cared what I thought.

My 'bid', at something over £4 billion, was only an increase of a few percentage points in cash terms on my existing budget. It meant we would have to lose some of the transport improvements we had wanted but I thought the bid would, or at least could, be seen as reasonable. It was certainly defensible.

But I had a big problem. The department was pushing forward the privatisation of British Rail. This was an unbelievably complicated process – made worse (which can be another way of saying 'expensive') by the manner an earlier Cabinet had chosen to establish privatisation. That decision was before my time so I had had no say in it. Some who did subsequently tried to distance themselves from the form of privatisation which collectively they had agreed. I wish they had had their 'second thoughts' at the outset.

Personally I strongly favoured moving British Rail – then a national laughing stock and monument to inefficiency – into the private sector. For forty years, each year, fewer and fewer people used the trains. All my predictions that a privately run system would result in enormous increases in investment and passenger use have been proved correct. John Prescott MP, my Labour opposite number, derided the idea that this would happen. His judgement in opposition turned out to be an accurate foretaste of his judgement in government.

The form of privatisation was just too complex. In my view the Cabinet should have agreed a form that reflected the former regional railway structure and did not separate train services from control of the track. This would have been less complicated, almost certainly less expensive to set up and generally more acceptable to the public, as long as the principle of competing train services had been included in those areas of the country where it was possible. However, my colleagues did not choose that option and by the time I was in my post I had to implement what had been decided. So I did.

Neither during my time as Transport Secretary, nor subsequently, did I say whether I approved the actual form of privatisation. My response was always the same: the question was not useful. We were where we were and my sole focus was on delivery. 'What if' speculation was just an indulgence. Had I indulged myself the resulting controversy would have caused a serious distraction, making my technical and political jobs even more difficult. Now, my view is of interest only to historians.

I digress. In that particular year the probable costs of privatisation were equivalent to a very substantial percentage of my total departmental budget. Normally such costs were borne centrally by the Treasury. However, we had received no formal assurance from HMT that they would pay that year, despite repeated requests. Any shifting of privatisation costs from HMT to the department would have caused mayhem. It would have wrecked our ability to fund, much less improve, the nation's transport.

My officials were concerned, but resigned. They had been through this annual process many times. The Treasury, they indicated, always had a somewhat bullying instinct and we were 'powerless'. In any head-to-head battle, HMT would always be the winner. My officials asked only that I draw this fundamental discrepancy to the committee's attention. I was determined to do more.

We gathered in the Cabinet Office and the Chancellor invited me to begin my presentation. Before I got into the budget details, I told the Committee I would be grateful if the Chancellor assured us that HMT would pay separately the costs of rail privatisation. 'Without that assurance there is little point in my proceeding. If rail privatisation remains a top government priority, as I know it does, then it has to be funded. If any of that funding were to fall to my department then we would have no ability to advance a viable departmental programme. And certainly we could have no confidence in my budget proposals.'

I paused. Ken, not amused, told me off for raising the issue. He thought the matter was not appropriate for this meeting! 'Please proceed.'

I started again and repeated my initial comments. I added that I thought it was entirely appropriate for colleagues to understand not only the pertinence of the issue but that I was raising it here because for weeks we had failed to get a definitive response from the Treasury.

Ken was now seriously irritated. He thought my behaviour 'intolerable'. I was told to behave. I then dressed up my request for an assurance in different language. By this point Ken was very and visibly annoyed. Tony Newton, the Leader of the Commons, whose instinct was usually to seek compromise, tried to persuade me to do as Ken demanded.

This nonsense went on for about thirty-five of the sixty minutes set aside for my session. With Ken ready to explode and my point made so clearly that everyone in the room understood the problem, Michael Heseltine gently told me it was time to move on. So I did.

Twenty-five minutes was not nearly sufficient for proper consideration of my budget proposals. A furious Ken warned me that I would be recalled and that next time he did not want any repeat of this disgraceful performance. I was dismissed.

On my return to the department I discovered two interesting things. Treasury officials had already briefed my officials on what had happened and had conveyed their boss's anger. No secretary of state had ever behaved so disgracefully in budget meetings nor shown so little respect towards the Chancellor etc. etc. Sometimes government can move very efficiently! Secondly, my officials were delighted that I had gone to bat for the department in such a robust fashion. No Transport Secretary had ever argued his corner or defended his officials so robustly etc. etc. I was a 'hero'.

I took it all with a pinch of salt. Flattery normally has a limited lifespan. Those who praise you one minute can just as easily be criticising you the next. As for the financing I was sure the Treasury would pay, would have to pay, but I needed this in writing both to keep the department's financial accounts clean and to underpin our transport programme.

A date for the resumed meeting was set by the Treasury, without consultation. I told my private secretary to agree it and add that I wanted a written assurance from the Chancellor himself, before the meeting, that HMT would cover our privatisation costs.

Days passed. No letter arrived, despite reminders.

On the day before the meeting, I told my private secretary to mention to Treasury officials that, without the reassurance of a letter, I was wondering if it was worthwhile attending tomorrow's meeting. Maybe I should just take the issue to full Cabinet instead, an idea I knew the Treasury would hate. Una O'Brien looked hard at me and wondered out loud if this was not a step too far. I thought her instinct was probably right but I was fed up with Ken and his officials. What a stupid way to run a government. For once my cautious instinct was set aside.

We dispersed at the end of the day none the wiser about what would happen tomorrow. First thing the next morning we asked again for a letter. I had decided, assurance or not, to attend the Cabinet committee and, if necessary, repeat my mantra, but told no one other than Una. I did not want my intention to reach the Treasury thereby reducing the pressure on the Chancellor, for I did not plan to be the one to 'blink' first.

I sent a message to my driver George that I would not need his services that morning. This was sure to get back to the Treasury, via one of their drivers, thus strengthening the idea that I might take the issue straight to Cabinet. Anyway, it was a pleasant morning for a walk.

Forty-five minutes before the committee was due to convene Ken's letter arrived.

I started the meeting by thanking the Chancellor profusely for his letter. My budget was approved with little damage and no evidence of vindictiveness from any of my colleagues. From then to the end of the parliament my personal relations with Ken were civilised, businesslike, occasionally friendly, occasionally less so. But we were never buddies, especially in the twelve months immediately prior to the 1997 general election, during which Ken became even more 'difficult' than usual over the issue of Europe.

I only had two other difficulties with HMT while at Transport. Each year the government had to agree with British Rail the range of fare increases. Government was involved because of the taxpayers' subsidy. I found it hard to square my repeated public assurances that passengers would benefit when nationalised British Rail was replaced by private operators (which overwhelmingly has proved to be the case) with the usual annual, inexorable, above-inflation fare increases. Why should passenger benefits not also include the fares?

My officials were sceptical. Since the nationalisation of British Rail, services had been in a downward spiral and fares in an upward one. Their view was that HMT would never agree a different fare regime and certainly not one that was more generous to passengers. They never had.

Eventually I proposed an increase in commuter fares and the fares most used by people going to and from work to inflation *less* I per cent. This real-term *decrease* would signal that the new rail system not only promised but also delivered benefits to passengers. The other fare increases were kept as close as possible to inflation. British Rail would have to improve its efficiency to cover the funding gap.

When our plan was sent to HMT for approval we were told a meeting would be necessary. The Chief Secretary could not agree this subtle form of extra expenditure without examination. Other political colleagues with an interest in transport and public expenditure would also attend.

When I arrived at the meeting the Chancellor himself was present. Perhaps he surmised that my proposal would seem politically appealing to our colleagues. If so, he was right – once they were convinced that my plans were not financially irresponsible.

There is no need to go into the sort of detail I did earlier. Suffice to say, Ken was not easily persuaded nor was his inch-by-inch movement towards agreement characterised by excessive grace. But we got there. A historic first. The fare news was announced and explained by me as the first fruits of privatisation.

Perhaps this is an appropriate time to inject some balance into my account. One of the dangers associated with reporting moments of political tension is creating the impression of constant warfare between Ken and me or between our departments. That perception would be as unfair as it would be untrue. Our normal everyday interactive business progressed without incident or serious dispute. Constructive daily communication was normal. We were two colleagues and two departments working together for the common good – as the government defined it. Our cooperation was both routine and effective. Nevertheless these incidents did happen and illustrate the occasional but often unseen tensions in government. In that sense they give a more rounded picture of how government works. For my part, I was and remain one of those who appreciate and admire Ken's political persona.

My final moment of discord arose out of government plans to build a new, high-speed rail link between the Channel Tunnel and London. I inherited this proposal and was required to make only two decisions, apart from the actual route.

Should the new line also terminate at Waterloo, as was then the case, or did we need a new terminal; perhaps one that was not on the 'wrong' side of the capital as far as the majority of the UK was concerned? Eventually I decided that a rebuilt St Pancras should be the new terminal. This was opened during the Labour government's time in office but, as is often the case in public life, the person who actually made the decision was not invited. It is an excellent example of a modern railway station and worth the money invested in it.

The other decision proved more controversial. Should we build another station on this new line at Stratford in the east of London? The arguments – pro and con – were both philosophical and about investment, jobs and money. An extra station would make the whole Channel Tunnel Rail Link project more expensive. Could that extra expenditure be justified?

The 'pro' argument was that this was a once-in-a-lifetime opportunity to open the East End of London to new investment and regeneration. Such help was badly needed. The 'con' argument was that a Stratford railway station was not needed in passenger terms. Its probable initially sparse use meant it could not be justified by any cost–benefit analysis. And our experience of railways was that they normally cost more than anticipated, and produced less. In addition this government favoured private-sector-led regeneration and, anyway, regeneration was not part of the Department of Transport's responsibility. Railway projects never were a favourite Treasury idea.

I was strongly 'pro'. My sense was that over too many years governments of both political parties had ignored the needs of people living in the East End of London. They had been hard done by when it came to the public purse. This was an opportunity to help redress the balance. I believed that Stratford station would facilitate much-needed private-sector regeneration.

While at Health I had similarly acted on my belief about the East End's need. I indicated that extra money had to be found for the Homerton Hospital and I worked hard with local GPs to improve primary care services, which required considerable help.

Ken and the Treasury were firmly on the 'con' side of the argument. There was no conceivable cost–benefit case to justify spending so much taxpayer's money on this project. 'Regeneration', no matter how laudable, was simply aspirational.

The issue was referred to a Cabinet committee for resolution.

Before we met I had, for me, a bright idea. Michael Heseltine was probably Ken Clarke's closest friend in Cabinet, but Michael and I had always got on well, personally and politically. He had been my choice as guest of honour at the dinner the Peterborough Conservative Association gave to mark my first ten years in Parliament.

I talked to Michael about Stratford. I acknowledged his closeness to Ken and his commitment to sound money but reminded him that a lot of his political reputation rested on driving the private sector regeneration that had transformed inner cities across the country – and mentioned Liverpool. Here was perhaps our last opportunity to transform another major inner city area. I told Michael that whichever way he 'jumped' in committee would decide the outcome. See you tomorrow, I told him, without seeking any commitment.

I have walked through the splendid new Stratford station.

The footnote to this story is an excellent example of the political law of unintended consequences. In July 2005 the East End of London was awarded the role of hosting the 2012 Olympic Games, to take place in a large area centred around Stratford station. Tony Blair, Lord Coe and their colleagues deserve great credit for this highly competitive success. The East End will benefit in ways which exceed people's dreams. There will be previously unimaginable regeneration. Seb Coe has told me that, without the station, the bid would have failed.

After I left Transport to become Party Chairman I had no further official dealings with HMT though, of course, I had many with Ken as a Cabinet colleague. The intransigence of his views on Europe contributed significantly to the political difficulties I had to handle within the party and to the tensions which afflicted the Cabinet, but then so did the equally intransigent opposing views of others.

Ken's great political skill has given him a formidable political career and an impressive reputation, not least as a normal, friendly bloke. He also has an admirable ability to pick just the right word, phrase or moment maximally to wind up his opponents, an ability he used memorably when addressing doctors and occasionally even within Cabinet. Ken's fixity of purpose and steely yet laid-back character meant that he did not just survive the rows which inevitably followed his more outspoken interventions; he often prospered from them and even gave the impression of enjoying them. On the other hand no Prime Minister (or even Party Chairman) welcomes discord within Cabinet or government. This appeared not to bother Ken unduly, though he clearly understands when to 'stop digging'.

I hope these stories convey a taste of the crucial, though sometimes 'uneven', relationship which exists between HMT and other departments. Governments cannot function without raising and spending taxes. Both are divinely inspired and practical requirements. The trick is to seek the best balance achievable between economic and financial arguments on the one hand and political, ethical and public service arguments on the other. But the force of the political cliché 'it's the economy, stupid' is massive. The public like governments which respond to their wishes but they also expect them to handle tax-and-spend competently and sustainably, as Gordon Brown learned to his cost.

12

Two Prime Ministers

Margaret Thatcher and I got off to a bad start – entirely my fault. She spoke at a Conservative meeting in East Anglia in the late 1970s and I made a total hash of introducing her. My serious embarrassment was heightened by local Tories who were forthright and uncomplimentary. Margaret looked amazed that I had been selected to stand for Parliament. Years later I could not shake the feeling that Margaret still viewed me as that raw flop from years back. But we did eventually become friends.

John Major and I were first elected to Parliament on the same day – he for Huntingdon, me for 'next door' Peterborough. We are very different people. John left school at sixteen, with a 'vague wish' (his words) to go into politics. He developed successful careers in banking and local government before entering the House of Commons. He is very good with people – charming and courteous – with admirable communication skills and a very astute political mind.

I remained in education – school, undergraduate, postgraduate – until I was twenty-seven. Then I taught medical physics and radiation biology to medical students in Iowa (USA) and London. Being an Ulsterman, a confessing Christian and something of an introvert meant, political commentators opined, that I was a bit 'dour' for the modern political, secular taste. Of the two of us John is the more naturally gifted and affable politician, especially given my greater tendency to call a spade a spade.

Some of those distinctions were evident in our first meeting a few weeks after our election. Conservative councillors on

Cambridgeshire County Council wanted to meet the county's two new MPs. John charmed and flattered them, assuring them he would work constructively with them.

My contribution was not well received. Over the preceding weeks I had written to a number of them about issues troubling my constituents which were their responsibility. Not one bothered to reply. I responded warmly to their welcome. Then, reciting my experience, I made the not unreasonable point that if we were to work well together, which I hoped we would, the process had to be reciprocal.

The contrast with John could not have been greater. Councillors, shocked by my forthrightness and the exposure of their failure, became irritated. None of them addressed the concern I had expressed on my constituents' behalf. Bad start.

John hardly spoke to me for weeks other than to chide me for upsetting colleagues. He too never mentioned the legitimacy of my constituents' concerns. My aggressive reputation had started to take root. So had my genuine concern to try to help constituents.

My second early experience with John further defined and illustrated our difference. As new MPs we went together to see a minister about some Peterborough issue (in 1979–83 John represented that part of the city south of the river Nene). I can remember neither the minister nor the issue but I remember well our walk back to the House. At one point John and I started speaking at exactly the same moment – and then stopped, at the same moment – each pausing to give way to the other.

When we had smiled politely, I said, 'Do you think we will get what we want?'

John said, 'What do you think he thought of us?'

The few who have heard this story have all told me that those questions are thumbnail insights into both of us.

Of course, John was right. None of us should be unduly cavalier about how others see us. Equally I have always been less concerned about creating warm atmospheres of goodwill than I have been on effecting positive change. Over the next fifteen years John and I maintained a good, if not particularly close, friendship. We got together, ate and politicked from time to time and exchanged friendly views whenever we happened to meet. He was the high flyer who moved in more exalted government circles. I showed less camaraderie to other MPs, being more private. And, of course, I spent six-and-a-half years as a minister in Northern Ireland, which took me out of the Westminster mainstream. However, I always kept John informed of matters that might be of political interest to him. And we both enjoyed sharing our different but complementary perceptions of events and people when we did get together.

Many years later, my being Party Chairman enabled us to deepen our friendship as we learned to trust each other's political skill and judgement. In that regard we only had one real moment of tension – but an important one.

'Could you be ready for a 6 February election?' John asked me at the start of 1997.

'Yes, if you want,' I replied, 'but it would mean seriously accelerating work on the manifesto and on the logistical arrangements CCO [Conservative Central Office] has to put in place.' He told me to plan on it.

The next morning John rang to say there would not be a 6 February election. Apparently he had thought that that early date might spring a surprise on Labour. At that stage of the parliament, however, no election date would have been a surprise either to the opposition or to the media; they all knew the pros and cons of each Thursday in the following few months. When he had realised this John had decided we should take enough time to make proper arrangements and complete the manifesto.

The second date examined was 6 March, mainly because we had had an unforeseen problem. Barry Porter, Conservative MP for the Wirral, had died suddenly. In keeping with parliamentary convention we had to move the by-election date. After a lot of hesitation, our initial thought was 27 February. We had hesitated, not because we were looking for a 'winning' date but because we knew the general election had to be held by early May. The prospect that the last piece of political theatre (and reality) before the general election would be a huge electoral defeat was not enticing and we wondered if and how we could avoid it.

On reflection there seemed to be two options. John could call an early general election (6 March) before the Wirral date was announced, thus removing the need for the by-election. Or he could call one for 20 March, after the Wirral announcement but before the by-election vote, thus terminating it. If we did the latter the opposition would accuse us of being afraid of losing and ask why, if we knew we were not going to let the by-election run its course, we had started it. In the prevailing atmosphere, I believed we could make the row over the general election date a 24-hour wonder. John wanted more reassurance.

Both the sixth and the twentieth of March had their advocates. The Chief Whip, Alastair Goodlad, wanted as early a date as possible. Throughout our discussions with the Prime Minister (by then Alastair, Michel Heseltine, Tony Newton and I were his 'core' consultants) he argued that the political sub-plots in Parliament were detracting from our broader message.

Michael Heseltine and I were 'as late as possible' men – to give the improving economy more chance to influence voters favourably. Tony Newton, as he frequently did, saw both sides of the argument. After long meetings, 6 March started to emerge as the chosen date. This meant that there would be no Wirral by-election. CCO staff would be pleased; they were dreading another electoral pounding.

Then the Prime Minister called me to say we would not 'go' on 6 March. No explanation. 'You and I need to talk more about this,' he said. We did.

On 29 January, by arrangement, I went to see John in No. 10 about 9.30 p.m. He was sitting in an easy chair in his bedroom working, with piles of papers on the floor around his feet. We examined again the arguments for 6 and 20 March. John said he had little confidence in our ability to survive beyond 20 March. We had no working majority in the Commons and the Prime Minister believed it likely that Tony Blair would move a vote of no confidence in the Commons on the grounds that we were simply clinging to office, not governing. John was not wholly confident of winning such a vote, bearing in mind the disloyal behaviour of some Tory MPs, although given my strong relationship with James Molyneaux, I had reason to be confident the Ulster Unionists would not vote against us.

But John thought going beyond 20 March was risky. He was determined not to be driven into an election, as Jim Callaghan had been in 1979. To this day I still do not understand why Tony Blair did not put down a 'no confidence' motion. If it had failed Labour's position would still have been very strong and they could have claimed, with some credibility, that Conservative MPs only supported the government to avoid the prospect of losing their seats – not because they had confidence in the government.

We studied historic data about the length of time that had elapsed between the dissolution of a parliament and the consequent general election. And we worried about how long it would take Norman Blackwell to finish the manifesto. I told John I had recruited David Willetts MP to help Norman.

Eventually we decided that 6 March was too soon, so 20 March it had to be.

There remained two irritants. Choosing 20 March meant we would have to terminate the by-election, about which neither of us was comfortable. Secondly, the parliamentary party was over-whelmingly in favour of 1 May. To a man (and woman) their instinct was to put off defeat for as long as possible. The first of May was the near-unanimous view pressed on me when I had addressed the 1922 (backbench) Committee.

John remained concerned about giving the impression of simply clinging to power, which waiting until 1 May might imply, so he decided that 20 March it would be. He ended that part of our conversation with the words 'now that that's settled'.

We turned to practical election details. Who would travel with John? Where would the campaign start: St Albans, Hertford, Basildon, Croydon, Battersea or Huntingdon? (In the event it was Luton.) The date of the announcement. The credibility of our political messages. And so on.

About 10.30 p.m. Norma came in, gave us both a look and said that whatever the two of us were planning, she planned to go to bed. So would we please move. Now. We retired to the living room.

My diary record of that evening reflects: 'I do not often feel "historic" in this job, though I do realise that what we decide can have historic implications. But I went home on Wednesday night feeling that I had been a little part of history and wondered again how all this had happened to a simple Belfast boy.'

A couple of days later the Prime Minister called me to say he had changed his mind. The parliamentary party's expectations were too fixed on 1 May (which meant he had been lobbied on the date since our meeting). I told him 'Fine'. The following week I asked for a private word with John after a routine sub-Cabinet meeting. Rightly or wrongly I adopted an ironic tone; on reflection it was probably wrong. Maybe I was more annoyed than I was willing to admit.

> Prime Minister, constitutionally the calling of a general election is your prerogative. I support you in that and thank you for including me in the process. I have only one request. The next time you decide on an election date please will you stick with it. I have no problem not going to the country on 20 March and affirm again this is your decision to make. But your change of mind has cost the party probably well over £1 million. Do not worry about that, Phil Harris and I will set about replacing it – but this is not good practice. So, next time, please could we stick to the chosen date.

John was doubly upset and did not hide it. He made clear he did not like my tone, then focused on the substance of what I had said. 'Why the cost?' he demanded.

> What do you think I have been doing since our last meeting? You have been doing what Prime Ministers do. I have been doing what Party Chairmen do. I have been booking poster sites around the country. In the weeks leading up to 20 March we have leased about

70 per cent of all available sites. They have been leased through a number of agencies so no easily identifiable political message has gone out about election timing. Now we have thousands of sites we do not need. Worse, I will have to spend hundreds of thousands of pounds with Maurice Saatchi to put out an unplanned message on those sites I cannot get rid of, to little useful purpose. All this we can handle and no serious harm has been done. But, please, next time, can we stick to the agreed date.

John was not amused and I was probably out of order in speaking as I did (though the message itself was valid). But our friendship and working relationship were strong and I believed my robust loyalty to him in public gave me some occasional licence to speak forthrightly in private. Nevertheless, on reflection, I should probably have given more weight to the huge problems John was dealing with and decided to handle issues around a new date with a little more delicacy.

There then followed yet more meetings about the election date. Those who wanted to go 'long' prevailed. The first of May was chosen and announced. We were trounced in the Wirral by-election, but it would be impossible to argue convincingly that this result seriously influenced the general election outcome. It was simply a foretaste of things to come.

†

Backbenchers have little personal exposure to any Prime Minister, so my contact with Margaret was limited. But one day was memorable. The 1985 Finance Bill Committee sat for ten weeks. We started about 4 p.m. every Tuesday and worked through the night until lunchtime on the Wednesdays. We reconvened on Thursday afternoons and worked until between 10 p.m. and 1 a.m. on the Fridays. Both Barney Hayhoe MP, a Treasury minister, and I, his Parliamentary Private Secretary, were on the committee. As our normal busy lives continued each week alongside the committee meetings we all became pretty exhausted.

Normally we would adjourn about 8 a.m. on the Wednesdays for a 45-minute breakfast break. One morning in July we went down to the tea room to find the Prime Minister waiting for us. Someone had advised her of our long hours and thought we would all appreciate a visit from her to say 'thank you'.

So there she was, full of vim and vigour, looking immaculate. She sat at the middle of a long table and we were encouraged to join her. I was near the front of the breakfast queue and just followed my colleague to a table where I found myself sitting opposite Margaret.

She was at her argumentative best. No matter what anyone said, about anything, she argued. She was, or seemed to me to be, loud and dominating. She made no allowance for the fact that we had just missed yet another night's sleep in defence of her government. If she did say 'thank you' I do not remember. What I do remember was the argumentativeness. It was both wearing and irritating to my sleep-starved mind.

I cannot recall my contribution to the conversation but I do remember her disagreeing sharply with a couple of my exhaustion-driven comments. Whatever I said, she was in no mood to accept it. I withdrew into myself, with the consoling thought that, though this woman could be impossible, it would soon be time to return to the committee.

Finally, I could take it no longer. I knew I had to move for otherwise I would say something that definitely would not be career enhancing! 'Please excuse me, Prime Minister, I have one or two things I must do before the committee reconvenes.' I left the table, the first to do so, in what seemed even to my exhausted sensibilities to be a stunned silence. Too bad. She was driving me nuts – for obvious reasons not a sentiment I could express. This was certainly not my experience of or reaction to Margaret when I was getting my six hours (if lucky) of nightly sleep.

Notwithstanding the above, Margaret could be very supportive both of those who worked in No. 10 and sometimes of her colleagues. One of her kindest gestures, as Prime Minister, was to host a drinks reception at No. 10 on each evening that a summer garden party was held at Buckingham Palace. MPs get invited to one of these garden parties each year, with spouse. Finishing the afternoon with the Prime Minister was a much-appreciated treat for MPs and their spouses.

It so happened that on the day of this particular Thatcher breakfast Betty and I were going to Buckingham Palace and then on to No. 10. Betty arrived at the Commons after lunch to find me in very bad form. In my exhaustion I was still fed up with Margaret and her insensitivity, no matter how well meaning she had intended to be. Why could she not see that a 'thank you' together with some soothing, supportive words would have fitted the bill perfectly?

In my view her ill-judged behaviour well reflected one aspect of Margaret's personality – on occasions she was simply a steamroller. I fumed to Betty, who tried to soothe me with some of the common sense I was seriously lacking.

Each year at her receptions Margaret, with Denis beside her, greeted her guests at the door to the State Reception Room. This is at the top of the main staircase, on which hung the pictures of her predecessors. She would hold out her hand and, when you took it, she would abruptly whip you across to Denis. In this way she could choose who to talk to.

Had Margaret not done so, garrulous MPs would have kept her talking all night. But this sensible process had the effect of making the person on the end of the lightening handshake feel that they were not of great importance to the Prime Minister. No one, least of all MPs, wants to be made to feel that they are of little consequence to their leader.

As I contemplated our No. 10 visit, a befuddled plan emerged. When I shook hands with the Prime Minister I would plant my feet and refuse to move when she sought to whip me across to Denis. If she broke her wrist in the process – too bad!

How irrational could anyone get?

Betty, when I told her, wisely did not argue. She could see I was exhausted, knowing that, when the moment came, I would relent – at least sufficiently to avoid an assault charge.

As we mounted that famous staircase I could see Margaret posi-
tioned in the doorway. Betty never said a word but she did give me
a warning look. I stopped myself in front of Margaret as she took
my hand. Instead of moving it along to Denis she held it with a
gentleness that was real and clearly meant to feel so. She leaned
towards me and looked into my eyes.

'Did you get any sleep last night, Brian?'

'I got enough, Prime Minister, thank you.'

'Yes,' she said and nodded, 'you got enough.' She then handed me
on to Denis with what I can only describe as tenderness.

What a remarkable, sensitive woman.

In the space of less than half a day all the personality traits that
made Margaret such a formidable leader and so loved and admired
were on display. She was tough, fully briefed and strong willed
and had a well-developed instinct to try to stiffen the resolve of
colleagues and others. She was thoughtful in her kindness and,
sometimes, tender and caring towards those who worked closely
with her. In truth she could come across as dominating, irritating
and beyond correction. Yet most of the time most people thought
that handling those aspects of her personality was an acceptable
price to pay for all her many strengths and virtues. Thatcherism's
place in history already seems to support that analysis.

I knew John better than I knew Margaret, not least because she
was a political half generation ahead of me. Margaret and I were
never friends as John and I were, though we grew closer after I
became Party Chairman.

Relations between Margaret and John began to become edgy
while he occupied No. 11 Downing Street and started to deterio-
rate around the time John moved into No. 10 following Margaret's
historic and emotionally charged ousting. The rift between them,
which was politically real, slowly and irreversibly widened. Much
has been written about their strained relations. In my view too many
of these media interpretations owed more to the writers' political
sympathies than to the facts. I liked (and still like) both of them,
appreciated their strengths and tried to understand their weaknesses.

Part of my job as Party Chairman, as I have explained above, was to help prepare the party for a general election which was always going to be held in 1997. I say 'always' because the Prime Minister, his Deputy (Michael Heseltine) and I all subscribed to the mantra that while good economies did not ensure victory, bad economies were electoral bad news. Our economy was improving and people's personal disposable income was rising. They needed as much time as possible to feel the benefit, if we were to benefit.

My simple view was that our prospects of winning that election would also be improved if the present and past Prime Ministers conveyed the same message, comfortably together. Party unity is important to the electorate. So my task was to make Margaret again feel part of the mainstream of the party, not just connected to her band of Commons supporters, which was a serious challenge. Margaret's dismissal from office, though not from the affection of many party members, had had a seismic effect on her.

Understandably John Major believed his victory in 1992 gave him the right to govern as he saw fit. He insisted he was not elected simply to be a clone of Thatcher. In his view the inescapable conclusion of Margaret's removal from office was that he was free to be different.

John regularly reminded those close to him that Margaret knew how politically damaging Ted Heath's constant drip-drip of criticism of her had been. As a consequence he believed she should have been loyal to him both in public and private and, perhaps more importantly, made her advisers and right-wing colleagues behave similarly.

Neither happened.

Margaret, on the other hand, was traumatised by her unprecedented removal from office. You only had to be with her to 'feel' her pain. Three times the public had endorsed her, after which she found herself removed by 'frit' MPs. She was still aggrieved when I became Party Chairman five years later and her close supporters remained unforgiving. The party was split between the two of them with many wanting to support and love them both. And, without the salutary experience of having to deal daily with Europe, the Treasury and the party in the Commons, Margaret's views increasingly diverged from John's – as did their leadership styles.

To be fair, Margaret never once even hinted to me that she believed John was complicit in her 'downfall'. However, we humans have a natural inclination to turn on the messenger because we do not like the message. My sense is that John was sometimes the victim of this sort of instinctive behaviour from some of Margaret's followers.

Part of the difference between them was indeed one of style. John did make difficult, contentious decisions but he obviously valued being thought consensual more highly than Margaret did. In that sense he had more need to be personally appreciated. Whether she was liked or not seemed less important to Margaret, she was driven more by conviction (which sometimes had to be reined in).

Their rhetoric too was different. John's was more nuanced, always looking for that consensual approach even when it was difficult to find. Margaret's rhetoric was more robust and intransigent even when subsequent events belied it.

Today's Europe – like it or not – was primarily shaped by decisions taken while Margaret was in the Council of Ministers. She signed up to the single market and, in the public's perception, got 'our' money back. The fact that we are still opted out of the European single currency is John's achievement, with, it is only fair to recognise, a little help from Gordon Brown, who thwarted Tony Blair's contrary intentions.

As I said, trying to effect some mending of fences between these two big political beasts was a serious challenge. Obviously as John's Party Chairman, I saw him more frequently. On a regular basis he would talk to me about Margaret – always when we were alone. My listening mode must have encouraged him for his comments became more frank as time passed. I became a sounding board for his reflections and, sometimes, for his anger at what Margaret was alleged to have said or the fact that, apparently, she refused to control her acolytes' criticism of him.

I paid a formal visit to Margaret soon after my appointment as chairman to seek her advice on how I should set about my new job. This was well received. (As opposed to my visit to Ted Heath, who received me courteously but was not interested.)

Initially she was reserved or at least cautious. However, as my visits became regular events we both became more relaxed. We chatted – usually just the two of us – about what was happening in the party, government, country and world. She gave me her assessments frankly and sometimes in terms which were less than appreciative. Normally these were variants around a constant theme. Britain, especially in Europe, needed leadership which was strong, clear and consistent with our history, values and convictions. Slowly she also became less restrained in her comments about individuals, including some who had served in her government.

In the early days she made only an occasional direct comment about John and his performance as PM. Sometimes she was complimentary; at other times she could be critical and would champion a simpler, robust approach. I responded calmly and circumspectly, even when I was disagreeing with her and 'defending' John. As time passed her comments became more frequent, analytical and biting. I still responded calmly and made it clear that I was not some sort of prize to be won in a political tug of war. As a member of the Cabinet I explained what we were doing, and why, and that I supported our collective approach. I gently deflected some of her criticism and listened to the rest, stressing that I respected her views both when I agreed with her and when I did not. That straightforward honesty seemed to be well received. We never approached a slanging match and this too, I think, she appreciated. I adopted the same attitude in conversations with John that related to Margaret.

My regular meetings with Margaret, initially scheduled for about forty-five minutes, started to stretch to sixty then to ninety minutes and very occasionally to two hours. Once in a while Denis would drop in to be friendly. Otherwise for the most part we were left alone – obviously on her instructions.

Neither John nor Margaret ever gave me an explicit message for the other. Neither probed my conversations with the other. I was a sponge for their views and both left it to me to decide how much I should 'drip' on the other.

In our early meetings I had the sense that Margaret expected to read about our conversations in the media and that if she did she would react negatively. But I had no intention of talking. Vanessa Ford, my outstanding PA at Conservative Central Office, knew where I was but no one else. Most of the time I did not tell John about my appointments and I never discussed the substance of my conversations with either of them with anyone else. I was privileged to know what each thought of the other – both their strengths and their weaknesses – but neither pressed me to reveal what I knew. My judgement is that they both cared what the other thought but neither would demean themselves by asking.

Margaret seemed to believe that as John was the inheritor of Thatcherism he should be its defender. Knowing John, I was always surprised that Margaret saw him, or was persuaded to see him, as being at heart 'one of us'. While that may have been broadly true on economic policy my perception was that, at least on social policy, John was politically to the left of Margaret. I think Margaret's realisation, over time, that her views and John's did not precisely overlap helped to unsettle her and undermine her confidence in his ability (or desire) to continue her specifically Thatcherite tradition.

Neither I nor anyone else will ever know how much the multiple conversations Margaret and I had mitigated the differences between her and John. I would like to think they did – but then I would say that, wouldn't I?

As Party Chairman I oversaw two major structural changes to the party's headquarters, then at 32 Smith Square, just down the road and round the corner from Parliament. Originally the research department and the press office were on different floors. We stripped out one floor and built the first-ever integrated department with researchers and press officers sitting side by side. Traditionalists did not like the change but it made sense, reduced mistakes and overlap, and made our contact with the real world more effective. Proximity in politics is hugely important, just as access is a prized asset.

I also appointed new heads of research (Danny Finkelstein) and media (Charles Lewington). Each excelled in his vocation, was a good leader and communicator and they worked well together. Incidentally Danny, a good Conservative, came from an SDP background. Some old-time Tories were disgruntled by the appointment but I decided that merit not tribe should be the determining factor. He was certainly a huge improvement, in relational and political terms, on his predecessor, Andrew Lansley, who went on to become a Member of Parliament and a Cabinet minister. My judgement was further vindicated after they left the service of the party. Danny is a much-respected editorial commentator with *The Times*. Charles set up his own business, Hanover, which continues to prosper.

The second structural change involved building a new and disgracefully expensive modern press conference facility. It was designed like an intimate theatre within CCO with separate access from the street. John was impressed by this new facility, was comfortable using it and held his general election press conferences there.

Sometime after John had first visited this restructured headquarters I invited Margaret to come and see the changes. She had not been to CCO since leaving No. 10. Her evident pleasure on receiving my invitation made me think that she had thought she would never again enter the door of No. 32.

There was a large media presence to greet her. She rejected all my suggestions about what she might say on the doorstep and talked instead about trade unions, their influence nationally and on the Labour Party. It was vintage Margaret – though as a result of her government's legislation, trade unions were not as big a public issue as previously they had been.

I walked her through the whole building – not just the new bits – for old times' sake. She was interested, impressed and reflected on days past as we went from room to room and met people she knew. But she was excellent also with the new, young people she did not know. She approved of the changes and was very talkative in the tea session organised to conclude her visit, even if some of her views were a little off message. That afternoon helped improve my relationship with Mrs T mainly because she left us feeling that, again, she was part of the party.

The next day John wanted to know why Margaret had been to Central Office. I reminded him that I had told him in advance about the visit – I am sure I did! He nodded but said nothing. I told him why she had been there and what we had done and I made it clear that it was my call as Party Chairman. John left me with the impression it would not have been his call.

Whatever Margaret's personal assessment of John – which oscillated depending on the latest Prime Ministerial response to events – she was at the centre of a perpetual tug of war for her 'affections' which influenced that assessment. On the one hand there were those, mainly on the right of the party, who considered themselves the guardians of her legacy. So whenever John did or said anything – no matter how sensible, important or in the national interest – that they thought varied in any way from what Margaret might or would have said or done they pressed her to be critical. Sometimes she was too swayed by their prejudice.

On the other hand there were plenty in the party who, recognising her continuing importance to the hearts of party members and to the minds of the general public, continually pressed her to speak out in more robust support of her successor. They wanted her to appreciate John as much as they did. As Party Chairman naturally I preferred the second option and thought John deserved it. If that was not available then 'no comment' or silence were the next best things. When, occasionally, she chose the first option life quickly became difficult.

Unlike, apparently, all Prime Ministers I have never been much interested in creating a so-called legacy. To me it was more important to do things because, at the time, they were the right things to do. I thought then, and still do, that this is the most solid foundation for legacy and is likely to be endorsed by the judgement of historians. I remain to be convinced that politicians in office can 'spin' future historians.

I remember one speech Margaret made – I think it was the first Nicholas Ridley Memorial Lecture – which well illustrates the point. It included some not too coded criticisms of the Prime Minister and his policies and therefore was not helpful. The speech, which was to be delivered that evening, arrived in Central Office in early afternoon. For me the timing was awful. I had back-to-back meetings, each one more difficult and demanding than the previous one. From about 3.30 p.m. Vanessa kept popping in with notes saying that Margaret was going to make a speech that evening, that it was 'unhelpful' and that I needed to read it – quickly.

Like when? I ignored the notes.

Then Charles Lewington arrived in my office followed by Danny Finkelstein and after him Michael Trend. My office was like a train station, crowded with people passing through. I became increasingly irritated. 'That woman' was becoming a pain.

Eventually, some time after 5 p.m., I had to give up my meetings and read Margaret's speech. I was very cross at this, to me, totally unnecessary intrusion and my unhappiness was soon enhanced by parts of her speech that were simply unfair to John. This could prove to be very difficult. Her silence would definitely have been preferable.

The team and I quickly decided we needed to set up, in advance, a public response or framework for media reporting of the speech, to reduce the speech's anti-John sting. In politics, as in other walks of life, getting your retaliation in first can be an advantage. It provides media distraction and, normally, guarantees that some element of balance gets conveyed in media reports.

Next we agreed that I should give the response, not the Prime Minister. Frankly we were afraid he would not be as balanced as I would be, mainly because I was not the one being criticised. If our fears about the Prime Minister's reaction were to be proved correct then, instead of shutting down the story, his response might just give it new legs.

The above may sound very dramatic but in fact decisions about who should handle media stories were a standard part of our lives. That helps explain why, in a Conservative government at least, the Prime Minister and Party Chairman are the most publicly visible politicians.

Soon a message arrived from No. 10. The Prime Minister too was not much impressed with aspects of Margaret's speech and wanted the chairman to handle the response. Clearly officials in Downing Street had been having the same sort of discussion we had.

Charles was told to alert the electronic media at Millbank, who of course had had an advance copy of Margaret's speech, that I would soon be down to respond to what she was planning to say. My remarks had to be carefully judged. If I openly rejected those aspects of her speech which were critical of government policy I would upset Margaret and set back or, depending on how strident I was, maybe destroy the relationship I was building with her – one which was important to the party. A strident rejection would also give the story more publicity.

On the other hand government policy, for which I had collective responsibility as a member of the Cabinet, was being criticised. And part of my job as head of the Prime Minister's larger private office was to ensure that John was treated as fairly as it was possible to achieve.

So we decided that, in my media replies, I would concentrate on those aspects of Margaret's speech which supported what the Prime Minister and Cabinet were doing. I would simply ignore the rest, the critical paragraphs. If questioned on them – as we knew I would be – I would divert back to the issues on which we agreed. That great crooner Bing Crosby had it right: sometimes it is best to 'accentuate the positive, eliminate the negative'.

I spent about seventy minutes doing television and radio interviews. The fact that I undertook them was in itself, of course, a media signal that we were concerned about Margaret's remarks. However, what I said did have the effect of calming the atmosphere and reducing potential damage to the government. The episode did not improve Major–Thatcher relations. John was seldom effusive in his thanks but he clearly appreciated the handling of Margaret's speech and the damping down of its potentially incendiary consequences.

That evening had a rather ironic ending. I was due to be having dinner with Michael Heseltine. We ate together every three or four weeks to talk politics, policy and the way forward, having agreed previously that if we both offered the Prime Minister the same advice then that advice became stronger and therefore more likely to be adopted. As Michael and Margaret had often differed, fundamentally, I got little sympathy from him when I explained how fraught my day had been.

Michael and I had a strong friendship which had grown with time. We were close before and while he contested the leadership of the party. Every political generation has one or two politicians who could have made good Prime Ministers had they achieved that high office. In my opinion Michael is one such.

†

Perhaps the most significant public handling challenge posed by the two Prime Ministers' relationship occurred at the 1996 Party Conference. Margaret had indicated that she would attend the start but would not be able to remain to hear the Prime Minister's speech on the final day. By tradition the Party Chairman's speech was the main speech just before lunch on the first morning. Margaret and John would make their initial appearances in time for it.

After a lot of CCO planning I went to see John. I proposed that there would be two John–Margaret 'meetings' on that Tuesday. The first would be for my Conference speech. The suggested choreography was that the Conference chairman would escort Margaret to her seat on the platform earlier in the morning session. In this way Conference could focus on her alone and give her a warm welcome – which it did.

Later I would escort the Prime Minister on to the platform. We would both walk over to Margaret. John would give her a peck on the cheek. I would follow suit. The session would then continue and I would recognise both of them in my speech. John's reaction was positive about the appropriateness of cheek pecking.

On the day John's reception was, if anything, even warmer than Margaret's but neither could have complained about the show of affection. In my speech, when lauding Margaret, I borrowed from an American politician. Tony Blair, as opposition leader, had been claiming to be the heir to Thatcher. Having praised Margaret I added: 'Mr Blair. I know Margaret Thatcher. Margaret Thatcher is a friend of mine. You are no Margaret Thatcher.'

The Conference erupted and Margaret smiled broadly. They all loved it and John applauded robustly with everyone else. In the hall only he and I knew that, when I had told him I was going to use that quote, he had wanted to add it to his speech – but I had declined to withdraw.

It was not easy to know what to say about John that might elicit an equivalent response from Conference. I need not have worried. I spoke of his upbringing, his success in business and politics, his decency and concern for others, his leadership and how he put his country first.

Anthony Seldon in his book *Major: A Political Life* summed up the Conference thus:

> By Tuesday, a feeling of cautious optimism was beginning to spread among the (Conservative Party) leadership ... Mawhinney, delighted at his brokering of peace between Major and Thatcher, himself delivered a strong speech, saying 'Mr Blair, you are no Margaret Thatcher'. He had high praise for his leader: 'This man, this tough fighter, this compassionate, decent man, this true Brit, this is the best man to be our Prime Minister.'

The Conference rose to John – literally. This was the only time during my thirty years at Conferences that one politician was given a standing ovation in the middle of another's speech. Margaret applauded enthusiastically with everyone else.

For me the more fraught part of the Conference was still to come. Despite some CCO reservations about the plan being too high risk, I had decided that, because in the general election I wanted John and Margaret to do something together, we ought to have a 'dry run'. What better setting could there be than at a Party Conference where everyone revered them both?

They agreed to make a joint appearance at the London Conservatives Reception one evening. Literally hundreds of people attended including some reporters and TV crews, privately briefed earlier, who added to the crush.

Agreeing arrangements for the event had been delicate. John, as Prime Minister, would speak second, but my nervousness lay primarily in what each might say. The story I wanted was harmony, unity and mutual respect. The danger was that policy and personality differences might derail those good intentions.

So, tentatively, I asked them (separately) if they would write out their five-minute speeches and let me read them in advance, which to politicians of their standing could be considered a serious insult. To my amazement Margaret immediately agreed. John did not take so kindly to the suggestion and insisted he would speak without notes. Then he looked at me, smiled, nodded and said he was in favour of what I was doing and would be careful and supportive. He promised to say nothing that would cause me unease. He kept his word.

Margaret and John spoke well and were mutually reinforcing. The event was an outstanding political success – John and Margaret could undertake joint events – and was reflected as such by the media. London Conservatives were happily boisterous and everyone went off to dinner in good spirits.

That 1996 Conservative Conference can claim a small footnote in political history. John always excelled in question and answer sessions, in my opinion more so than sometimes when making a set speech, and I often told him so. He was more knowledgeable than people expected and explained issues clearly and with charm. He answered questions directly and never got flustered.

One day I had a proposal for him:

Will you do a massive question and answer session as part of the Conference itself? Spontaneously. Microphones around the hall.

Any representative present can ask whatever they like. No advance notice of questions. The media must be convinced that this is a real spontaneous initiative and not a set-up job; otherwise we will be blasted for trying to 'con' people.

Only you and me on the platform. I will introduce the proceedings, call the questions and keep an eye on the time. You do the answers. Mobile microphones mean you can move around the stage as you wish. I will stay close, but not too close, and promise not to get in your way.

John, surprised, agreed relatively quickly and with a degree of enthusiasm.

Very few in CCO knew what was planned and the official programme gave no clue to those attending Conference. On the preceding evening John and I had paced the Conference stage. It was then we decided to shed our jackets, the next morning, to emphasise that we were relaxed but getting down to business.

The media remained in the dark. For once we genuinely surprised people, which added to the positive impact. Today, question and answer sessions are commonplace at party conferences. David Cameron did the first leader's speech without reading from a script and did it exceptionally well. But in 1996 this Q and A initiative was a big step into the unknown. John Major should be commended for taking the political risk and for enhancing the democratic process. He showed he was the master of his brief. Everyone could see that he was good.

†

In the weeks running up to my first Conference as chairman in 1995, there was much media speculation that John Major might be awarded the Nobel Peace Prize for his work in the Northern Irish peace process. The announcement of who had won the prize was due to be made on Friday 13 October, precisely while John was delivering his end of Conference speech.

The name of the Peace Prize recipient is a closely guarded secret. Even No. 10 had no information about the likely outcome. Clearly we needed a handling strategy in case John won. I raised the subject with him two or three weeks prior to the Conference. He refused even to discuss it. On a couple of other occasions I got a similar dusty response.

Finally, a few days before we left for Conference, I met with him and Howell James (head of his political office) and insisted that we agree a plan. Incidentally Howell, who was sensible, politically astute and charming, did a fine job and handled the Prime Ministerial pressure of the job, and the tantrums, impressively.

John finally accepted that we did need a plan while remaining a reluctant participant in the conversation. There was no point wasting time on the possibility (probability, in his view) that he would not win. But what if he did?

Our first thought was to do nothing until after he sat down. Our second thought was that this was not an appealing plan. If he won, word would soon spread through the hall, either via the media or by Conservatives outside bringing the news inside. If that happened we thought it likely that those in the audience that heard the news would simply disregard protocol, get to their feet and start cheering. Not everyone would rise, however, because not everyone would hear the news or hear it at the same time. So it would be a mess and would look like a mess to television viewers. More importantly such a momentous event merited a more measured announcement.

Even if Conference physically restrained itself until after John's speech had finished, once they heard the news they would start talking and stop listening and responding to him. Again, television would reflect this disturbance and, perhaps, wrongly attribute it to a bad attitude to John's speech.

Finally, in the circumstances, it seemed a pity to waste a good speech and significant policy announcements, bearing in mind that they would be drowned out by extensive public coverage of the Peace Prize.

Finally John agreed to be bold. Howell, who was to be in charge behind the scenes, would send me, on the platform, a written note telling me the outcome. If John won it was agreed I would step forward and join him at the rostrum, move to the microphone (he would step aside because he would know why I was interrupting him) and simply announce the good news. I decided to couch it in terms of my being the first to congratulate him. I would then shake his hand, return to my seat and leave him to deal with the mayhem that would follow. Our strong advice to him was to abandon his speech and use his skill, experience and natural courtesy to close the Conference and get off the stage.

Howell's note duly arrived. For obvious reasons few in the hall would have focused on my briefly leaving the stage. I had decided it would be too embarrassing to make a mistake. I wanted Howell to tell me the result personally.

John's speech was well received and got positive media coverage. The fact that he did not win the Peace Prize was not a distraction. As one well placed to say so, I think John's outstanding efforts in Northern Ireland, which included transforming our relationship with the Irish government and paving the way for the Good Friday Agreement, should have been recognised more widely. If not then, later.

Although my relationship with Margaret was much improved by election time, she and I did not always see eye to eye. She kept her word and campaigned effectively with John and other candidates during the election, but trouble occurred at the candidates' meeting in CCO on a Sunday morning just after the election had been called.

With John's agreement I had invited Margaret to address the candidates, before him. Margaret spoke well and made only a side reference to Europe, but in acceptable terms. John was excellent and answered questions with great mastery and calmness.

On the previous day the Grand National had had to be postponed because of a published IRA threat. During that Sunday morning with the candidates we learned that the race had been rescheduled for the following day.

My diary takes up the narrative.

On being told, John immediately said he wanted to go and that he would announce it to the candidates so that Blair could not get in ahead of him. I [was very enthusiastic but] cautioned him to wait a few minutes while I checked the logistics. As I came back to the room to report I was met by Robert [Lord] Cranborne who said that, in my absence, they had all agreed that John would invite Blair and Ashdown to go with him. I retorted to the effect that I was not much impressed! I then entered the room and told John we could handle the logistics and that he could go if he wanted and that he was free to announce his intention. Margaret then told me they had all decided – Denis and Margaret Thatcher, Howell James, Alastair Goodlad, Robert Cranborne and others that Blair and Ashdown would go too [be invited to go]. John said nothing. I said this was a very bad idea and that I was strongly against it. It should not happen. It was ridiculous to enhance the act of evil men in this way.

Robust discussion followed.

John quickly backed off from inviting the other two.

Others in the room were concerned that John should not jump the gun by announcing [his intention] too early. They had security concerns. Some thought he should say nothing and just turn up. Knowing that he [John] was concerned not to be politically outflanked I said he should go ahead and announce the visit. I was absolutely clear in my mind that the police would make sure there was a ring of steel around Aintree on the Monday. There would be no trouble. Anyway the idea that the Prime Minister would get blamed for a bomb or someone getting killed by the IRA was an argument I was very willing to have. Margaret Thatcher suddenly lit into me. She was standing beside me and turned her face about twelve inches from mine and issued a loud protest about how irresponsible I was. It was irresponsible for the Prime Minister to announce [in advance] that he was going to go; we had not consulted the security forces;

what would I say if his going created another bomb or people got killed. How would I feel then? It was totally irresponsible etc. etc. What sort of a chairman was I etc. etc.? In other words she had a mega Thatcher rant.

I fixed her in the eye and did not blink throughout the whole thing. Did not give ground. Did not even move. I held a poker expression and gave her no indication that I was either impressed or intimidated. I think eventually she got the message because she moved away and said, 'Straight from the shoulder, just expressing my views, hope you don't mind.'

'I do not mind at all, Margaret. I just think you are wrong,' I said. 'I do not happen to agree with you, that's all.' There was a stunned silence in the room. Even John looked perplexed. Margaret did not say a word. John then had the idea of ringing the chairman of Aintree and getting himself invited. It was left like that.

As we walked out he gave me a strange look. I rolled my eyes heavenward and got a reassuring smile in return.

The rest of the morning's programme went well. Margaret was clearly worried that she had gone too far with me. She was solicitous and kept saying to whoever would listen that none of them had thanked me for all I had done and for organising the candidates' Conference and what a great success it had been.

I guess all those hours we had spent together had fostered a proper positive relationship with Margaret after all. Or maybe, as John had told me, she just valued people who 'stood up' to her and argued with her.

Those meetings with Margaret made possible both the joint Conference events in 1996 and the election efforts. Two extracts from my diary underline this view.

Early in my chairmanship: 'She is fine [with what we are doing] on everything except the Euro on which she is still opposed.' However, 'she was able to check herself when I made it clear that I simply was not going to discuss the issue with her.'

And later, in 1997, 'Our relationship has improved enormously.

She said generous things about the way I was running CCO and genuinely contributing to the party. She clearly sees me as a real Conservative as opposed to Michael Heseltine and Ken Clarke about whom she is scathing and dismissive.'

My relationships with John and Margaret were not evenly balanced. John was a contemporary and a personal friend. We entered the Commons together. We ate Indian meals together in London and in the Bombay Brasserie in Peterborough (an excellent restaurant run by my friend Roni Choudhury). Margaret appointed me a minister but John promoted me, made me a Privy Counsellor, took me into his Cabinet and made me Party Chairman. (Shortly after doing so he apologised privately to Betty for having given me this 'poisoned chalice'.) We did not always agree in private but in public I was totally loyal to him, nor did I ever forget that he was Prime Minister. John was appreciative of my efforts on his behalf though he is not by nature a flatterer. On three occasions in the weeks preceding the election, he asked me what Cabinet job I wanted in the event we won. I took that as a sign of appreciative friendship. I never did reply. Had I done so I would have chosen Business Secretary.

Given the nature of Margaret's relations with John, my conversations with her were more restrained and constrained. I treated her with the respect due to a distinguished former Prime Minister. Eventually she treated me with the appropriate respect, and degree of affection, which she thought a Party Chairman who treated her well deserved. I became her friend but, as with John, we were never particularly close.

Margaret and John; two Prime Ministers – two friends – it has been my privilege to know and with whom I was honoured to have worked closely.

A postscript

In light of today's political scene and the relevant lessons that can be learned from our pre-1997 general election experience, I am adding an extra story which reflects a lot of hard work but sadly not the outcome I wanted to achieve. I hope some will find it helpful.

I tried, and ultimately failed, to make the 1997 general election the first in which a debate was staged between the two main party leaders. Personally I admire the American presidential debates. Voters can benefit from seeing how their potential leaders prosper under the unique sort of pressure which a debate generates.

When I first raised the matter with John Major he was not enthusiastic. In fact on the first couple of occasions I tried, he did not want even to discuss it.

Eventually we engaged. He was worried that, if he agreed to debate, this willingness would be interpreted as concern about the election's outcome. Rather bluntly, I fear, I asked if he had read any of the recent polling information we at party headquarters had been forwarding to him.

Eventually he agreed in principle to debate, the first Conservative leader to do so. We then both said, independently, that we each had one condition. Any debate must be between him and Tony Blair only. Neither of us would agree to any three-way debates, to include Paddy Ashdown, leader of the Liberal Democrats.

Our reasoning was identical. Despite their own party-political hype there was no prospect of a Liberal Democrat Prime Minister being elected in 1997. So there was no justification for including him in a Prime Ministerial debate.

Secondly, as a consequence, there would be no restraint on what Ashdown might say in such a debate. He could make attractive promises, no matter how far fetched they might be or sound, or claim anything which might have the effect of unreasonably and unfairly damaging the two real Prime Ministerial candidates. Ashdown would know that, because he could not win, he would never be held to account for what he might say. In a three-way debate, one candidate who could say anything he liked, just to please the electorate, would always hold an unfair advantage over the other two, bearing in mind that one of them, when elected, would be expected to deliver what he had promised.

So we agreed, only Major and Blair. However, the rules govern-ing broadcasters' impartiality meant that some way would have to be found to accommodate Ashdown. Those rules were important for they bolstered the electronic media's requirement to be politically impartial. How well that impartiality is maintained in practice is an entirely different issue.

With John's approval, I entered detailed and secret conversations with a senior ITN executive. In those days we had more confidence in their political even-handedness than we did in the BBC's. We spent many hours on the phone and at two very private lunches – at a hotel in Bournemouth and a small restaurant in Hampstead, north London.

After the former we had an amusing moment on Bournemouth railway station when we discovered we were both returning to London on the same train. In order to avoid being seen together, which could have set political tongues wagging, we agreed to travel in different coaches.

Eventually we reached a conclusion which satisfied us as well as John Major and ITN's leadership team. There would be one ninety-minute televised programme. ITN wanted two and I agreed to leave open that possibility. The views of the BBC and the other parties would need to be taken into account – and I would need to persuade John, who was in a one-debate frame of mind.

Our agreement included an initial thirty-minute debate on home affairs by Major and Blair and a similar thirty-minute debate at the end on foreign affairs. One would be moderated by a BBC broadcaster, the other by someone from ITN. The parties could not pick the moderators but they could veto the broadcasters' nominees.

The middle thirty minutes would be devoted to a one-on-one interview with Paddy Ashdown who would have a say in the choice of interviewer. Our lawyers and ITN's agreed that such a format was acceptable under broadcasting rules. All that remained was to persuade all the others!

When I went to see the BBC they seemed somewhat nonplussed by the suggested format but they did not reject it. Their questions were entirely reasonable and predictable. Had I spoken to ITN? Yes. Were they in agreement with this proposal? Yes. They thought it both achievable and worthwhile. Had I spoken to Alastair Campbell (Labour)? No.

I heard later that Alastair was unenthusiastic about the very idea of a debate, never mind this format, so the BBC quickly became equally unenthusiastic. Before long the whole idea had foundered.

Partly to satisfy media pressure for a debate, representatives of the three main parties met with broadcasters. Michael Dobbs (the distinguished author and now a peer) represented us, very professionally. This was not a surprise. It was in anticipation of his skill and charm being put to effective use that I had recommended him to John in the first place.

I explained to Michael beforehand that we would not countenance a three-way debate or debates. He told me that, on the basis of his conversations, we would have to. I did understand how uncomfortable this restriction made his position but holding a three-way debate was not going to happen. I offered to let him hear the same message from the Prime Minister but he graciously said that would not be necessary. Labour's lack of interest in debating slowly caused the wider talks to wither, which protected us from being blamed for exercising our caveat.

The first party leaders' debates were held before the 2010 general election, three elections later. They were three-way debates. I do not know to whom David Cameron turned for advice on the format. Whoever it was gave him poor advice.

Betty and I watched the first debate (ultimately the only one that mattered) on television, as did many others. At the end she asked me what I thought. I told her, using the sort of undiplomatic words which husbands and wives use when they discuss issues in private.

Gordon Brown was never going to win either the election or the debate. He had too much negative baggage for the former and none of the skill or charisma necessary to achieve the latter. Sadly for him the debate simply emphasised both his fundamental weaknesses.

David Cameron was the one put at risk by the three-way process, especially bearing in mind that he entered the first debate with poll ratings which could and should have been translated into an overall electoral majority. But he could not cope with a slick, visually appealing and politically irresponsible third debater who knew he could not win so had nothing to lose. Caution in a Prime Minister can sometimes be praiseworthy, but it is usually much less so in a debater.

In my judgement Nick Clegg behaved exactly as John Major and I had feared his predecessor would have done, except that Paddy Ashdown had, and still has, much more gravitas. My precise description of Clegg's performance does not bear repeating but words such as 'opportunistic', 'populist', 'unfair', 'untrue', and 'irresponsible' came to mind.

The media loved it. So, too, did the public. They liked the idea of the 'little man' bashing and ridiculing the big boys. They seemed to give little, if any, thought to what Clegg was saying except perhaps at the most superficial level. Clearly they did not expect him to offer political coherence, pragmatic credibility or deliverability. Nor were they disappointed.

Liberal Democrats' poll ratings rose. Conservatives' fell. And the prospect of Cameron's overall majority melted away. The whole episode became a quick lesson in cause and effect. That first debate laid all the necessary groundwork for a coalition government.

David Cameron did better, later; but later was too late. What should have been the inevitability of a Tory government was gone. In its place, when ministers should have been concentrating on sorting out the mess of the country's finances – bequeathed by Labour – and focusing on raising the poor standards of education – bequeathed by Labour – they had to be distracted by Liberal Democrat proposals for alternative vote schemes and constitutionally wrecking the House of Lords. The word 'reform' has seldom been so abused by politicians, mainly of the Liberal Democrat variety, as it was on these issues.

Today many Liberal Democrats must rue what has happened to their political credibility over the last couple of years, especially as so many were impressed by their leader's first debate performance. Certainly many Tories rue the fact that he was given the opportunity to debate and as a consequence feel frustrated.

Had someone in the Conservative hierarchy thought to take soundings from those who had previously wrestled with the three-way debate issue, today we might be enjoying being governed by a Conservative government with greater clarity and accountability.

By the way, after the 1960 inaugural American presidential debates between Kennedy and Nixon had taken place several more such elections took place before there was a second set of debates. In other words, the precedent of having debates did not require all future presidential elections to include such debates. Personally, I hope David Cameron will reflect on that American lesson, on our judgement in 1997 and on his experience in 2010 and then insist on setting a new precedent in this country, when consideration next turns to the issue of future general election debates.

13

How to Lose an Election

Thursday 22 June 1995 was sunny. John Major held a press conference in the garden of 10 Downing Street, after Prime Minister's Questions, to announce that he had tendered his resignation as leader of the Conservative Party. He would be a candidate in the election to pick his successor. The outcome of that election would pitch me into running a general election. Anthony Seldon's *Major: A Political Life* has an excellent account of those days.

During the sixteen years John and I had been MPs, to that point, we got together maybe twice a year specifically for a meal and chat – as friends and political next-door neighbours do. Sometimes we indulged our shared enjoyment of Indian food in the Bombay Brasserie. The national press heard about our meals – not from me – and created the impression that these sessions carried more political weight than ever was the case, though our political views were broadly similar.

When we were first elected John already had many friends and admirers in the party and Parliament. I knew no one, had never even been in the Commons and my personality was less outgoing and sophisticated. As John said of me later, 'he is hard to get to know'; kindly adding that, as a result, my political alliances were slower to evolve. We shared mutual respect but were not family friends as John was, say, with Baroness Blatch and her husband John.

One evening in May 1995, while in the voting lobby, John told me it was time for another meal and chat. He decided on No. 10 for security reasons, despite my suggestion that his being seen eating out in a restaurant would be a political plus. But he insisted – security.

Nothing happened in May – despite a couple of reminders from me. Another conversation with John Ward MP, John's PPS, in early June also produced nothing. So I decided to give up. If the Prime Minister really wanted us to eat he could make it happen.

Then without warning on Tuesday 20 June John Ward called. The PM would like me to come to No. 10 for dinner the following evening and details would be confirmed the next day. He stressed repeatedly that I was to tell *no one* (apart from Betty) – obviously on instruction – and warned that I was not to approach No. 10 from Downing Street but use the inter-connecting door from the Cabinet Office.

While it would be nice to have dinner with the Prime Minister, I was less encouraged that he wanted to keep it secret. He probably did not want to appear to be favouring one minister over others was my guess. In the event it turned out I was doing my friend an injustice.

John Major makes no mention of that evening in his autobiography, nor does Anthony Seldon in his book. The latter knew about it but, with typical grace, honoured my request not to mention it. When Anthony and I had talked, details of those days had not yet been made public and we agreed that John should have the first option – one he did not choose to exercise.

We met in his flat's sitting room on that Wednesday evening and soon relaxed into friendly chat. (When talking to John privately it always took a few minutes to get past the fact that he was Prime Minister.) We enjoyed a delicious meal served by a female member of the armed forces.

During the main course John said he wanted my opinion on a serious matter. It was private. The party was in turmoil over Europe and he was not prepared to change government policy. He believed his policy was right for the country, if not for everyone in the Conservative Party. And he noted that there was strengthening talk of a leadership challenge to him in October.

There were, he said, three options. First, he could continue with the same policy and by his unwillingness to change 'dare' his colleagues to produce a leadership challenger – real or Trojan horse. A challenge would not be good for party unity and our electoral prospects, he said. My strong sense was that he thought the party would not vote a second Prime Minister out of office, particularly so soon after the first. If there were to be a challenge, however, then he would expect to win but, probably, would emerge as electorally 'damaged goods', his phrase, not an attractive prospect in the run-up to a general election.

His second option was to resign as Prime Minister and lay claim to his successes; he particularly mentioned the euro opt-out. He would make it clear that someone else could wrestle with the European issues and get covered with the reputational flying mud. From the party's point of view he doubted that his colleagues would find this an attractive option, ahead of a general election.

His third option was to resign the party leadership while remaining Prime Minister, and fight for re-election. He thought this could have two advantages. It might shock the party sufficiently to enhance its loyalty and therefore our electoral prospects. Also, the leadership election would be called by him at a time of his choosing which would give him an advantage. Other candidates would have little time to organise. He thought this option could be seen as an act of leadership and that his winning would be electorally positive. He did not explore the consequences of losing.

As he explained the three options I knew he was not really 'consulting' me. He had already decided what to do and was simply interested in my reaction. So I suggested he choose option three, which he then confirmed was his preference. As we discussed the matter over dinner his language became increasingly firm in favour of this choice.

Seldon's book reveals that my experience was not unique. Apparently after I left No. 10 that night, John saw Robert (Lord) Cranborne and told him, 'You are going to have to be pretty persuasive if you are going to dissuade me from the third option.' Cranborne agreed to lead Major's re-election team. When the Cabinet met the following morning, apparently about half of us knew what the Prime Minister planned and half did not. No one said a word.

My immediate reaction on hearing the news was that John ran a possible risk of highlighting his weakness rather than his leadership. But his other options were less appealing and would have highlighted weakness more, so I supported his choice. Anyway there was no obvious alternative candidate who would make a better or more acceptable leader than John.

During dinner John's principal private secretary arrived. He hesitated when he saw me but John told him to proceed. He conveyed responses to the proposed course of action from Buckingham Palace, Lambeth Palace and the Head of the Civil Service.

I have been a senior politician long enough to know never to quote the Palace. Lambeth's response amounted to little more than an acknowledgment of the news. The Head of the Civil Service replied in terms which were unenthusiastic about the proposal but using more colourful language.

All three responses were interesting (at least to me) but none affected John's decision.

We returned to the sitting room where I gladly accepted John's invitation to help in his re-election campaign. He also invited me to observe the next day's press conference, which, weather permitting, would be held in the garden. On the day Ian Lang MP was the only other Cabinet minister present, with Norma, on the balcony outside the Cabinet Room.

Just before I left No. 10 that evening, I asked John if he had told the Party Chairman of his intention. As I left the room he was picking up the phone to speak to Jeremy Hanley MP.

Robert picked Alastair Goodlad MP as his second deputy alongside Ian Lang, who was John's choice. Although a Cabinet minister I was definitely the outsider. Robert explained my attendance at the first team meeting as being John's choice, in a tone which suggested I would not have been his. As the campaign progressed Ian Lang and I concentrated on the press briefings and a significant number of the official media interviews.

On the Monday before the vote I missed the regular early-morning team meeting because of Transport business (I was still running the department through all this). The team discussed a request from BBC *Panorama* to stage a debate on that evening's programme between John and his challenger, John Redwood MP. The team decided the debate should proceed with someone substituting for John Major, who would not himself debate.

In my absence I was chosen as the 'someone'. Had I been present I would have argued strongly against the whole idea. In this election we were not trying to influence national voters. While the programme might benefit the BBC and interest its viewers I could see no benefit to John. Our electorate was Conservative MPs, most of whom would not watch, much less be influenced by, any such debate. And no matter how careful we were Conservative differences would be on show.

The programme went out live and most of the audience of Conservative activists thought it went well for John Major. Party members had much more loyalty to the Prime Minister than did some Tory MPs. Team members and others were complimentary about my contribution.

John Major was re-elected comfortably. On the following day he reshuffled his Cabinet. I was appointed Party Chairman and Minister without Portfolio in the Cabinet Office. I was also made a member of significant Cabinet committees where I could contribute a relatively independent (i.e. non-departmental) view. I was not a member of the Cabinet's Northern Ireland Committee but did receive its papers so I could talk knowledgeably to the Prime Minister directly about the Province, which pleased me.

During our reshuffle conversation, John said he had received a lot of pressure from both inside and outside the Commons to appoint me Party Chairman. Apparently people liked my focused and logical presentations and willingness to 'take on' Labour. He asked me to continue behaving this way and to get a grip on the party organisation, adding that he wanted me in the Cabinet so I could continue to offer sound advice and political insight, which was kind of him. On reflection those marching orders suggested to me that my place in his re-election team had been a test of my abilities, my willingness to work closely with colleagues I did not know well and perhaps my discretion.

The first few months as chairman were hectic. I reorganised party headquarters and appointed Michael Trend MP as my deputy, to take day-to-day charge. Michael Simmonds, my special adviser at Transport, strengthened the team. Both were real assets, on whom I depended greatly. I very much appreciated their hard work, insights and commitment. I also had to find new leadership for our research and media departments.

My other early priority was establishing strong links with No. 10. I had promised John that, 'in public, no one would ever be able to slip a piece of paper between us on any issue'. I kept that promise, as a Christian should, though understandably it took John some time to be reassured to the point where he fully accepted I meant what I said. In private I had greater freedom to express my views and used it, though often with discretion.

After my first Party Conference in October I summoned my initial 'top of the office' meeting to explore general election issues and organisation. I asked to see the preliminary planning done by my predecessor only to be told that none existed.

In the second meeting we looked at every published opinion poll since the 1992 general election. Then we had received just over 40 per cent of the votes. By 'Black Wednesday', the following September, we had dropped to just under 40 per cent. Within a few weeks of that disastrous day we were down to about 30 per cent, our core support, and remained there for the following three years. Nothing the government or MPs did in those years seemingly affected public opinion. This was a counterintuitive fact that never seemed to register with political commentators.

By the latter part of 1995 no one was talking about Black Wednesday any more. So the steady 30 per cent polling clearly suggested that the public had already made a judgement about us and were simply waiting for the general election to express it. Our aim had to be to find more effective ways to persuade them to renew their confidence in us. We had to hope this could happen – unless, of course, the judgement they had already passed was irreversible.

We planned a detailed and comprehensive election campaign strategy, aided by someone anonymously sending us the Labour Party's electoral grid programme of initiatives. We sought new ways to send personal messages to voters, over the heads of the media, from both the Prime Minister and me. This was hard to do effectively because, to my amazement, the party had no central record of names and addresses or email addresses. Conservative associations had proved very resistant to giving us access to their membership lists. They simply did not trust Central Office – a depressing state of affairs.

We also set up a new 'instant' rebuttal service to respond to Labour attacks masterminded by the ferocious but impressive Alastair Campbell. A Labour story immediately corrected or denied reduced negative press coverage and generated credibility for our own positive media output.

Two complementary strategies were discussed. Following the nadir of Black Wednesday the economy started to improve and people's disposable income increased. Usually these factors were politically favourable for the government. However, in our case, because the effect of Black Wednesday had been so dire, we got no credit for the fact that people were increasingly better off. Voters believed any improvement was due to their working harder and had nothing to do with the government. Our challenge was to convince them otherwise. We tried hard, but failed.

Our other strategy stemmed from the change Tony Blair imposed on his party. He jettisoned many of Labour's most strongly held beliefs, or principles, as he moved his party towards the political centre ground. Clause Four disappeared. Nationalisation was off the agenda (except for a late wobble over transport). Tax and spend, the historic speciality of Labour Chancellors, was to be a thing of the past (Gordon Brown cynically cancelled that promise immediately after Labour won). Trade unions were to be kept under tighter control and British business was seduced.

All this was wrapped up in a user-friendly name – New Labour.

Their agenda proved successful. New Labour moderated its rhetoric and sounded more conservative. Soon newspaper stories suggested there was little difference between the two potential governments. This was stunningly difficult for us because it implied New Labour was now safe to vote for. We needed people to understand the risk associated with voting Labour.

After a lot of research, discussion and help from Maurice Saatchi, we targeted the word 'New'. 'New' could mean fresh, remade, full of promise, different from the old – which was Labour's intention.

It could also imply untried, untested, dangerous – which was our alternative strategy.

Hence was born 'New Labour, new danger'. This idea held real promise if the polls were to be believed.

Unless we could quickly undermine New Labour we knew its potential credibility would politically 'do for us'. So we developed a strategy around the 'new danger' thought and started slowly to make progress until, led by John Major, the party suffered a collective collapse of political will. After only a little media pressure my colleagues got 'frit' – which was a bad omen.

Every branding exercise needs a logo. We chose red eyes. Our message was that under Labour 'Big Brother' would be watching every aspect of people's lives. Even we had no idea how accurately prophetic we were being. We used the eyes in a party-political advertisement. No one commented on them – save to ask what they meant. The explanation was accepted without question and certainly without criticism by the same media who went hysterical the second time around.

One day Clare Short MP – one of Labour's frontbenchers – lashed out at the 'new' bit of New Labour. Her attack summed up our message, but in words we would never have dared use. So we prepared a newspaper advertisement which read: 'One of Labour's leaders, Clare Short, says dark forces behind Tony Blair manipulate policy in a sinister way. I sometimes call them the people who live in the dark.' She said about New Labour, 'It's a lie. And it's dangerous.'

We superimposed our red eyes on a picture of Tony Blair's face, to illustrate her message, and sent it as an advertisement to the *Mail on Sunday*. Jonathan Holborow, the editor, told us how much he liked it. Later he rang back. He still liked the ad and wanted to use it but, he said, several of his colleagues thought it too 'spooky'. Did we want to think again? Central Office colleagues remained firmly in favour of its use. I tracked down Maurice Saatchi to his home in France (his company had produced the ad) and we spent a long time debating the issue as the *Mail on Sunday*'s deadline approached.

Before Jonathan's call, Maurice had been gung-ho about the advertisement. Nor was he worried about personalising the political attack on Blair. The words were Clare Short's and not from any Tory. Eventually, after dithering for two hours, he flipped and said we should pull it. My problem was that he did not advance any coherent argument in support of his wish to reverse our intention. Fairly or unfairly, I decided I was really listening to commercial concern.

I knew the ad would be controversial. That was positive. The greater the controversy the more the message 'New Labour, new danger' would be impressed on the public mind. At no point did anyone – me or anyone else – speak of the ad in the context of 'devil eyes'. Should the possibility of this interpretation have occurred to us? Why should it? When previously the eyes had been used it had not occurred to the British media, the Labour Party, the Prime Minister or any of us. Using the concept of the devil was not something I, a Christian, would do. Nor would I dream of linking the devil, in whose existence I do believe, unlike many of my critics, with any individual.

Long after the election Peter Mandelson told me that immediately he saw the ad he recognised its potential to cause trouble for New Labour. *He* decided to spin it around the concept of 'devil eyes'. A compliant bishop soon appeared on the media, not bothering to inform himself before opening his mouth. He made no enquiries of our party before expressing his judgement, he simply became the mouthpiece for New Labour spin about 'devil eyes'. However 'independent' is the status this bishop now claims in the House of Lords, then he came across as simply a Labour stooge. From there on the media die was cast. We were tarred and feathered. True or false, fair or unfair never entered the equation. 'Devil eyes' trumped 'New Labour, new danger'. Peter Mandelson told me that he had not been behind the appearance on the scene of the helpful bishop, as had been alleged. I choose not to believe him.

On the Sunday of publication I did two media interviews after which Betty and I left on a pre-arranged holiday. The party handled media accusations by telling the truth about the ad. Had I been around I would have done so with more vigour and faith-driven passion. I might even have mentioned New Labour, media and Church hypocrisy. No one would have gained the impression that we were sorry to have given Tony Blair and Clare Short exposure in this way. But the battle was lost long before we returned home.

John Major was also on holiday, in France, and so had not been briefed in advance. In reality any briefing would have made little difference. 'Devil eyes' was not part of our script – as already explained – and there was little about the ad, apart from Clare Short's stunning indictment of her own party, to catch anyone's attention. We simply gave her charge air space. And, of course, John had already seen the eyes used earlier, without comment.

Some Conservatives sent messages of complaint to No. 10 – based on hearing the Mandelsonian bishop's nonsense. John was cross and, because he had been unsighted, reacted badly. Without any discussion with me, he said the party would not use the ad again. I was tempted to generate an internal row on my return but chose not to do so. We had enough on our plate, even though John's 'shoot from the hip' response did damage our collective confidence.

Someone reported us to the Advertising Standards Authority. As often happens when an official finding does not sit comfortably with an earlier media crusade, by and large its judgement elicited little comment. There was *no finding* against the substance of the ad. The main criticism was that we should have asked Tony Blair's permission to superimpose the eyes on his face! How silly is that?

And how many hundreds of times has that 'principle' been ignored by the media in the years since? Have you heard of the ASA being perturbed by those breaches? Form your own judgement.

The irony is that Clare Short turned out to be right. Eventually she resigned from Tony Blair's Cabinet.

In my view John Major's unilateral decision to ban the eyes was an electoral mistake. Polls showed we had indeed succeeded in lodging the concept of 'New Labour, new danger' in the public mind. But without being allowed to refresh the message it soon faded. Sadly that ad, with its well-targeted strapline, proved to be the only real evidence of 'success' in our two-year campaign for re-election. Had we continued using the eyes symbol to reinforce our message we might have made progress – but we were afraid. Never again were we able to come up with a short, pithy comment that challenged the 'New Labour' brand.

†

Any serious attempt to understand why we lost the 1997 election must start with the infamous 16 September 1992, likely to be referred to as 'Black Wednesday' for a very long time.

That day, after growing financial and currency turmoil, Britain suspended its membership of the European Exchange Rate Mechanism (ERM), but only after billions of pounds of our reserves had been spent and interest rates had risen from 10 per cent to 12 per cent to 15 per cent in just a few hours as government tried to maintain our currency relationships, primarily with an eye to the German deutschmark. Like everyone else I was amazed and depressed by the interest rate rises. For me, with little economic knowledge but some political nous, ours was always a policy that was unlikely to prosper and would probably not even be sustainable.

When Chancellor of the Exchequer John Major took Britain into the ERM in October 1990, Prime Minister Margaret Thatcher was not enthusiastic. Whether this divergence was for financial or political reasons, or both, it certainly began the process of clouding their subsequent relationship.

Less than a week before Black Wednesday Prime Minister John Major, in a speech in Scotland, committed himself to defending the pound and its exchange rates within the ERM. That speech had left him no loophole against negative, much less calamitous, contingencies. To be fair, had he not done so his 'weak' speech (as the commentators would have described it) would itself have added to the pressure on sterling. He had got himself or been forced into a no-win situation. No wonder relations between No. 10 and the Treasury were strained. John told me later that he had meant what he said in Scotland and, in the circumstances, believed it was important to say it.

Our exit from the ERM represented a huge Treasury and political failure. The original ERM concept had been built on flexibility. If currencies diverged beyond pre-determined, reasonable levels of variability it was supposed to be possible, in fact essential, to affect realignments without undue political stress. Such changes would have required nations to cooperate with each other in determining the new exchange rates and variabilities but, after all, was not such cooperation what this European adventure was supposed to be about?

What actually happened was that the deutschmark became increasingly dominant while, in parallel, the ERM's flexibility decreased. There is evidence to suggest that it was German intransigence in defence of its national interest, despite ERM rules, which helped to precipitate Black Wednesday. Whether HM Treasury's behaviour made it harder or easier for the Germans to cooperate will be a point of argument for years to come. I tend to the former view.

One of the Treasury's main failures, we all discovered to our cost, lay in not protecting the ERM's inherent flexibility, which was fundamentally necessary for its proper functioning. Flexibility was the elasticity in the system. Without it the system hardened. Under pressure the relationships could no longer flex, they could only crack – and they did. If the Treasury alone was powerless to prevent this loss of flexibility it should have highlighted the potential dangers in a way that, politically, would have forced their earlier, broader consideration.

Tories traditionally do not like referenda. We live in a parliamentary democracy which has served us well for centuries. Unlike some of my colleagues, however, I am willing to make exceptions. Given that public opinion has played its part in the evolution of our unwritten constitution, over many years, I can support holding a referendum if a particular issue would significantly affect the working of, or the distribution of power within, our constitution. The Maastricht Treaty, with its associated European framework, agreed by Major, and the Single European Act (1986), heralded by Thatcher, would both have qualified in my opinion. Entering the ERM with its widely perceived, albeit misjudged, signal that we were thinking of embarking on the road to a single European currency would not have qualified for a referendum in my view – a single currency proposal most definitely would.

Later, Eurosceptic Tories believed that Major, given his history, was only being pragmatic, not principled, in his opposition to a single currency. This distrust or simple misinterpretation of Major's intentions lay at the heart of the party's European split. Their behaviour in pursuit of their instinct simply made our political position worse and weakened Major's ability to defend the national interest, as he was seeking to do.

The Prime Minister was adamantly opposed to granting a referendum on any European issue, in principle. He told me so, repeatedly. The fact that Thatcher called for one may have strengthened his opposition to the idea, though I know he was not beyond hoping the result of the later French referendum on Maastricht would provide an escape route for the British government and ease our party tensions. Again he told me so.

One final observation on the politically damning consequences of Black Wednesday. The awfulness of the preceding days' inexorable progress to an apparently unpreventable climax, and of the events on the day itself, are impossible to convey; at least they lie beyond my capability.

Interest rates on a 10–12–15–12 per cent moving stairway, with all the predictable consequences for mortgages, small businesses, investment and employment, were catastrophic. Inevitably this sequence of events had an unprecedented effect on both the public pocket and the public psyche. Trust in government and its economic and financial policies disappeared. Trust in our European policy, and our European partners, was similarly shredded. And the negatively resigned public mood was electorally of huge importance. Public disillusion was quietly but determinedly transformed into a decision to be rid of us when the time came. It was so strong no one even talked about it. It was a 'given'. The 1997 general election was irretrievably lost on Black Wednesday.

One thing might have reduced that negative transformation of the public mood but would probably only have 'reduced' it. To quote Anthony Seldon again: 'The government never apologised for ERM and there was no official enquiry into what went wrong.'

An apology for entering the ERM on the basis we did was not required. On the contrary, at the time there was widespread cross-party and media agreement that entering the ERM was 'a good thing'. Our political opponents typically soon forgot their support for the government's initiative when the going got tough.

The apology that *was* needed was for our conduct of the ERM and the political failure of our exit. We had been unwilling seriously to contemplate fundamental alternatives when experts could see how the ERM was actually developing. The political arguments advanced in defence of our policy were that advocating a radical alternative to or within the ERM would have upset our partners, or would have called into international question our 'European-ness', or would have raised questions about our sense of being *communautaire*, or any combination of the above. The Treasury arguments for maintaining the status quo can safely be left to the experts – who will not agree! The harsh, ultimate reality was that we ended up outside the ERM in the worst possible circumstances.

Even worse, the public decided they 'knew' why we did not say 'sorry'. Our silence suggested to many of them that, for us, international approval outweighed our sense of domestic public responsibility – a hard charge. The populace were not consumed or persuaded by the intricacies of international finance. They were just left with the unfair but distinct impression that we were unrepentant about the financial damage which had happened to tens of millions of them.

Equally, we were unapologetic for the moral failure which this episode reflected. I know this, too, is a hard charge but I have little doubt it occurred to the public mind. Saying 'sorry' involves taking some share of the blame, conveying some understanding of the damage done and a determination not to be found wanting again. That sense of repentance is certainly morally based but it is also good politics. Had we said 'sorry', we as a party and a government, as well as the public, could more easily have come to terms with what had happened and thus have moved forward more confidently.

Could anything have been worse in the circumstances of Black Wednesday than not saying 'sorry'? Well, perhaps, yes.

No one taking responsibility was just as bad, if not worse. I quote again from Anthony Seldon. 'The facts and motives behind Lamont's continuation in office [he was Chancellor of the Exchequer] are exceedingly muddy … Whatever the truth, Lamont did not see why he should take sole responsibility, and did not insist that he resign.' And 'Major certainly was not keen for Lamont to go.'

The public rightly believed someone was responsible and that he should have owned up. So when no one took responsibility for the ERM failure, the public decided that no one was really sorry, with all the induced cynicism and devalued moral purpose this reflected.

Following Jim Callaghan's example in 1967 (when Harold Wilson devalued the pound), Norman Lamont should have left the Treasury. His real friends might have hoped he would insist on going. If not, John Major should have insisted. Neither did. Nor did either say 'sorry' because this, if meant, would have required the Chancellor to move.

On Black Wednesday I had no economic responsibilities so was never in the loop. And there was no compelling reason why John should have sought my views or shared his with me. However, these views, formed then, remain my opinion. And, for the record, I told John privately at the time that I believed Norman Lamont had to move or be moved. He resisted my suggestion.

Anyway, and again for the record, I am sorry for what happened on Black Wednesday and the government's part in it. And I am saddened so many people were hurt. Years after Black Wednesday I discussed its effect on the 1997 general election result with Peter (now Lord) Mandelson, one of the authors of New Labour and later one of its Cabinet ministers. His analysis of the electoral importance of Black Wednesday coincided precisely with mine. He told me that New Labour's polling guru, the late Lord Gould, held the same view.

In 1996, and looking back four years to Black Wednesday, it was apparent to those of us trying to deliver an election victory the following year (1997) that we had a mountain to climb. Looking back eight years after that watershed, it was clear that this mountain never was conquerable. But in politics, as in football, hope springs eternal even when, rationally, there is little or no hope.

However, Black Wednesday turned out not to be just about finance. The sixteenth of September 1992 had a second fundamentally unhelpful effect on government policy. It crystallised the growing division in the Conservative Party over our relationship with Europe. Although some party Eurosceptics had been challenging Major's European policy before that date, the vigour and sometimes aggression of their challenge increased thereafter, reaching a crescendo when the Maastricht Treaty was given its detailed consideration in the Commons the following year.

The inter-governmental meeting held at Maastricht in December 1991 was widely seen as a seminal moment in the development of the so-called European vision. Ahead of it Major ruled out a series of proposals being strongly advocated by other countries. He would not support a federal Europe, transfer of foreign or defence powers, a common currency or the Social Chapter, which he believed would 'undermine the ability of Britain to compete'. These positions were widely supported by Parliament and the media.

On the day, Maastricht was a Major triumph. He combined political skill, resolve, good relationships, calmness and, occasionally, obstinacy in our national interest, to achieve all his main objectives. Parliament gave him a great welcome home. Even most of the Eurosceptics cheered.

The euphoria did not last. The negotiating skill John had used to such good effect was 'reinterpreted' – or 'spun' if you prefer – as evidence of his pragmatic, rather than principled, opposition to the Maastricht proposals. I know of no supporting evidence for this Eurosceptic 'analysis', then or now. To a significant number of Tories, however, the threat of Europe became the next big political crisis.

At which point a seminal question had to be answered. To become 'law' the Maastricht Treaty had to be endorsed by all the European parliaments involved. When should that happen in the UK?

There were two options. Either we should act 'immediately', taking advantage of the goodwill generated by Major's success. This would have meant jettisoning other Bills in order to pass the Maastricht Act before Parliament was prorogued prior to a 1992 general election. Even under those circumstances the timing would have been tight.

The second option was to wait until after that election when, hopefully, electoral success and the passage of time would have taken the heat out of the issue, or at least most of it. What actually happened was that Eurosceptics returned to the House of Commons released for five years from the constraint that an early election always generates. This was entirely predictable.

The second option was chosen. Buried as I was in work in Northern Ireland I played little part in the party's internal debate on this at Westminster. I recall only one short, chance conversation with the Prime Minister. In reply to my query about legislative timing he set out the two options above. I muttered something about striking while the iron was hot. Unfortunately I cannot remember his precise words but he left me wondering if the Cabinet was not in danger of underestimating the level of Euroscepticism and hostility in the party. When to legislate was a matter of judgement and the

Cabinet had made its judgement. I kept my own counsel. I wanted John to prosper and did not wish to say anything that might give him a contrary opinion.

With not insignificant help from Margaret Thatcher and Norman Tebbit, the party was asymmetrically divided by the time the Maastricht Bill arrived in Parliament later in 1992 and this remained the case until its passage through the House of Commons was complete in July 1993. By then the public had seen its government withdrawing from a European economic/financial framework, which earlier had been heralded as a necessity for economic stability in the single European market, and openly, and at times aggressively, be in dispute with a minority in its own party over its future in Europe.

It is a well-established political fact that the public is more persuaded by political parties that are united and whose members are comfortable with each other. It strongly dislikes division and the distraction it causes. Not unreasonably it takes the view that if politicians cannot agree with each other, why should the public believe them? Indeed which fragment of the party should they even think of believing?

So by the time the Maastricht Bill became law, European divisions were entrenched in the party and government. If those divisions had eased after the passage of the Bill we might have done better as the memory of conflict faded. Instead they ebbed and flowed right through to the 1997 election. They also reinforced Black Wednesday in persuading voters it was time for us to go. After all why should they support a government that was not believed by a significant number of its own MPs on one of the really big issues of the day?

John Major always had the right to drive this legislation on to the statute book, given that Parliament had endorsed his objectives in going to Maastricht and had warmly welcomed his success, including the currency opt-out, as had the British media, on his return. Twenty-plus years and three governments later, the country remains outside the eurozone. Overwhelmingly people remain grateful for John's foresight and political courage in achieving this, though historians may wonder why, given Margaret Thatcher's

instincts and John Major's vision, David Cameron was the first
Conservative Prime Minister to wield a veto on economic matters
that were troubling all member states.

Some people believe there was a third reason we lost in 1997,
so-called 'sleaze'. In the years running up to that election some
of our MPs behaved improperly. Their unacceptable activities –
media-labelled 'sleaze' – appeared (too) frequently in the news. The
level of shock was high, and some were outraged. Notwithstanding
this, I suspect that lasting political damage was limited because the
public understood that some of their MPs were behaving as some
of them behaved, daily, and therefore deemed the electoral significance of their behaviour less important than they would if, say, the
bad behaviour had involved money rather than sex. Most, however,
believed MPs should live to a higher standard.

†

The Maastricht Treaty will never be only about politics or governance to me. As the Bill's legislative passage through the Commons
progressed it was profoundly to affect us as a family.

That passage through the Commons was a nightmare. Eurosceptic
Conservative MPs fought a prolonged battle against their own
government, clause by clause, during which the government agreed
that there should be a separate vote on the Social Chapter aspects
of the European debate once the main legislation had been agreed.

The crucial votes were set for just before the House rose for the
summer recess. The Maastricht Bill finally received approval on
20 July 1993. The crucial additional vote on the Social Chapter was
scheduled for Thursday 22 July.

During the summer of 1992 our son David met Susan from St
Paul, Minnesota. One month later Betty and I were on holiday in
Kenya when we received a phone call from David telling us he was
engaged to an American girl! They were both working in China,
teaching English as a foreign language, and had decided to get
married in Hong Kong on Saturday 24 July 1993.

The family and I had agreed to fly to Hong Kong on the previous Sunday (arriving Monday morning). Betty had already met Susan during a special trip primarily to see David but the rest of us had not had that pleasure. We wanted to spend some time with her before the wedding.

I had told the government whips well in advance that I would be away that week. Given the exceptional circumstances (David was our first to be married) they allowed me to 'pair' with Eddie McGrady MP – an SDLP Member from Northern Ireland who was and is a valued friend.

Tickets were bought and bags packed. Then less than twenty-four hours before our departure the government changed its mind. I would have to vote on the following Thursday – two days before the wedding. No, it was not negotiable. Everyone, without exception, had to be present; no matter where in the world they had hoped to be.

Our family options were simple. I could resign as a minister, miss the vote and possibly be expelled from the parliamentary party. I was up for that but Betty persuaded me that David would not want me to take such drastic action. He was secure in his knowledge of our love and Christian support and did not need a dramatic demonstration.

The second option was for everyone else to fly on the Sunday with me flying on the Friday, after the Thursday night vote. There was a lunchtime flight which would land in Hong Kong at Saturday breakfast time – in time for me to get to the 2.30 p.m. wedding. A third option was to fly with the family on Sunday, fly back on the Wednesday overnight flight, vote on Thursday and return to Hong Kong on the Friday lunchtime flight.

While this was a punishing schedule, especially at the end of a heavy parliamentary session during which I had been a very busy Minister of Health, for me it had two big advantages. First, it would allow me to meet Susan before the wedding. And if for any reason I missed the wedding – I was thinking in terms of aeroplane delays not lost votes – then at least I would have had some chance to get to know her a little before she became Mrs Mawhinney. In addition, my undertaking two return trips in a week to Hong Kong gave me a way of demonstrating how much I valued my son and his wife to be.

I chose this option, with Betty's blessing. We spent three happy days all together in Hong Kong before I set off back to Heathrow. A dear friend, David Parry, met me at Heathrow and took me home. On the Thursday evening the government lost the vote on the Social Chapter because more than twenty Tories voted against their own government. The Prime Minister immediately announced there would be a vote of confidence in the government on the next day, Friday, at 4 p.m.

My plan to return to Hong Kong on the Friday lunchtime flight was aborted.

I rang Betty and told her the grim news. There was a 6 p.m. flight on Friday but whether I could vote at 4 p.m., get through London's pre-weekend traffic and catch the plane was questionable. But I had to try.

I just made the flight, though only because British Airways kindly allowed me to board late thanks to the good offices of Thomas Cook. The flight was due to land at 2.30 p.m. – precisely the time of the wedding. The family did not even know if I had caught the plane because BA refused to tell them.

The flight landed in Hong Kong on time. Emotionally I was in less good shape. After clearing immigration I literally ran through the airport, jumped in a taxi and drove to the church, arriving about 3.20 p.m. I was distraught because I thought I had missed the wedding service. That was one of the worst emotional moments of my life. Sixty seconds later my feelings of surprise and delight were equally strong.

When David had learned what had happened to me, he and Susan immediately reversed the wedding procedure because they wanted me at the service. So at 2.30 p.m. the minister told a surprised congregation that the service itself would be delayed until my arrival. Instead they would proceed with the reception, the cake cutting and speeches in the church hall – after which would follow the church service.

I, of course, did not know this. I ran into the church foyer, noted the empty church, decided I was too late and burst into tears.

Betty and David met me, told me what had happened and after

drying my tears told me to hurry into my wedding suit – I had a speech to make. In a total daze, and with no planning, I made my contribution. The fact that I was doing so spoke far louder than what I said. In due course, after a hugely emotional service, Mr and Mrs David Mawhinney went on honeymoon; the rest of us flew home on the Monday.

There was a political footnote to all this. In response to a press story which mentioned which ministers had been brought back to London from foreign destinations for the vote, the *Daily Mirror* demanded to know if the taxpayer had paid for my flights. No, I said, I paid.

A few days later the Health Permanent Secretary stopped me in Richmond House. Without any preliminaries he told me bluntly that the department would not pay for my extra flights. I would have to foot the bill myself. His tone was unusually officious. My irritated but restrained reply was that I did not remember asking him for reimbursement. A few days later he came to see me in my office. He had been wrong. It was permissible for the government to pay for my flights. He was sorry he had misinformed me. If I would just tell him how much I was owed … I interrupted his and said I would maintain the integrity of my response to the *Daily Mirror*.

†

Difficulties arising from and associated with the Maastricht Bill, which affected the party, the government and the country, also affected individuals. We were one such case. Others fared much worse. The political divisions exposed by the legislation revealed the split foundation on which the party had been resting since Black Wednesday, and, indeed, before it. That foundation neither settled nor became more secure during the rest of the parliament leading up to the 1997 general election. Its result was entirely predictable and the evidence pointing towards a massive defeat was there for all who would see.

We lost the 1997 election within four months of winning the preceding 1992 one and then spent the rest of the parliament fighting,

thus making sure that a majority would never vote for us. It is greatly
to the credit of John Major, many in the Cabinet and most of our
MPs, that so much energy, innovation and hard work was expended in
support of the party to which we were all committed. That includes the
superb team in Central Office, and especially the excellent colleagues
who worked directly to and with me, including Michael Trend MP,
Michael Simmonds, Tim Collins, Danny Finkelstein, Tony Garrett,
Charles Lewington, Andrew Cooper and Vanessa Ford.

Reflecting on all the infighting of those years, the so-called
Maastricht Bill (the European Communities (Amendment) Bill to
give it its proper title) epitomised the irrecoverable splits in the
Conservative Party which burst into so much prominence following Black Wednesday. As Party Chairman I was still dealing with
the ensuing discord years later.

Which explains why the word 'Maastricht' has become symbolic
in the context of why we lost the 1997 election. It was not the
primary cause of us losing, it just helped ensure that we never had a
chance of winning. Michael Howard MP once said in No. 10 that it
was so obvious we were never going to join the euro, why didn't we
just say so? That neatly summed up the issue for many.

John Major talked to me privately and at length on several occasions about the pros and cons of possible radical changes to our
European policy. He was clear. What Michael Howard wanted
would not solve the dilemma. As no Prime Minister can bind his
successor or indeed any future parliament, saying 'never' would
mean only that *he* would not take this action. In that context using
Michael Howard's formula would have made no positive difference
to our party or its standing. Both factions in the party would simply
have maintained their high-voltage barrage to try to force a party
position for future years.

In reality there was no easy formula to bridge the deep philosophical divide within the party. John becoming more Eurosceptic might
quieten some unpleasant colleagues (it would never silence them
because of their lack of trust in him) but it would equally certainly
inflame the rhetoric of those in favour of closer European unity.

Also a change of policy in a Eurosceptic direction would probably have resulted in Cabinet resignations, themselves a bad reflection on government. The status quo, even though it was unseemly, was at least reasonably stable (apart from John Redwood). A sense that the Cabinet was disintegrating was the last thing a Prime Minister (or government) wanted.

John ultimately concluded that, in the country's best interest, the policy should not change. Nevertheless much policy examination continued out of the public gaze, up to and indeed into the election campaign. To me he sometimes seemed tempted but eventually he was never convinced.

The effects of our public discord coupled with partisan, internal, private briefings to favoured journalists (especially by some special advisers), were toxic. Trust between colleagues diminished and ministers contradicted each other in public. We had no agreed handling strategy for Europe – and the public knew it. Things would have been even worse had not Michael Heseltine, a Europhile, not been such a staunch and loyal supporter of John, in contrast to the unhelpful instincts of too many other senior colleagues. Michael was superb and I thank him for all his support of me too.

Coupling Michael's support of John with, at times, the crucial importance of good communication and trust between Michael and Ken Clarke, John and me and Michael and me enabled the government to go about its daily business with apparent tranquillity. Though whether we were a good advert for collective responsibility is debatable.

Policy-wise we should all have agreed to laud our opt-out and flatly refused to speculate on what might or might not happen in the next parliament. This would not have brought peace but, perhaps, some calm. At least it was credible and defensible. But mine was a lonely voice.

Black Wednesday, a refusal to say 'sorry', a divided party and Maastricht were the realities that ensured we were defeated. Personally Maastricht still reminds me of one of the most emotional weeks of my life. It signifies to me collective political failure and our collective family strength.

14

Even God Allows U-Turns

Tony Blair was congenitally deceitful, but he lied so fluently and with such ready charm that he escaped censure time and time again.
Peter Oborne, *Daily Mail*, 1 December 2007

I think Margaret Thatcher followed the same routine as John Major. In his day, Prime Minister's Questions (PMQs) occurred twice a week. Afterwards he would go into his Commons office with a few senior officials and colleagues. Sometimes, as Party Chairman, I attended those debriefs.

We would check all his responses in case he had unintentionally said something untrue or used words which might imply a change in government policy. We also listed any commitments which needed to be pursued. If an answer could have implied a policy deviation, the relevant department was contacted to agree an explanatory statement which would be common to its Secretary of State and No. 10. If John had said something inaccurate (he seldom did because his memory was so good) then as quickly as possible a way was found to put the record straight.

The Prime Minister was perfectly content to defend his policies, robustly, in the face of strong opposition disapproval or awkward questions. PMQs were seldom about getting cross-party political agreement. At various times they were ill tempered, dramatic, sombre or knockabout as conflicting personalities, ideas and occasionally ideologies battled for supremacy.

The Prime Minister was also content, from time to time, to

answer a different question from the one asked, or to respond to just
one aspect of a question. In the latter case, being selective allowed
him to defend his government's position, while at the same time
ignoring those aspects of the question which sought to highlight
his government's weakness. Sometimes his replies were aggressively party political, Madam Speaker allowing, when he tried to
highlight the opposition's weakness, division or lack of a sensible
policy alternative.

What he did not do was deliberately tell untruths. He did not
lie (a forbidden word in Parliament); that would not have been
honourable. As the quote from Peter Oborne suggests, Tony Blair
appeared to many to operate from a different perspective.

Losing the 1997 election was a traumatic experience for those of
us who had been in government. One day we were Cabinet ministers, with all that that implies, the next we were on our own. As
soon as those election returns became clear, the blame game started,
for blame is an inevitable part of politics. In our case the search for
scapegoats was tempered by the size of our defeat. It was so large
that few believed it could be traced to one or a few individuals who
had failed in their responsibilities.

Prime Ministers, of course, carry the ultimate blame that goes
with leadership. In 1997 only two journalists tried, very half-
heartedly, to blame me as Party Chairman. Their thesis was that our
electoral organisation must have been deficient or we would not
have lost. I told them I was flattered by the idea that I personally
had had the power to overturn a negative majority of over 160 if
only the party had been better organised – and not to be so silly! In
addition I was spared blame because of my obvious efforts to ensure
that the party was in good shape and because of the conduct of the
election itself. I also took the battle to the opposition, which party
members (and some journalists) liked.

The personal trauma of defeat was heightened because we were
all exhausted. After a physical examination I learned, like other
colleagues, that we had been living on our adrenalin for too long.
Our depleted adrenalin levels were likely to normalise over time,

but they were unlikely ever to recover fully. My doctor told me I was clinically exhausted and would need a year to recuperate. He was right.

For me, at least, there was an additional component which added to the discomfort. All political parties celebrate winning general elections. Success is always pleasant and the emotional release of victory is natural. It makes all those hard, volunteered hours seem worthwhile. New Labour, on the other hand, was blatantly triumphalist, always a less appealing spectacle.

In one sense this was understandable. They had been in opposition for eighteen years, having lost four general elections in a row. They had gone through the internal conflict of jettisoning historic, strongly held beliefs in an attempt to make themselves electable – they hoped.

I say 'they hoped' for two reasons. First, opinion polls predicted they would win in 1992, right up to election day, but they lost. That loss badly dented their confidence. In 1997 they worried that history would repeat itself. My second reason for saying 'they hoped' was reflected in one of the more pleasant political compliments ever paid to me. I have always tried to maintain good working relations with journalists, even those whose reporting was not supportive. Some time after our defeat I was talking with several parliamentary lobby journalists about the election. They generously complimented me on our campaign and especially on the fact that it was not until the Monday of election week (less than seventy-two hours before polling began) that they finally decided that John Major and I knew we had lost. Given the final result, keeping the issue open that long in the minds of cynical, seasoned journalists seemed no mean feat so, given their political anxieties, the relief of winning probably added to Labour triumphalism.

The new government revelled in the media praise heaped upon it. If the hopes publicly vested in them were overdone, again this would be understandable in the circumstances. People were relieved to see the back of us. As a government we had been tired and out of ideas. The economy, which had been poor, was now in good shape and had been getting better for quite a while, though much else was contentious and politically disjointed. We simply did not have a coherent story to tell. The party was fractious and had lost its sense of unity and self-confidence. We needed a break from office – another thing it is difficult for politicians to say in public and, often, even in private.

The size of the election result underlined the fact that the country wanted change. The electorate thought we needed time to reflect, learn, recharge our batteries and formulate fresh policies which would be appropriate to the twenty-first century. They also thought we needed new leadership, while retaining their sense that John Major was a decent man.

Throughout his premiership, Tony Blair gave many the impression that the votes of confidence he received from the public and in Parliament somehow set him apart from the norms which had governed his predecessors. Which brings me back to the way he handled PMQs; he changed the time-honoured twice-weekly sessions to once a week, for his own political convenience.

Initially I did not feel like sitting in the Commons Chamber listening to Blair's triumphalism, so I either set myself other tasks on Wednesdays at noon or watched proceedings on the television in my office, while multi-tasking.

Gradually I became disturbed that Tony did not 'calm down' with the passage of time. Too often his answers seemed to me to be tangential to the truth. Of course he was entitled to give a party-political slant to his answers, as his predecessors had done. I believed, however, that he should have paid more attention to facts than appeared to be his instinct.

After some weeks it became clear that Blair had set a pattern from which he had no intention of deviating. I decided privately that just as he was responsible for his behaviour, so I was responsible for mine. I would not go into Prime Minister's Questions as a protest about what I believed, too often, was Tony Blair's lack of truthfulness. This, sadly, turned out to be a perennial feature of his premiership.

My decision was not an overt party-political stunt. I did not tell a soul. I sought no political advantage from my self-imposed absence. If constituents asked me about something Mr Blair had said in PMQs, I replied simply that I had not been present, though I did try to respond to the point they had raised. No one ever pressed me to elaborate.

Nor did I brief friendly journalists in the hope that they would write up the story of my non-appearance. After the aggression of Alastair Campbell and the undoubted charisma of Tony Blair, not to mention eighteen years of Conservative rule, the media in the early years would not have countenanced any questioning of the Prime Minister's word. That became more commonplace later.

Why am I making such a fuss about truthfulness, especially in a politician, you may be wondering. There are times in politics, as in our daily experience, when giving a straight yes-or-no answer to a question would be embarrassing or, worse, misleading. In those situations, politicians duck and weave, evade the central question, answer a different one or filibuster. The public do not like us doing this, but in fact each person who reads this acts in the same way every day in his or her private life.

Having acknowledged that, there remains a fundamental difference between not fully answering a question, which can be exasperating, and answering a question untruthfully. The latter simply reflects a politician's or indeed anybody's lack of inner integrity. Most listeners can tell the difference. Peter Oborne's words are a harsh reflection on Prime Minister Blair. Had I written them I might have been accused of a 'political hate crime'. But Peter's judgement, factually, has much to commend it.

In case you think this uncharitable, let me quote Tony Blair's biographer. In *Blair*, Anthony Seldon wrote:

> Blair's particular skills were his oratory, courage, personal magnetism and self-belief (which ultimately was his undoing) ... Blair is like a tragic hero, a good man who tried to run his country wisely and well. But his character flaws, above all his hubristic belief in his own

powers of persuasion and the rightness of his own 'principled' course of action, damaged him greatly.

So for the eight years I was in opposition I never once attended PMQs. No one noticed my silent protest in quiet support of truth and Tony Blair was undamaged by me. Over time he damaged himself. The handling of the death of the government scientist Dr David Kelly, the untruthful highlighting of weapons of mass destruction in Iraq and the apparent amending of intelligence advice to ministers in the run-up to the war in Iraq are just three of the more memorable examples. Whatever the facts, as time went on the British people formed a view about their Prime Minister and his government.

There is a commonly held belief in British politics that a party needs a full set of detailed policies and defined aspirations before it enters a general election. It certainly does need to give the British public some idea of its proposed purpose and an indication of the issues on which it hopes to legislate. But a comprehensive menu is neither appropriate nor necessary. No party can or should attempt to set out its views on every conceivable matter which might arise, not least because things which do require government action but, years earlier were inconceivable, will happen.

Margaret Thatcher had a relatively thin policy manifesto in 1979 – indeed only two major commitments remain in the memory. At the time, her manifesto was criticised precisely because so-called political experts thought it was too general. Yet her party won comfortably.

Matthew Parris, a former MP, and now a distinguished journalist, who worked in Margaret's Westminster office for two years prior to the 1979 election, wrote later (*The Times*, 25 April 2009) reflecting on the manifesto: 'I don't remember there being anything much about privatisation, doubling VAT or the cruel salami-slicing of welfare benefits that was to follow. Even on the broad theme of "taming the unions" the extent of our declared ambitions was unclear.'

Elections are seldom, if ever, won by a detailed list of policy proposals. Instead the British people listen to and observe politicians who wish to govern and form a view on who to vote for. That view starts forming long before an election is called and owes much to the public's appreciation of the character and values of the politicians, including their vision, competence and ability to communicate. One or two seminal policies may play an important part in this process but manifestos primarily shine a light on politicians' beliefs, values and priorities. The best ones underline ideas.

In 1970 the public remembered the devaluation of the 'pound in their pocket' by the Wilson government a couple of years earlier and believed Ted Heath's commitment to deal with the unions. They surprised everyone (perhaps even themselves) by voting Conservative. I say 'perhaps even themselves' because few were willing to concede this possibility to pollsters even a few days ahead of election day. Few remember the details of the manifesto.

In February 1974, the country voted against the government which had introduced the three-day working week. The British claim to like the prospect of firm government, but when push comes to shove we can be persuaded that necessary toughness may be unfair to a minority. If this happens then the innate British sense of fair play (which, like others, I recognise but find hard to define) kicks in and toughness becomes secondary. Most voters could not have given a policy analysis of the pros and cons of the dispute other than that the three-day week had something to do with miners' intransigence, or with their principles. Without personal involvement, they just did not like it. If this level of everyday disruption was a consequence of government policy then the policy, or the government, should be changed. So the election became a referendum on the government's behaviour, not the miners'. Manifesto details were largely irrelevant. Harold Wilson became Prime Minister – just – not because he offered better or more coherent policies but because he was the alternative to Ted Heath.

The second 1974 election democratically enforced Labour's reasonable desire to have a working majority, which any government needs if it is to govern properly. The British public understood that and responded accordingly. No one remembers any of the manifesto promises.

In 1979, Margaret Thatcher became the country's first woman Prime Minister. Ironically, Labour Prime Minister Jim Callaghan helped set up the Conservative win. In September 1978 he encouraged people to expect an autumn general election, not least because opinion polls were showing neither huge support nor antipathy towards Labour. If it had been held then, the election's outcome would have been in doubt.

Jim Callaghan then caused public confidence in his government to decrease. Not only did he dither about calling an election, and then not do so, he teased the public about his intentions. The British people do not like politicians trifling with their emotions. They do not like being led to the top of the hill (expecting an election) only to be told, when they get there, to make their own way down. Later Gordon Brown did the same thing and discovered the same antipathy. When a leader behaves this way he forfeits public confidence, and when that happens confidence is hard, maybe impossible, to reclaim, because people have long memories.

In the winter and spring of 1978–9, the outcome of the upcoming election was also influenced against Labour by the behaviour of militant trade unions. They seemed out of control. Too many union leaders gave the impression they thought they were bigger than the law or Parliament. Then, in the midst of industrial unrest, Jim Callaghan, just back from abroad, made things worse by saying, in effect, that he could not see what all the fuss was about. The British people were offended. The government's inability to persuade union members to bury the dead or remove garbage from the streets was widely thought to be symptomatic of lost authority.

In 1979 my majority was over 5,000. Had we gone to the polls in the autumn of 1978, before the so-called 'winter of discontent', it would not have been anything like that. The overall election outcome might not even have been the same, because Margaret's commitment to 'deal with the unions' would have seemed less compelling before that winter of discontent and more like a 'promise' of months of social unrest, with echoes of 1974.

By May 1979, people had formed a view. Many were opposed to having a woman Prime Minister but felt, in the prevailing circumstance, that gender was less important than curbing trade union power. This issue overwhelmed all other considerations. I spent every day of that election, except Sundays, on the streets of Peterborough and its surrounding northern villages. Not one day passed without people approaching and telling me that, though they seldom if ever voted Conservative, this time they would be voting for me. 'Somebody needs to do something about the unions' was their recurring theme.

Only one other policy initiative may have influenced voters in 1979: our excellent commitment to sell council houses to sitting tenants at discounted prices. Given the popular perception of UK politics, it is ironic that it was the Conservative Party which was responsible for the single largest redistribution of wealth in modern times.

In 1983 the election outcome was influenced primarily by the successful reclaiming of the Falkland Islands, which had demonstrated Margaret Thatcher's toughness and patriotism. In case that was not sufficient reason, many could not bring themselves to vote for Michael Foot. Other specific policies simply paled as issues, even though, earlier in that parliament, Geoffrey Howe's handling of the economy had been hugely contentious while he laid the foundation for economic growth.

Speaking of Michael Foot, he came to Peterborough to support Labour's election candidate. Arriving late, he discovered that he had been locked out of the meeting hall. Poor Michael was reduced to walking around the outside of the building, with the media, banging on windows trying to attract attention.

In 1987, people decided that the Labour Party, under Neil Kinnock, had only begun to reform itself and, as a consequence, was still not fit to govern. Meanwhile Margaret Thatcher's government was admired for its strength of purpose. It was returned to power, but no great policy initiatives helped that process. The people just 'formed a view' about the two parties in the persons of their leaders.

The outcome of the 1992 election was a surprise. Margaret Thatcher had been replaced by John Major as Prime Minister and he was not expected to win. Thatcher's government had introduced the community charge to replace domestic rates. It soon became known as the 'poll tax', which from the very beginning was damaging PR for Conservatives. The tax was first introduced in Scotland, at the urging of several north-of-the-border Tories, a year ahead of England. It caused many Scottish voters to become mightily antagonistic to our party. They still are.

The principle of the poll tax was defensible. The government announced that, for the initial year, 1990/91, the average community charge would be £278 per capita in England. Individual local authorities added to this basic figure so that the actual amount turned out to be £363. For many, the level of poll tax in that year and subsequently was more (for some, considerably more) than they had been paying in rates. The scheme carried little popular support. It was too complicated and its administration was a nightmare. People did not, could not or would not fill in the necessary forms, or do this on time. Local government was unable to cope with the significant, constantly changing, personal movements which mark our society, not to mention the myriad financial amounts owed by and to millions of people. These numbers constantly varied as people's individual circumstances changed. The resultant backlog of calculations, often coupled with an individual's misery of circumstance, enhanced the more general anger at the tax. Doubts about its fairness simply added to the growing toxic mix. It was a tax mess pure and simple, which, in turn, led to a political mess.

The 'final straw' for many came with the rising levels of tax levied. These led to claims that individuals could not afford to pay what they owed. In response, Margaret only sanctioned marginally greater support from the Treasury. She viewed significant help, i.e. more public expenditure, as a major U-turn – and the lady was not for turning.

My Peterborough constituents were as upset as those who lived in the rest of the country, though they were never minded to riot. Nevertheless, those poll-tax-dominated months were the nadir of my twenty-six years as an MP, not least because it was 'my' government that was responsible.

The Conservative government's popularity sank, along with the local popularity of Conservative MPs, leaving many wondering if they had any political future. And Margaret got the blame. The lady making clear that she was not for turning simply added to public fury. Even the devotion Margaret engendered in rank-and-file Tory volunteers was strained.

By the time of the 1992 election, the poll tax had been removed and its toxic political effect had been mitigated by John Major and Michael Heseltine – but only after one of the twentieth century's great Prime Ministers had been 'retired' by her parliamentary colleagues, without ever having lost any test of popular electoral opinion. The public decided that John Major should be given a chance to show what he could do, mainly because most had formed the view that he was a good and decent man who could be trusted.

Three other issues influenced the public's voting intentions in 1992, but none had much to do with specific government policies. At the time, the country was caught up in a worldwide economic downturn. People accepted that this had not resulted from any economic incompetence by government. In the privacy of their own homes they asked themselves who they trusted more to look after their money, deciding equally privately, and maybe selfishly, that they trusted the Conservatives more than Labour, and determined to vote accordingly. Whether they were embarrassed by the prospect or simply thought it was 'uncool' to be supporting Conservatives so soon after the poll tax debacle, many kept their intentions to themselves. Secondly, we were seeking a fourth consecutive term in office, unheard of in recent political history and thought by some to be unhealthy for our democracy. Whatever the true reasons, decisions quietly taken by millions of people were not discernible prior to election day. As a consequence there was a sense of shock when the result was announced.

In Peterborough I could not understand why Conservative colleagues were so gloomy. My *personal* canvassing, measured against 1987 figures, was holding up well. Party officials sent two national journalists to see me in the final week of the campaign. They were not convinced by my figures and took the view that I, a member of the government, would say, that wouldn't I? Well actually, as a Christian, no. Both had the grace, after the election, to apologise for not believing me. My predictive figures turned out to be remarkably accurate.

The third 'quiet' issue was Neil Kinnock. The country, apart from Labour stalwarts and many Welsh people, saw him as a 'windbag' – more words than substance. To make matters worse he held a 'victory' rally in Sheffield during the actual election, which led many to question his judgement. His policies were secondary, people just formed a view about him.

So the 1992 election result was made possible by people's reaction to the demise of the poll tax and their private convictions about how best to protect their interests in a recession. It was also influenced by the personality of the new Prime Minister, and that of his opponent. Manifesto promises? What manifesto promises? John Major's soap box was more influential than his manifesto.

In 2001 and 2005, the election results were 'pre-ordained' by the British sense of fair play. Tories had governed for four parliaments. It would not be 'fair' to think of removing Labour after just one or two parliaments. In addition Mr Blair was smooth and charming and the Tories in opposition did not show much sign of having refreshed themselves for government. The British public quickly formed a view. Labour was doing well and coming across persuasively. Mr Blair should remain in No. 10.

After the 1997 election, I remained Party Chairman for the few weeks it took the parliamentary party to elect a new leader and for him to pick his own team. (I was made shadow Home Secretary.) Therefore candidates for the leadership had to lodge their candidacy papers with me. To ensure that all were treated even-handedly I devised a standard response when each told me he planned to stand for election. 'I will play no part in the process, nor express any preference. I will ensure that Central Office remains neutral. And I wish you well.'

Only once did I 'amend' my formula. When William Hague told me of his intention, I added a question. 'Should I presume that this means you are comfortable with the timing of your bid to be party leader?' He said he was. I remained silent. Even then I had no doubt that whoever succeeded John Major would not win the 2001 election, but I kept my own counsel. The British sense of fairness would prevail.

If political manifestos are one of the great 'givens' of British politics – albeit overrated in their importance, in my view – the other great 'given' is political advertising. In 1979 the Tories' poster 'Labour isn't working' was credited by some with winning us the election. This media mantra that a poster depicting a queue outside a job centre was the key factor in winning the election is nonsense.

One of my predecessors as Conservative Party Chairman, Chris (now Lord) Patten, warned me against expensive full- and half-page newspaper advertising when I went to him seeking advice. He said it was a non-influential way to waste money. In my judgement he was right, despite newspaper editors pressuring us to give something back to those who were giving us so much coverage! Personalised advertising in local newspapers for local candidates is too expensive for most constituency elections but probably has more selective merit.

I would go further. Personalised or individual candidate advertising is also more effective than posters on city centre hoardings. Such posters may provide a sound bite to help a few voters firm up their thinking, but the cost efficiency per vote gained is almost certainly low. Hoardings can constitute good public relations for some businesses but they contribute little influence in the democratic process. And, boy, are they expensive. I always resented giving the Saatchis so much money to produce posters – and it was a huge amount.

Some may be wondering why a story which started about the truthfulness of Prime Ministers has developed into a reflective election analysis. Let me explain. Truthfulness is a key indicator of integrity. When the public forms a view about which politicians to support, they are assessing their elected representatives in the round. A selfishly attractive policy is usually not enough to persuade many people to vote for it. If it were, the party which offered to cut taxes the most would win. Or, to quote a similar but opposite example, the public overwhelmingly support the death penalty but most of the MPs they elect do not. What the public want is to have a sense of the men and women to whom they are going to entrust their lives and wellbeing. 'Attractive' is good, obviously, but most people want more.

Elections in this country are often determined on the basis of character, values and vision, as well as intentions, i.e. by both political credibility and integrity. Of course parties also need policies, mainly because it is through them that they project their priorities. Taken together, policies indicate whether a party's thinking is politically and ethically coherent or simply a mish-mash of populist ideas. They convey a world view that will guide and temper legislation as well as influence foreign policy responses. They create or diminish public aspirations, ranging from personal care to security, and provide a framework for economic policy. In this sense, policies taken together as a whole are important. No party can or should be elected without them.

Parties can also be assisted into government through the occasional political slogan, especially if this coincides with the national mood. 'Education, education, education', 'tough on crime, tough on the causes of crime' and 'prison works' are good examples. The public can find them helpful when trying to decide how to vote and, later, when trying to assess a government's record of delivery. In the latter case, unless a government has integrity about its promises, what was once politically helpful can easily become politically destructive.

About thirty years ago, Margaret Thatcher made a speech which has had a profound effect on truthful intention and integrity and on the way politics has been conducted ever since. One phrase in that speech deserves special attention. In the early years of the first

Thatcher government, the Prime Minister and Chancellor Geoffrey Howe restructured the tax system by significantly increasing expenditure-related taxes. Our manifesto had indicated we would do this, but no one seemed to have been paying attention. Anyway, experiencing a policy is always more memorable than talking about it in advance.

VAT was raised to squeals of protest from every quarter. Perhaps understandably, tax reductions *never* produce the same noise level, nor did they on this occasion. As a consequence of those tax changes the party's popularity fell. Predictably, some political commentators and even Conservative MPs urged the government to reverse its decision. The Prime Minister was under real pressure. Margaret gave her response to them in a robust Party Conference speech. 'U-turn if you want,' she said, 'the lady's not for turning.' The Conference cheered mightily.

As a political slogan it was outstanding: clear, concise, moderately aggressive, confident and contemptuous. There was no need to 'spin' what the lady thought, this was what she thought. And she was comfortable with the words. They fitted her personality like a glove.

I have no doubt that, for many years, this message was a political bonus for Margaret. People loved it and many used it as a stick with which to beat her male contemporaries. Why could we not be as robust and forthright in defence of our country, its values and institutions as the lady was? It became part of the definition of the Thatcher premiership. It was the essence of Thatcherism.

Perhaps you sense a 'but' coming. Normally there is a 'but' associated with any deft political slogan once years have passed and circumstances changed. In this case there are two. During her years in office, Margaret delivered or tried to deliver a significant number of the commitments she made. She was truthful. She was not always successful, however, when she 'battled' with Europe – though, memorably, she got 'our' money back. Equally memorably, she was renowned for trying. Most people will be surprised to be reminded that, in Europe, the lady occasionally was for turning. Sometimes her nationalistic clarion calls before departure were out of sync with her reports on return, but her integrity was bolstered in the public mind because she did try to deliver her promises, and that effort was fundamental to high integrity.

Being strong, forthright and immoveable can be a political bonus. But politics is also the art of the possible, the art of finding workable solutions. No politician of Margaret Thatcher's standing can always be immoveable. Apart from anything else, the collegiate responsibility of Cabinet membership should ensure some appropriate flexibility to accommodate changed circumstances.

Refusing to turn when the decision to retake the Falkland Islands had been made reflected strength, conviction and patriotism. Refusing to mitigate the poll tax did not. The former was politically enhancing, the latter politically disastrous.

So a slogan that was hugely admired as a political defining moment of supreme importance, for both the lady and the nation, became over time a standard against which any failure to sustain her policy positions could be judged and magnified against her.

There turned out to be a second, and perhaps more serious, weakness in this famous declamation. 'U-turn' became more loosely defined as time passed. Governments govern for years during which external and national circumstances change. For example, I remember watching in amazement as the Berlin Wall was torn down – a world-changing event that was unimaginable at the general election a few years earlier. Whatever the prevailing manifesto said, this event changed foreign policy. A 'U-turn' was inevitable.

†

I was on the last British Airways flight out of Boston on the evening of 10 September 2001. The next morning (9/11), other flights left Boston and US east coast airports. I got home just in time to see one of them fly into the World Trade Center in New York – hijacked by terrorist fanatics. The world would never be the same again. International circumstances and homeland security changed fundamentally. Those events demanded policy and rhetoric change

– even U-turns – within government. The genesis of the invasion of Iraq occurred in those days, though it was unmentioned in New Labour's manifesto.

When governments enact legislation, they do so to give effect to their electoral commitments and aspirations. These, over time, change national circumstances so that new and different policies need to be devised. Government's problem is that too often it remains more or less bound into the initial framework of facts and perceptions which got them elected. Yet facts and perceptions do change with time. An unwillingness to 'turn', to adjust to these changes, can soon be seen as obstinacy, weakness or electoral fatigue, rather than strength. Trying to maintain the status quo, whatever is happening around us, can become politically counterproductive.

Over time the public perception of 'U-turn if you want, the lady's not for turning' shifted from an appreciation of admirable strength to, in some cases, a perception of stubbornness. Margaret's opponents spun the slogan by reinterpreting it to mean that change equalled untruthfulness or an admission of error. It was a spin that was as unfair as it was telling. It carried the danger of inhibiting sensible, necessary and politically advisable change, of causing government to become bogged down.

There was enough truth in Margaret's slogan to ensure that any charge against a politician of U-turning became a damaging political accusation, not an admiration of forthrightness. Changing your mind, and therefore your policy, generally became equated with weakness and being wrong, which of course sometimes it was. Unintentionally, Margaret's excellent mantra began to limit government action by making it difficult for ministers to adjust to new circumstances.

Three, or at the most four, consecutive parliaments are likely to prove the limit for any governing political party in the foreseeable future. Apart from familiarity breeding contempt and a public perception of too many broken promises or untruthfulness, governments require policy renewal and regeneration from time to time. Some of this renewal may break new ground, but some is likely to involve changes which cut across established policy and practice, not least because the world, the nation and their issues have changed in the intervening years. Government's risk these days is that those changes will be designated U-turns, the symbol of weakness, by political opponents. So good and necessary change is inhibited. As a consequence, governments soldier on, giving the impression that the world has not really changed in the years since they were elected and that no fundamentally new thinking is required. Such a position is neither credible nor sustainable. Change and U-turns may be necessary for the common good.

By 1997, the Conservative government was out of steam, in part because we were trying to solve problems at home and abroad with thinking and paradigms which stemmed from our last party policy review in 1975. And we were nervous of U-turns and of being accused of making them.

Over time, the New Labour government faced the same issue of increasing policy irrelevance and equally failed to solve it. For example, the issue of terrorism, which blossomed in the early part of this century, bears little relation to what was happening in 1997 (excluding Northern Ireland). Yet neither Blair nor Brown undertook a proper and detailed policy review on how to handle this massive change, other than an examination by Privy Counsellors, of whom I was one, of how terrorism legislation was working, forced on Blair by Parliament. They seemed concerned that holding a review might suggest they did not have adequate policies. So rather than doing so, they pretended that the number, tactics, determination and weaponry of terrorists and their sympathisers had not escalated, and just soldiered on.

Instead, these governments, being unwilling to contemplate considered change, passed laws in which human liberties were damaged. In themselves, these new laws were a U-turn from Labour manifestos and the principles on which we have long been governed. Consequently the liberal democratic nature of our country was changed, perhaps irrevocably, and certainly not attractively.

This country became great because its traditions and values were based on the Christian belief that men and women are made in the image of God. Terrorist behaviour will often require policy amendment, but that should not include abandoning the principles on which our liberal democracy is based.

Nor has this progression of illiberalism been a clear success. It has been described by some as simply a recruiting sergeant for more terrorist activity. Groups of citizens turn on each other out of ignorance or mistrust. Hate increases. As a society we claim to be inclusive, but increasingly our focus has shifted towards difference and the divisive while pretending that they do not exist, rather than towards the common good. We no longer provide room to accommodate proper freedom of belief and expression. Instead we are in danger of becoming squeezed into a centrally controlled, 'Big Brother knows best', politically correct surveillance society. Governments and politicians would be treated more sympathetically by the public if all of us were able to be a little more relaxed. Instead we convey the impression of being uptight, by our overblown rhetoric and a frequent inability to say sorry. 'Sorry' is too often seen as a sign of weakness, not strength. Yet David Cameron's apology over Bloody Sunday – for which he and his government had no responsibility – shines as a beacon of hope.

Perhaps politicians and others need to be reminded more robustly that God allows – even encourages – U-turns. In Biblical language they are associated with error, repentance and forgiveness.

In case you think the above criticism of the undermining of our civil liberties is overdone, let me recount one small vignette. In 2008, walking down Pall Mall in London, I stopped to talk to two policemen who had recognised me. They were involved in a street operation and were wholly friendly. In passing I mentioned, to save them potential embarrassment, that one of their vans was breaking the law. The reply was chilling. 'Since you people in Parliament passed the anti-terrorism legislation, Dr Mawhinney, we can do what we like.'

†

I wish I had devised, and said, 'U-turn if you want, I am not for turning'. It is so powerful.

I also wish that the rest of us had paid a little less attention to it when it was said. In the mouth of Margaret Thatcher it had real, if limited, positive meaning. For those who followed her, without her gifts or philosophy, it has been allowed to become both confusing and unhelpfully limiting.

After over thirty years in public life, I recognise more than ever the importance of telling the public the truth. What we say is still a good insight into who we are. It may seem old fashioned, but the Bible's encouragement to 'let your yea be yea and your nay be nay' is still a good yardstick by which to judge politicians.

15

In and Out

Although I played no part in the timing, from my point of view it was excellent. In 2001 I had been re-elected Member of Parliament for North West Cambridgeshire (which included about half the district of Peterborough) with a comfortable majority. This would be my second parliament on the opposition benches.

For over twenty years I had been, and had been seen to be, a conscientious constituency MP and I intended to continue that commitment. But, truth to tell, I was missing the demands of being a minister and felt the need of some additional challenge. On the other hand, I was not minded to go looking for a second job. I thought about approaching headhunters but did little beyond thinking.

As a grammar school boy in Belfast, my love of sport focused on rugby, cricket and golf. While living in the USA I followed American football and baseball. Enjoying watching soccer came later – when we were settled in England – and that, in turn, brought me into contact with Geoff Davey. He is the one who should be blamed by those who think politicians should stay out of football.

Geoff, now retired, ran several professional football clubs over many years. In 2002 he was chief executive of Peterborough United. I had been one of the city's MPs, and a Posh fan, since 1979. Geoff and I had become friends and we met occasionally for a chat over coffee. He would give me club gossip, useful to a constituency MP, and I told him what was really going on at Westminster. Our

September meeting that year was in his small office: a desk, with a chair either side of it, a filing cabinet and little else.

Geoff did most of the talking. Following the recent collapse of the Football League's media contract with ITV Digital, he told me, clubs were in chaos. The League's chief executive had been removed from office and the chairman, Keith Harris of Seymour Pierce, had lost the board's confidence, departing with the memorable phrase that he was leaving the asylum in the hands of the inmates.

Club finances were in meltdown. Most clubs, typically, had 'spent in advance' all three years' money of the ITV contract. That is, they had literally spent it or had legally committed it to player contracts. Unfortunately for them, only about eighteen months' money had actually been transferred to clubs – hence the chaos. A hastily nego-tiated, relatively small, new media deal, coupled with a financially limited helping hand from both the Football Association (FA) and the Premier League (PL) (an example of the so-called football family coming together, though the largesse had strings attached), while welcome, did not nearly fill the gaping hole in Football League clubs' balance sheets.

Geoff was giving me the gory details, being uncomplimentary about the League's leadership, reflecting on the need to find a new chairman and chief executive and saying how difficult it might be to get good people to fill these posts, when he suddenly stopped.

'You know, Brian,' he said, 'you have all the attributes we are looking for in a new chairman. I know from seeing you here that you are a fan. More importantly, you have the senior management experience as well as the public and media exposure we need. And you are not easily pushed around.'

Without saying anything more, he picked up his phone and called Peter Heard, who was then the League's acting chairman. Peter was also chairman of Colchester United and an FA board member. He has been one of the most influential men in English football over the past generation and, even in semi-retirement, remains one of the most respected.

Geoff told Peter that he thought I should be considered for the

League's chairmanship (without mentioning that I was sitting across the desk from him) and believed I might be interested! Peter told him to invite me to forward my CV, but in a tone which to me suggested he was underwhelmed by the prospect. I thanked Geoff and said I would reflect on Peter's suggestion. Then we went on to put The Posh and the wider world to rights.

Thus started my seven-plus years' football administration adventure. Though to be honest, it was not my first venture into football land. While I was Northern Ireland's sports minister, and following crowd trouble at a number of English club grounds, Margaret Thatcher, then Prime Minister, was persuaded that the game would be safer and more orderly if fans were to carry identity cards to matches and use them to enter grounds. With little or no knowledge of football crowd control, she could not see why turnstiles should not be adapted appropriately.

The game was adamantly opposed to her initiative. Fans were incensed. Eventually she agreed to meet with senior figures from the FA around the Cabinet table so that they could press their case. All four sports ministers in the government, along with more senior ministers, were invited to be present.

This was my first exposure to the FA. Its leadership was unbelievably poor at arguing its case. They seemed to believe that, because they were the football people, the politicians had to take their word that identity cards were a bad idea. They made no attempt rationally to convince a conviction Prime Minister that she was wrong – a huge mistake when dealing with Margaret.

To the politicians present, the FA mandarins were embarrassingly unpersuasive. Margaret was disparaging in her private summary of their advocacy.

Eventually the football identity card scheme was shelved; not because of the FA's opposition but almost in spite of it. It was some of us in government, treated with disdain by the football world, who made the persuasive case not to proceed. Years later, even as an FA board member, I was seldom persuaded that the organisation had improved much.

Back to 2002. Driving away from The Posh that day, I thought about Peter's offer. Write or forget it? Like most football fans, though one who has never claimed to be a football man, I knew little about the game's management and cared even less. Certainly I had never had a burning desire to run anything in football. On other hand, my friend obviously appreciated my skills and thought they could add value to the League.

Eventually I sent Peter a letter simply because not sending one would have been an unchristian and churlish response to Geoff's act of kindness. After all, at this stage, it constituted nothing more than an expression of interest. On reflection, my relatively short letter possibly indicated that I too was a little underwhelmed at the idea of 'running football'. Anyway, the chance seemed remote.

About three weeks later Peter rang. The League's board had decided (correctly in my view) to run a transparent appointment process; the job would be advertised nationally. The board did not need me to apply, he said. They would regard my earlier letter as an application.

After a preliminary 'interview' (in truth it was more of a general chat with a couple of board members), I and one other candidate were interviewed formally by the whole board in early December. I have no knowledge of that other candidate, but at least in my case the event was neither testing nor memorable. Except for one question.

Was I in favour of chief executives running organisations? The very strangeness of the question prompted caution. 'Yes,' I said, I favoured chief executives. Organisations need clear decision-making processes, sensitive handling and an easily identifiable chain of responsibility. Of course I knew that other management arrangements did exist. However, I added, I did not know enough about the Football League to judge whether it was best suited to having a chief executive or not, if that was the thought that lay behind the question.

Later Peter Heard rang to say I had been elected chairman unanimously. An appointment letter would follow. I still have it

– the only legal piece of paper which covered my 2,653 days in the job. To my surprise, the appointment did not need to be confirmed by the clubs, then or at any other time.

Apparently this omission had nothing to do with me personally. It represented more of a 'political' judgement by the board. In recent months, clubs, understandably, had been very critical of the board's handling of the ITV contract debacle. As a result, the board was nervous that clubs might use this opportunity, afforded by the appointment of a new chairman, as an excuse to claw back some responsibility for running the League. The board was determined not to allow any interference in its right to appoint the chairman.

Years later I asked Peter why my letter had had no exit strategy built into it (other than a sentence about three months' notice on either side). His answer provided an insight into the then demoralised state of the League.

'We did not expect you to stay as long as six months,' he replied. 'We all agreed you would have neither the patience nor the willingness to put up with seventy-two club chairmen, all with different views of what should happen next. We wanted you to stay but feared you would decide only to be a transient.'

Obviously the board had given thought to how the League's reputation would be damaged by losing a second chairman within a year – but seemed unable to address the risk other than by hoping they had underestimated me. They could not even bring themselves to talk to me about it. In fact they never gave me an in-depth briefing about what I was inheriting.

I quickly began to learn about the League. My first press conference, the first lesson, was a revelation. Two questions predominated. The first was, chairman – a politician? A Conservative politician? (in tones which parodied John McEnroe's famous 'you can't be serious!') This was an early warning of football's disdain for government and politicians. On that first day, some of the cream of English football reporting had great difficulty in progressing beyond the box labelled 'politics'. There was no recognition that I may have any skills – inherited or learned – relevant experience or personal commitment. Indeed the continued use of the word 'politician' too often sounded as if it was accompanied by a curl of the lip. English football fans deserved something a little more analytical and, dare I add, more objective.

The second question was how many clubs I thought the Football League would lose by the end of the season. The reporters' downbeat assessment was that six to eight clubs could go out of business. I told them I did not have a crystal ball and would not guess ('speculate' is the polite word).

Many football journalists are transfixed by speculation; perhaps because so much about football revolves around prediction, passion, prejudice, hope and injury rather than hard fact. To be fair, they have to explain a game where the past is never a reliable indicator of the future. Some journalists thrive on substituting 'what-if or maybe' in place of informed judgement. They talk and write as if feelings are a solid basis for factual analysis – or indeed even for guesswork. 'How do/did you feel' has become the lazy substitute for proper questioning in football, as it has throughout the media. 'What do you think?' seldom gets examined. Fortunately there are outstanding exceptions to this slightly unflattering generalisation. Each of us will have our favourites. Mine include, but are not restricted to, Patrick Barclay, David Conn, Charlie Sale, Martin Samuel, Henry Winter and Jimmy Armfield.

In the event, no club was lost in that five-month period, nor during my seven-plus years as chairman – though I admit there were some close calls.

My second introductory lesson about the League was much more worrying and important. A few days after I started work, Peter Heard summoned me to his professional offices. We were joined by John Elsom, a Leicester City director, League board member and another good man. 'We have a serious problem,' they said. 'The job of League chief executive has already been advertised and four men have been shortlisted for interview in the January board meeting.' When Division One clubs (as they were then called) had learned this, they had become very angry. The

behaviour of the League's previous chief executive had so upset them
that they were adamantly opposed to having another one (hence
the strange interview question). Peter and John told me the clubs
had decided to convene a Division One club meeting at Leicester
City a few days later to hold their three board representatives
(one of whom was John) to account for agreeing to appoint a new
chief executive.

Peter and John agreed it was 'wholly unacceptable' that they and
others had withheld this fundamental dispute from me during my
appointment process, presumably because they were afraid it might
put me off. I never forgot that insight, which was by no means
unique, into the way the League conducted its governance.

However naive, forgetful or duplicitous board members had been,
the looming showdown had to be addressed. It was clearly my first
leadership 'test'. 'Tell them', I said to John, 'that I plan to attend the
Leicester meeting and look forward both to meeting them and to
starting to learn about the League's current issues. Please stress I do
not want to chair the meeting, sit at the head table or even speak.
I just want to observe and learn.' John, obviously unnerved, said he
would convey the message. He did not look happy. Peter, on the
other hand, looked impassive, which I was to learn was normal. He
is not easily rattled.

Two days later we were back in Peter's office. The Division
One chairmen did not want me at their meeting. I would not be
welcome. John looked embarrassed. Clearly he had not robustly
argued the new chairman's case with his colleagues. Indeed, in the
circumstances, why should he further antagonise them? The tension
in the room was increased by the fact that Peter was leading those
board members who were determined the League should have a
chief executive.

In my political world, such challenges are routine and routinely
resolved. The lesson learned from those experiences was that it was
best to start as you meant to continue. 'Tell them, John,' I said, 'that,
because the meeting is about the League's management structure,
as League chairman I will attend. But if the first item of business

is a properly moved and seconded motion for me to leave, and it is carried in an open vote, then I will go quietly.' What the consequences would be of my removal in this way were left unexplored. Some thoughts exert a more powerful influence if left hanging.

John looked stricken by my bravado. On the day, the club chairmen welcomed me warmly. No one mentioned a motion.

The meeting was a revelation. Its substance was seriously rebellious against the board. The number of times chairmen swore that, no matter how bad things were, they would not break away from the League simply underlined how dominant that possibility was in their thinking. The conduct of the meeting was disgracefully 'illegal' if set alongside League regulations.

Theo Paphitis, then chairman of Millwall and a prominent businessman (later of *Dragons' Den* fame), talked us through a PowerPoint on what he and others thought was wrong with the League and what needed to change. It included some interesting ideas around the concept that Division One clubs needed to be and to feel more important within the League. The three existing Football League board members were then 'fired' by acclamation – forced to resign if you want me to be technical – and were replaced by Theo, David Sheepshanks (Ipswich) and Terry Robinson (Sheffield United). All this was done outside the League's regulations for board appointments. On this first outing as chairman, I chose discretion rather than valour and said nothing. At least there was no mistaking the mood or the will of the Division One chairmen. When invited to address them at the end of the meeting, I stood up, thanked them, said I looked forward to working with them and sat down – thirty seconds max – to their evident surprise. You could see them thinking that maybe I was not such a 'toughie' after all, which was fine with me.

This still left us with the issue of four prospective chief executives coming for interview to the board meeting the following week. In the intervening days, David Sheepshanks, speaking for Division One clubs, rejected outright the idea of a chief executive. He made it plain that if I insisted the board went ahead with the interviews, he and his two colleagues would walk out. I believed him, but thought the reaction distasteful.

Peter Heard, on behalf of Divisions Two and Three, insisted the board had followed proper procedure. The League needed executive leadership. Andy Williamson, the long-serving director in charge of football, did not want the job. Four men were expecting to be interviewed. This must happen to preserve the League's reputation and future. I may have been new to football but this sort of political stand-off was second nature to me.

I spent hours on the phone alternating between David and Peter. Eventually, thirty-six hours before the board meeting, I told them separately, but in identical terms, what I thought of their intransigence. Stripped of the emotion of the moment, the summary was not complicated. The board was split 3–3. I had the casting vote and in due course would let them know my decision. Both made it robustly clear that they were not used to being treated in this way – protests which were ignored.

When the board met, the interviews did not take place. I explained that this was not because I had chosen to take sides within the board. Interviews could not take place because, in the circumstances of stalemate, no one could explain to the interviewees what would be required of a new chief executive. I told my colleagues that, collectively, they had created this mess, so it was their job to sort it. While they were doing that, I would work with the senior executives to keep the League running. My tone discouraged dissent.

By the quarterly clubs' meeting in March, no progress had been made towards resolving the impasse, so the clubs got the same message as the board. They and their representatives had to resolve the dispute themselves. At this point I declined to intervene. If, however, there was still deadlock by the June annual meeting then I would propose a solution and expect them to vote through any consequential regulatory changes. The downside of them not agreeing was again left hanging.

In June, with the matter still unresolved, everyone agreed that I should become executive chairman (the first since the League began in 1888), to what appeared to be the considerable relief of most of the clubs. Their confidence in the 'traditional' board seemed limited. In addition I promised Division One clubs a director of their own – to try to raise more resources for their clubs and to argue their case when League policy was being drafted, to work with them but to be answerable to me. Division Two and Three clubs were reassured that I personally would look out for their interests. I also decided, privately, to become the first chairman to be able to claim to have visited every club in the League, a goal I achieved.

Early lessons in football reality – unsustainable debt, governance problems, clubs' insatiable demand for more money, legal problem solving, big egos and selective information – coupled with the need for sensitive, individually based leadership and foresight, together with occasional toughness, continued to dominate my chairman-ship. They are fundamental to managing all professional football, as I was to discover, but are by no means exclusive to football – which is why football leadership does not *have* to be entrusted only to football people. Sometimes my unwillingness to blink first also helped.

In May 2005 I decided to relinquish the great privilege of being a Member of Parliament. Two months later, on the day that London was announced as the host of the 2012 Olympic Games, I was introduced into the House of Lords as Baron Mawhinney, of Peterborough. By that time my two days per week contract with the Football League had already stretched in practice to nearly three days. It soon became four.

†

Seven years on and it was time to think about going. Only two of the 'original' directors were still on the board – David Sheepshanks and Terry Robinson – though, at that time, the latter did not know he was in his last few weeks of service. I say 'original' but in fact none of those who had selected me in December 2002 remained, David and Terry having joined the board 'unconventionally' at the

Leicester meeting. Seven-plus years is a long time to be running any organisation, especially when one individual, as chairman and chief executive, is carrying most of the management weight. Occasionally board members said they wanted more individual governance responsibility or policy involvement in the running of the League. I tried to accommodate them. Sometimes, however, this did not happen because they quickly learned they had under-estimated and/or were daunted by the amount of work involved. Ivor Beeks (Wycombe Wanderers), Peter Heard (Colchester United), Mark Arthur (Nottingham Forest) and Tony Kleanthous (Barnet) were honourable exceptions. Incidentally, Ivor Beeks and Peter Heard are excellent examples of the many fine chairmen who lead League clubs. They are sensible, balanced and dedicated. They work hard, understand financial sustainability and are not easily conned. I salute all such chairmen, not least because often they get crowded out of the public mind by the less desirable antics of some of their colleagues.

So 'time for a change', for me and indeed for the League, was the first reason for contemplating moving on.

Since the beginning of 2003, when I started, there had been about a 70 per cent turnover in League chairmen and chief executives. The upward trend of that percentage also suggested to me that it was time for the League to plan ahead for the next five years and, if it so wished, to give a new mandate to a new chairman.

In the Football Association and Football League, directors, by regulation and custom, stand down at the end of the season in which they turn seventy. In the Premier League they retire on their seventieth birthday. Overwhelmingly, for most club chairmen my retirement was not an issue. They wanted me to leave in June 2011, not on my birthday, July 2010. Some even talked about voting a regula-tion change to allow me to serve beyond 2011. I greatly appreciated this spontaneous compliment, which had not been encouraged by me. My view has always been that no one is indispensable, as indeed I had demonstrated when choosing to leave the Commons. On the other hand, as some FA and League chairmen have discovered, club confidence in them is a vital ingredient if any football organisation is to prosper. Acting as I was thinking of doing, while still enjoying that confidence, gave me time to think long and hard about what was best for me and the League. My decision was not rushed.

Only a very few people in the League showed me any personal antipathy. I suspect, but cannot prove, that this was encouraged by some in the senior ranks of the Premier League. They argued for ignoring League 'custom' about my retirement date and sticking to the 'letter of the law', i.e. my seventieth birthday. This first surfaced in Charlie Sale's column in the *Daily Mail*, the best-informed gossip column for sport, and impressively accurate. However, their mischief making did not fly.

Terry Robinson told me he was in favour of David Sheepshanks succeeding me on my seventieth birthday. Championship clubs, he said, would have more confidence in one of their own as League chairman. I knew from my own experience that he was talking nonsense. He was dressing up his (and David's?) views as if they represented those of all the other clubs. They did not. I was simply not pliable enough for him, nor did I pay sufficient attention to what he wanted. Nevertheless that fundamental divisional tension in the League, at which Terry was hinting, was and remains a serious issue.

Meanwhile David Sheepshanks informed me, and later the board, that Championship clubs had lost confidence in the whole board – which again was absolute nonsense. The only real consequence of his making that remark was that people started wondering what he was scheming.

The reality was that clubs strongly supported my chairmanship, for which they all have my sincere gratitude. After my retirement, they and the clubs in Leagues 1 and 2 unanimously created the new position of Honorary League President for me as their 'thank you' for my service to them – a huge honour. And I conscientiously displayed my appreciation by attending over 100 games in my three-year appointment.

I can truthfully say that, for me, the League chairmanship was always about what was best for the clubs and never about me. In the world's terms, my reputation had already been made in politics before I ever entered the world of football. What drove me in football was my assessment of what was in the clubs' best interests. The thought of swatting away the distractions caused by a few – it was never more than that – with personal agendas for twelve months or longer did not appeal to me. The majority of Football League chairmen deserved better, even though it was not in their nature to deal with this sort of juvenile politicking themselves.

Holding the League together – the only specific board request on my appointment – was beginning to chafe with a few greedy Championship chairmen. They wanted to be free of the lower leagues to associate with the Premier League – and I was in their way. They were accumulating debt, spending money they did not have, and as a consequence were starting to cast increasingly covetous eyes on the Premier League's riches. In their fantasy world, this was described as 'living the dream'. They were being openly encouraged in that thought by Phil Gartside, chairman of Bolton Wanderers, who was advocating a Premier League Second Division (to be composed mainly of Championship clubs). He, in turn, was not being hampered in this effort by his friend, the Premier League chairman, Sir David Richards.

Then and in recent seasons, clubs like Blackburn, Bolton and Wigan have struggled to maintain their standing against the bigger and better-financed clubs in the Premier League. Relegation for them would mean a significant drop in income, which in turn would entail getting rid of some star, and expensive, players. The threat of administration could not be ruled out. So, from a financial point of view, the attraction of being in the top league was obvious. Perhaps Phil Gartside had a premonition and that was what lay behind his idea. At the time of writing, Blackburn and Bolton are hardly dominating the Championship.

Gartside's proposal was simple. There should be two Premier Leagues – One and Two – each consisting of eighteen clubs, with promotion and relegation between them but not between them and the lower divisions. In his plan the proposed PL1 and PL2 would consist of the twenty Premier League clubs, Celtic and Rangers from Glasgow and sixteen of the twenty-four Football League Championship clubs.

Richard Scudamore, the Premier League's chief executive, told me regularly that it was not supportive of Gartside's proposal. David Richards said likewise while at the same time 'unofficially' helping his mate Phil. The Football League board, even without all the incendiary information above, was against the idea in principle. That did not deter one of our number, Terry Robinson, from supporting Gartside.

In the year Middlesbrough was relegated from the Premier League, Keith Lamb, its then chief executive, stood for election to our board to become one of its Championship representatives. This was an unusually quick nomination but within the rules. I invited Keith to sit with me for dinner at his inaugural annual meeting. During our conversation I asked Keith why he had decided to stand for election given that he had had no Championship experience. 'Oh,' he said, 'David Richards and Terry Robinson urged me to do it so that, if elected, I can help then drive Phil Gartside's idea of Premier League Two.' I said nothing but thought a lot.

Sir David Richards is a complex man whose word I learned to take seriously but never trusted completely. His manner is folksy, forthright (as befits a Yorkshire man), aggressive (at times) and independently minded, with a noticeable ego. His mind, once decided, is very hard to turn. Combine all these characteristics with a willingness to work diligently for long hours and a well-developed sense of ambition and it is no wonder that people sometimes interpreted – or misinterpreted? – his persona as bullying. But, undoubtedly, he has contributed to the success of the Premier League. Officially that league was not in favour of PL2, yet he asked me if I would meet with Phil Gartside privately so that I could understand better what he had in mind. 'You never know,' he said, 'you might be persuaded!' I agreed that the two of us should meet, without publicity.

Phil set out his ideas about two divisions in the Premier

League, with all the money generated being divided between the thirty-six clubs.

When invited to comment I confessed confusion. I said it sounded as if he intended to gut the Football League, founded in 1888 – the very sporting arena in which his club had developed its potential. I think I added that Nat Lofthouse, Bolton and England's legendary gentleman of football, would not have been impressed by such an attitude to the Football League.

Gartside's reply was breathtakingly frank. 'The days of four professional football divisions have passed,' he said. The econom- ics of the game, including involvement in European competitions, for the few not the many, dictated that only two divisions were viable. The other two were a financial drain and not sustainable. The Football League's two remaining divisions, Leagues One and Two, together with the remaining eight Championship clubs, should add Conference teams and all become part-time, semi-professional clubs – and forget about financial support from the Premier League.

I told him he was selfish and wrongheaded and was nuts if he thought that I would be the League chairman who presided over the demolition of the Football League. No deal. Nothing worth discussing. We agreed we would not brief our respective boards at that time but, for obvious reasons, I made no commitment to keep Phil's views confidential. I know he told David Richards about the content of our conversation.

The huge financial difference between the two leagues continues to divide and add stress to relations within the Football League. Unless great care is taken at board level, those deadly sins avarice and envy will undermine the Football League's solidarity.

Talking of solidarity, recent multi-million-pound 'hand outs' from the Premier League to the Football League, with suffocat- ing long-term strings attached, are already stirring discontent. They are referred to as 'solidarity payments' – a good spin. In reality they appear to knowledgeable outsiders as designed primarily to strengthen the Premier League's grip on the English game. The fact that they were offered to the Football League by Richard

Scudamore on an alleged 'take it or leave it' basis tends to heighten that perception. It is no longer his job to decide what is in the best interests of the Football League, so his 'strings attached' need to be treated with considerable caution, more than I think they received at the time.

In my view it is no coincidence that Richard temporised about revealing his latest solidarity offer to Football League clubs, despite my prompting, until after I had left the chairmanship. Richard knew I would have called his bluff big time and encouraged our clubs to decide their future on a different basis. I would not have allowed his 'all or nothing' to fly, but I declined to comment at the time, for the League's leadership was no longer my responsibility. My successor did not seek my opinion or advice and had no basis to judge whether or not Richard was bluffing.

But I would not want to leave the impression that Richard and I were constantly at daggers drawn, for that would be untrue. More often than not we were in broad agreement, except over aspects of England's World Cup bid. David Richards once told me, with obvious chagrin, that I was the only person who had a sixty-minute private meeting with Richard every month, without any formal records being kept. In fact we often worked in tandem to advance our separate causes and the general good of football.

Richard is a gifted man with impressive political and commercial skills. The obvious success of the Premier League is his success, and it involved management flair, toughness, commercial acumen and political skill, all of which he added effectively. And he can be thoughtful. I will always appreciate the kindness he and his family showed Betty, me, our son David and his family when we visited their home in Massachusetts.

The grand prize for clubs, salvation through more money, is illusory. The problem for most of them stems more from too little cost control rather than too little money. They are driven by unrealistic expectations and an inability or unwillingness to harness the unrealistic passion of fans. Understandably, fans want success and sustainability for their club but focus predominantly on the former.

And this drift towards ever-increasing amounts of money is fuelled by rich individuals and corporations. I guess it must be an ego thing for most of them.

The history of the last fifteen years of debt-driven football is sobering. Memories of Leeds United (under Peter Ridsdale's chairmanship), Portsmouth, Cardiff City, Plymouth, Notts County and Sheffield Wednesday (whose multi-million-pound debt has only just been resolved, maybe twenty years after David Richards vacated the chairmanship) seem to have made little impression on how clubs are run. Accumulated debt in the Premier League is literally in the billions of pounds.

Over the same period, debt nearly did for Luton Town, Crystal Palace, Accrington Stanley, Stockport County, Southampton and Southend United among others. The list of clubs with what may prove to be unsustainable debt grows alongside the size of their debt.

Football clubs are no different from other small and medium-sized businesses. Debt is an integral part of their normal business management regime. In football, however, when people talk about club debt they are seldom talking about prudent financial management. Some clubs intellectually recognise the reality of unsustainable debt but emotionally push it into the future. This has been made possible, in part, by both leagues' management's success in increasing sponsorship and media contracts. Sometimes the Professional Footballers Association (PFA – the footballers' union) lends money to clubs to pay players' wages in the short term, knowing it is protected by the iniquitous 'football creditors' regulation. Sometimes rich owners make loans to clubs to tide them over – a practice which should be banned, for it undermines clubs' long-term stability. Owners should be restricted to gifts and/or equity involvement only, or, at most, loans which must legally be repaid within twelve months and cannot be rolled over.

Financially irresponsible management behaviour makes life impossibly difficult for those good, fiscally sensible chairmen and directors who have the genuine long-term best interests of their clubs and fans at heart. They are great people, pushing against the gravity of spend, spend, spend while being burned by others' bad behaviour. Nonetheless, Dickens's Mr Micawber, with his hope that 'something' would turn up, must surely have been invented with a football club chairman in mind.

Any sensible analysis of unsustainable debt must associate the problem with players' wages and agents' fees. For years we worked hard laying the groundwork for team salary capping. Where once I was practically a lone voice, now the issue is front and central in football. Progress has been made. Even some Premier League leaders are beginning to be interested. Positive change will probably come, although a number of clubs may have to fold (an unattractive thought) before genuine reality dawns in this new age of austerity. But dawn it will – with or without the involvement of outside forces. UEFA has taken a lead and this has been embraced by the Premier League and the Football League Championship. Its weakness is the number of caveats and 'exceptional' escape clauses it contains. Leagues One and Two put some player salary limitation in place years ago. I did not find them hard to persuade.

Trying to help so many clubs who were reluctant to make the necessary but really hard economic decisions was wearying, especially while holding my own emotions and instincts in check against the wave of their excuses. And the strong sense of community spirit among clubs – where the well-run ones were loath to take up democratic 'arms' against those who were profligate – added to the sense of stalemate. I grew tired of being the hamster running on that particular wheel. Stepping down from the Chair started to seem less unattractive, despite the intellectual and political stimulation it gave, my huge enjoyment of it and a lifelong tendency to be attracted by challenges.

The spring of 2010 provided a window of opportunity for a change of chairman. All the League's outstanding sponsorship deals would have been concluded – as it happened, with record-breaking increases in income due to the League's enhanced standing in the commercial marketplace – and colleagues would only be starting to think about the next competitive media bidding process, not a process on which I was particularly keen to re-embark. In the event it produced a significant decrease in income.

Also, a spring change would enable the next chairman, if he wanted, to have three or four months to set his agenda for the 2010–11 season. With this in mind, over a period of months I talked to and sought confidential advice from my wife, Betty, and from my friends Ivor Beeks, Peter Heard and Charlie Sale – making clear that the decision had to lie with me. Ian Ritchie, the board's other independent director, agreed to chair any transition process.

Andy Williamson, privately, declined an invitation to let me have his view on what should happen to the League's leadership during the following eighteen months. But in refusing, he stressed strongly that now was not the time for change – which may have been a personal compliment or a reflection of his conservative (small 'c') nature. He never did say when would be a good or even proper time for change. Otherwise, he helped me so much and in so many ways. 'Thank you' seems a rather inadequate response. It is very sincerely meant.

Eventually, I told the November 2009 board meeting that my tenure would end in or about March 2010. From the reaction round the table, this was obviously a big and unwelcome surprise. I am grateful to Tony Kleanthous, Peter Powell (Colchester) and Lorraine Rogers (Tranmere Rovers) for their genuine support and their efforts to persuade me to change my mind. Terry Robinson did not join the chorus of those who wanted me to stay but spoke warmly of my tenure. David Sheepshanks was not present but subsequently sent a gracious letter. Ian Ritchie said little and easily contained any sadness he may have been feeling.

In the discussion that followed my announcement, I made clear I would play no part in the choice of my successor. That being the case, I took the opportunity to underline three issues of good governance on which I hoped the board would reflect deeply. Before thinking about a replacement they should (1) debate at length whether they wanted another executive chairman or should revert to a non-executive one – by implication coupled with a chief executive (2) remember the League regulation (a good one) which required the chairman to be independent of football and (3) take as many hours as they wanted to interview me in order to understand the nature and challenges of the job. This would enable them to develop the most accurate and compelling job description, thereby enhancing their chances of picking an excellent and appropriate successor.

Seven years of my stressing within the League the importance of good governance evaporated like dew in the morning sun. Ian Ritchie called a meeting and the fundamental issue in point one was decided in minutes, without examination or even much comment. Point two was agreed even more quickly and point three never did take place. To this day I do not know if the primary responsibility for this unimpressive process lies with Ian or the rest of the board. I did hear what board members said to me about the process, but the reality is that when they should have stood their ground they did not do so. The only real debate apparently was whether to use headhunters! In my view the rush was a big mistake, and so was their decision not to seek to be guided by my experience, especially as they knew I was willing to stay for an extra couple of months if they needed that time to complete the choice of my successor.

Greg Clark – my successor – has had a long international business career, run large companies and made big decisions, which others obeyed. He was an impressively high-powered business executive, though senior executives in his world have seldom had significant experience in the collegial decision-making process of trade associations.

The Football League is one such trade association, run by a board on behalf of its members. It requires a unique form of leadership – more 'will you' than 'you will' – with an emphasis on relationships, small-'p' political judgement, educated instinct, persuasion and sensitive handling of individual members. Achieving change, particularly radical change, requires careful preparation so that clubs find it easy and rational to vote in favour of the common good even if, initially, it did not seem that good. Dissent has to be resolved not feared.

No one can run either government or a political constituency for any length of time with a 'command and control' mindset. Incidentally, this may help to explain why so few industrialists shine when transferred to high levels of political governance.

Greg has reshaped aspects of the League, particularly in its relations with the Premier League, and worked hard visiting clubs. He has made it clear publicly and privately that he has his own form of leadership and is not a Mawhinney clone. Good for him. I told him on his appointment that I was willing to offer advice, should it ever be sought, but otherwise I would not 'interfere', for he was now in charge. Nor have I. That offer remains in place though sadly, apart from a quick lunch in June 2010 and an occasional social acknowledgement *en passant*, so far we have not talked. I say 'sadly' because I have always believed in the strengthening effect of continuity of experience in organisations.

Unlike me, Greg had football in his background. I am told he made clear at his interview that he is a Leicester City and Championship 'fanatic'. Indeed, he served on the Leicester City Holding Company board during autumn 2002 when that club went into administration.

This administration was historic in the League's 125 years. It wiped out about £50 million of debt. The relative advantage enjoyed by Leicester City, using this entirely legal and regulatory-compliant move, so outraged the other League clubs that, with my encouragement, they grasped the nettle and acted decisively. My proposal that a deduction of ten points be imposed on any club going into administration was overwhelmingly endorsed by the clubs, and subsequently followed by the Premier League (which chose nine points). It was only the magnitude of Leicester's debt which made this positive governance development possible. Like most aspects of human activity, football enjoys its share of irony.

Incidentally, the decision on what should be an appropriate level of sporting sanction was arrived at democratically. At the clubs' meeting, once the decision in principle had been made, each club representative was invited to write his or her suggested points deduction. I think they varied between three and twenty. The average was 9.7. The clubs unanimously settled on ten.

My final act as chairman was to write to all the League clubs, to thank them and to share my thoughts both about the previous seven-plus years and about the future. Although lengthy, it is a concise summary of issues which continue to confront the 'beautiful game'.

Dear Friend,

Having chaired my last board meeting, club meeting and official function, the time has come for me to move 'upstairs'. I thank all of you for the huge honour in inviting me to become the League's Honorary President. I will always seek to uphold the importance and integrity of our clubs, the key role of the board and the enhanced reputation of the League.

The last seven-plus years have been a privilege. I have enjoyed the challenge (and successes) and have derived satisfaction from shaping a more sustainable and confident League and working with some great people at board level and more widely. In 2003 the League had serious issues around finance, governance and its place in the world of sport. All have been addressed and improved. It has been a team effort and I thank you for allowing me to lead the team. Your support and encouragement have been greatly appreciated, as has been the professional excellence of our executives. Personally, I have learned an enormous amount (to my benefit) and made friendships which I hope will last for the rest of my life.

It has always been my view that it is better to move on when others are saying 'please stay' than vice versa. That time has come – though the prospect of still visiting clubs to watch games delights me.

Be in no doubt many challenges remain for my successor and the board. As for me, my experience and perspective are always available to any of you on request.

Looking back, I am encouraged that together we have addressed the need for sporting sanctions; we have promoted transparency (not least in relation to agents); the reputation of the FL has been markedly increased in the commercial marketplace, as has the standing of the FL in the world of sport. We were the first to introduce a 'fit and proper persons' test. We have emphasised our commitment to our local communities, including their families, and our moral responsibility by concluding a ground-breaking arrangement with HMRC.

And for the sixth successive season our attendances will top 16 million.

But much remains to be done. My advice, which as always you are free to ignore, is that together or separately you might want to think about the future and how it might be improved. On finance you might reflect on how you plan to be more sustainable. This will probably include finding ways to control players' wages and agents' fees – both of which are in danger of escalating even further; making more use (confidentially) of the League's knowledge of what players are paid before new club contracts are enacted; requiring directors who wish to give money to clubs to gift it or buy equity rather than make loans (which hang on as a future threat, as do multi-year player contracts where only the first year may be underpinned by a benefactor).

The FL brand has been enhanced over the past seven-plus years. My decision, with board agreement, to rebrand the League was one of the most significant of my time in office. To enhance the brand further you might want to encourage club owners and Chairmen to engage more with the League, in addition to their club. After all, this is your League and it depends on mutuality of interest.

Part of the strength of our brand is an emphasis on trying to treat everyone fairly. With that in mind, we need to be cautious about the world's assumption that, too often, might makes right. Revisiting the decision taken many years ago not to share gate receipts would entail some readjustment but might create a morally more sustainable and therefore more attractive brand. And talking about the moral strength of the brand, are we all comfortable that, in financial and debt terms, we treat football clubs more favourably than we do our local communities and their businesses, other taxpayers (to whom we have a civic responsibility) or St John Ambulance? The concept of football creditors may even militate against the most efficient financial running of our clubs. That is for you to decide.

Defending the integrity of our competitions is vitally important. Maybe you will decide to reflect on whether the League needs to adopt a 'Fit to Trade' framework in response to unsustainable debt. Failure to remain within it might even lead to strengthening sporting sanctions. Personally, I would prefer relegation to a lower division rather than a points deduction. I know, from conversations with the Conference, that this would not constitute a problem for them.

On one other issue I would urge you to remain strong. The FL should not be caught up in the transfer window saga. This was generated to 'protect' the integrity of European competitions. I hope you will continue to encourage the board to lobby FIFA, through the government and the FA, to pursue subsidiarity and exclude our domestic transfers from this restriction.

The agenda stretches into the sunset; responsibility for it now lies with others. I encourage you to show confidence as you did in me. For that, more than anything else, I really want to say 'thank you'.

With kind regards,

Brian

Before I close this chapter, I would like to go right back to the beginning and Geoff Davey. I think he is a good man to whom I was and am very grateful. Thank you, Geoff.

16

The World Cup Bid

'So what do you think?' Keith Mills said to me as we emerged from my first England 2018 board meeting in February 2009. You really want to know? It's got the smell of death about it ... Ultimately, the fault, I believe, lies with the awful dysfunctionality of the English game, its personalities and its politics ... The most difficult thing to contend with, however, was the internecine warfare at home. The FA distrusted the Premiership. The Premiership distrusted the FA, and Brian Mawhinney, as chairman of the Football League, wasn't comfortable with any of them.
Lord Coe, *The Times*, 31 October 2012

England's bid to host the 2018 World Cup finals began with Gordon Brown MP.

Gordon, then Chancellor of the Exchequer, had launched a feasibility study months earlier, on his own initiative, which had generated a lot of speculation and support. Cynically, perhaps, I thought he was just courting the football fan vote or, yet again, playing one-upmanship at Tony Blair's expense.

Fans welcomed the idea. Eventually 2 million of them 'signed' their support online. Many believed hosting the tournament was our 'right' (it was this sense of arrogant entitlement which had scuppered England's 2010 World Cup bid) and welcomed the prospect of no costly foreign travel. The more gloomy were encouraged by the thought that at least England, as hosts, would be guaranteed to be playing. Eventually the FA registered our hosting interest with FIFA and a World Cup bid board was established.

David, Lord Triesman, the FA's part-time chairman, became the part-time chairman of the bid board also. Although a relative newcomer to football administration, he was a football fan and Spurs season ticket holder. David had an excellent ministerial record and was a canny politician who found generating friendship easy, and satisfying. He had the sort of personality which many believed FIFA ExCo (executive committee) members would find attractive. I can understand why the FA endorsed David as the bid chairman, but I thought its reasoning suspect (not for the first time). It would have been better if a separate bid chairman had been able to engage with the FA chairman for the common good. This was my early judgement and one from which I have never resiled. I say that notwithstanding my personal friendship with David, both then and now.

The composition of the board appeared to have been entrusted by the FA to David, though I have no doubt he consulted appropriately. The Premier League was represented by David Gill, Manchester United's impressive chief executive. Sir David Richards and Richard Scudamore – respectively chairman and chief executive of the Premier League – held Triesman in such low regard, at times bordering on animosity and contempt, at least in private, that there was no initial prospect of either serving on the bid board though I know Triesman would have welcomed Scudamore.

David asked me, in a personal not a Football League capacity, to become a joint deputy chairman with Gill and to oversee the bid's enormous domestic agenda. This included choosing host cities, liaising as appropriate with local authorities, delivering the government guarantees which FIFA required and keeping an eye on the bid's governance. I worked closely with the excellent Simon Johnson. Like me, he too despaired at times of the standard of the bid's governance.

Before accepting the invitation, I had to clarify one issue. I told David it was my considered view that Russia would win the 2018 competition, though this would lessen neither my commitment to England's success nor my work rate. Within football there are some who believe that Sepp Blatter, the FIFA 'boss', has set his heart on receiving a Nobel Peace Prize for using football to enhance the lives of millions of people. Certainly football generates that sort of excitement around the globe; whether Blatter deserves the primary credit is a bigger debate. Personally, I have no idea whether this aspiration is real or merely an urban myth. In World Cup terms, however, the only major areas of the world likely to bid to host the 2018 and 2022 Cups which were not already seriously and positively exposed to his influence were eastern Europe and the Arab world. I chose to believe his aspiration was real (which, of course, did not make it so), hence my belief that Russia would win 2018. Using the same analysis I later judged that Qatar would win 2022. Both did. Triesman understood my analysis, accepted my assurances and confirmed the invitation.

Three lead executives were appointed. Andy Anson, a former Manchester United commercial director, hired from ATP tennis, became chief executive. He owed his appointment to the support of David Gill, with whom he used to work. Simon Johnson was chosen as chief operating officer and Ian Riley technical bid director. Simon came from the FA, where his support of the chief executive, Brian Barwick, had given a positively new meaning to the concept of loyalty to the boss. Fortunately for Simon, the bid interviewing committee was persuaded to judge him on his own merits. He turned out to be an excellent appointment. Ian, a South African, had helped his country land the 2010 World Cup and was technically expert and focused. Andy gave every indication of enjoying his worldwide travel schedule.

In June 2007, Gerry Sutcliffe MP replaced Richard Caborn MP as Sports Minister and joined the board. Caborn made his displeasure known – vigorously I am told – to the Prime Minister, who then appointed him his personal envoy to the bid. Shortly thereafter Caborn too wound up on the board with David Richards's backing – another example of the mutually reinforcing nature of Sheffield football, for good or ill. Why Gordon Brown needed a personal board member, when his government's Sports Minister was already on the board, was never explained. Gerry Sutcliffe was definitely not amused.

Unfortunately, both failed to influence the government for good.

It had promised the FA board a dowry of £5 million (this fact was reconfirmed to me much later by Brian Barwick). Despite endless talk and strong public backing for such a grant, Gordon's money never materialised. Meanwhile, in keeping with football tradition, the bid continued to spend more than it could afford.

Then the going got rougher. Government sought to 'redefine' its financial promise in terms of 'best endeavours'. Triesman argued unsuccessfully and, I understand, heatedly with Brown. Although I was supposed to relate to government, I was forbidden from approaching the Chancellor of the Exchequer. I was Conservative, he was Labour – as if that mattered in these circumstances. Anyway, money was not forthcoming. Given the Labour government's spending record, this was a bizarre decision, especially as the Chancellor had started the process and promised the money. In fact he told the bid launch at Wembley that he (by then Prime Minister) would do *whatever was necessary* to help the bid be successful.

Then Sutcliffe floated the possibility of a reduced government grant of £2.5 million for the bid, which left a bitter taste in the mouth. That grant offer soon became the possibility of a loan for the same amount, but only if the bid board agreed to repay the loan whether we were successful or not.

The time had come to draw a line. Our fiduciary responsibility as company directors had to mean something. When I brought this issue to a head at a board meeting, we had identifiable income of £4.5 million and a budgeted spend, if observed by the executives, of £10.5 million. Contemplating adding a further £2.5 million of debt – with no means of repaying the loan – was plainly unacceptable. With some reluctance, the board agreed to refuse the loan after an emotional debate but without a formal vote. To me, acceptance of the money would have been a resigning issue and I made that clear. Obviously the Labour government's attitude to the bid was 'cooling'. We turned to the FA for extra funding.

It is hard not to think of those running FIFA as anything other than control freaks. They did not just like to be in control, they wanted you to know it. I had met Blatter twice – once in his headquarters in Zurich, Switzerland, where I had gone, as Football League chairman, on a 'getting to know you' exercise, and once in the UK when we negotiated some flexibility in FIFA's rules about the eligibility of a very few Football League players to appear in the 2006 World Cup finals. On both occasions I had the same feeling. Monarchs grant audiences. Elected leaders talk with a palpable sense of authority. Blatter combined elements of both, but to me he seemed to be without the sense of reality and sensitive judgement which characterise good leaders and politicians.

FIFA's instructions to countries developing a bid book were inches thick. They were ridiculously detailed. Ian Riley, from his South African experience, interpreted any 'ambiguous' instruction conservatively, to be on the safe side, so the pile of paper kept on rising.

Our bid book – in three volumes – ran to about 1,700 pages. It is an impressive fact-based work of art of which English fans can be proud. We learned in Zurich, where the final decision was made, that only three ExCo members had actually bothered to read it! What a waste of the £5–6 million it cost to produce. What an indictment of the control freaks at FIFA and indicator of how the ExCo reached its decision. What a mockery of FIFA's insistence that decisions would be based objectively on facts. And what a con to threaten any country with non-compliance, leading to elimination, if they objected to any FIFA instruction on how this book should be compiled.

Equally daunting were the instructions governing FIFA's visit to check our suitability as hosts. Over about four days they demanded to see government ministers, locally elected politicians, major football stadia and personalities, in addition to enjoying trouble-free security and transport, not to mention the best hotels and meals. They insisted on a Park Lane hotel to house FIFA's 'great and good' if we were to be successful. The visit cost us £1 million, give or take.

Our post-visit report was glowing, as were our risk (low) and commercial case (good) assessments. Interestingly, both Russia (winner of 2018) and Qatar (winner of 2022) had high risk assessments. Our chins were up, for, at that time, we still believed that these matters were influentially important to ExCo members.

To help cover the deficit created by government's reneging, the local authorities of the twelve bid cities chosen to act as hosts were charged £300,000 just to bid. In fact the bid board decided £250,000 but, without reference to us, the FA board increased that figure. We were in no position to argue with our parent company and our chairman could hardly disagree with theirs.

The combination of the executives doing their thing with little or no reference to the board, and the FA board dictating our finances, meant that bid non-executives were kept pretty much in the dark. Sadly, neither the bid chairman nor the FA chairman ever satisfactorily resolved this problem.

Ten cities paid the £300,000 promptly. Only Plymouth and London needed my 'encouragement' to do so. To my regret, I have reason to believe that after we had been eliminated no local authorities received any in-depth report from the bid chief executive on the reasons why their money had been wasted.

The competitive selection process to determine our potential World Cup grounds, which I chaired, threw up only three issues of significance, apart from the need to disappoint three cities. On legal advice, Nottingham had refused to sign one FIFA required document. After private conversations during the interview process, the FIFA paper was signed before selection began. Mark Arthur of Nottingham Forest helped enormously to resolve that dispute.

Sheffield council's bid was unusual. It offered us both the United and Wednesday grounds but was written as if only a single application was being made. Richard Caborn MP told me later that the then council leader hoped to stand for election to the House of Commons within months and did not wish to alienate either set of Sheffield fans by choosing only one club. We were left to decide.

Kevin McCabe, chairman of Sheffield United, was furious that his ground was not chosen, which unhappiness was probably heightened by our choice of Wednesday's ground. United's application had contained a major flaw which our executives had drawn to the club's attention well in advance of the selection interview. On the day, the club's representative advanced a solution which, potentially, would have put fans' welfare and health at risk. His proposal was neither serviceable nor acceptable. Clearly McCabe had not been told. One of the fallouts arising from Sheffield United's rejection was an obscure linkage to the termination of Terry Robinson's contract with the club and thus his position on the Football League board. This was entirely a matter for the club and its owner and not one I intend to explore here.

The third problem involved London. FIFA insisted that no more than three stadia could be chosen in any city. London, knowing this, submitted four names and refused to budge. They were told repeatedly, by our executives and then by me, that we would not make our whole bid invalid by submitting their four names. As with Sheffield, to avoid local blame, they passed the ball to us.

Eventually we decided to include, as our third choice, the Olympic Stadium and Tottenham Hotspur's ground on an either/or basis (Wembley and the Emirates were no-brainers). This left FIFA to decide in 2013 – if we won – by which time the Olympic Stadium would have been tested. Everyone in London seemed pleased with this solution except Daniel Levy, the Spurs chairman. Through Andy Anson, the FA, the Premier League and the London Mayor's office, he demanded to speak to me to have the decision changed so that Spurs and Arsenal were treated equally (I rely on what others told me, as Daniel and I never did speak). Arsenal had an impressive new stadium with sustainable financing in place. Tottenham had no new stadium and no definite location for one, so no planning permission and no financing (all confirmed in the interview). Discussing 'even-handed treatment' of the two clubs – one a reality, the other a 'possibility' – did not seem a priority.

Simon Johnson did an impressive job in getting government to sign the guarantees FIFA required as a prerequisite to a bid. These were valued at an estimated £300 million and included amending immigration and border controls, permitting favourable taxation changes (for football) and reshaping money-laundering requirements. Simon and Ian Riley deserve considerable credit for delivering a first-class bid book – Ian for the technical contents and Simon for his general management, which, in fact, stretched across the whole bid. It is lucky he was willing to exceed his job description responsibilities.

The 'excellence' of England's bid owed little to the dysfunctional nature of the board. David Gill knew Michel Platini (UEFA) and some ExCo members. I knew none and neither did David Triesman, Baroness Amos (who was an expert on Africa) or Gerry Sutcliffe. David Richards knew some ExCo members but whether this helped the bid was a matter of judgement. No one was sure who Richard Caborn knew.

Lord Coe knew sport and Sepp Blatter, as did Sir Keith Mills. The latter and Sir Martin Sorrell between them seemed to know nearly everyone worth knowing in business around the world, which speaks volumes about their standing and expertise. All three were and are hugely impressive and influential individuals who should never be underestimated. They each have the 'wow' factor which otherwise is noticeably rare on the English football scene, especially off the pitch.

The board's governance was unimpressive. Frequent rewriting of board minutes, to bring them into line with what had actually happened, did not inspire confidence in the management. The significant exclusion of board members from informed consultation between meetings may have constituted a senior executive comfort zone or, maybe, a boost to their sense of power and importance, but it heightened tension and mistrust unnecessarily. It almost certainly resulted in poorer decision making and public presentation. Only a very few knew what was happening or, given the result, thought they did.

Personality politics were a real bugbear. Seb Coe was right. I was not comfortable with any of them. It would be a huge mistake to believe that, when Sir David Richards overcame his antipathy to David Triesman and to a lesser extent to me, his joining the board heralded a new era of goodwill. Sir David insisted on becoming a deputy chairman because, he told Triesman, he could not countenance a lesser status than the chairman of the Football League. Triesman knew the media would welcome this appointment as evidence of rapprochement and choose to believe that the Premier League was now wholeheartedly supportive. He also knew he should not be so naive. He was right on both counts.

October 2009 was a hectic month. FIFA vice-president Jack Warner of Trinidad and Tobago (whose football 'star' has since waned among much legal wrangling and accusation) told the Leaders in Football's London conference that our bid was creeping along when it should have been galloping. All hell broke loose. Football pundits who previously did not rate Warner suddenly chose to believe he spoke *ex cathedra*.

I thought what he said was nonsense and could not believe the resulting media hysteria. My alternative analysis was simple. Jack was worried too many people in the worldwide game thought he was backing England. As this perception would limit his 'leverage' with other bidders, he needed to engineer a rebalancing of what was thought to be his public position. What better way than to be uncomplimentary about his hosts while in London? This was only primary-grade politics; nevertheless it sailed over the heads of many in the FA and the media. But it did have an effect. More board remodelling followed. Had he asked me, I would have told the chairman that the board did need change but not in response to Warner. The timing of the change made us look both weak and guilty. In a frustrating way, at least to this non-executive, both were true.

Karren Brady, then running Birmingham City, and Paul Elliott, ex-Chelsea, added skill and experience to the board though Karren soon left, after yet another board change, without actually having managed to attend a meeting. Fifty bid ambassadors were named, though no one was sure why, or why them, or how many of them knew any of the ExCo members or what time they had committed to our cause or what their responsibilities were. Andy Anson never did provide us with comprehensive answers to these perfectly reasonable questions.

One ambassador – John Motson of BBC fame – told me a year after his appointment that no one from the bid had spoken to him, much less asked him to do anything to advance the bid, or even enquired how he would like to help. I am sorry my friend was treated in this shabby way and have told him so.

About this time, we had a boardroom fracas. Before the particular meeting in question, both the chairman and the chief executive had told me separately that Sir David and Richard Caborn would be confronted on the issue of privately briefing against the bid. In Caborn's case, I was told, the allegation came directly from the Prime Minister's office in No. 10 to Andy Anson. Both men were clearly and justifiably upset, as board 'leaking' had been a persistent problem.

At the board, Triesman raised the issue of leaking and kicked the ball to Anson. He was strong, but inexplicably did not name names or mention No. 10. That omission was a huge mistake. In this sort of 'political' discussion, striking only to wound by innuendo is naive and dangerous. 'Do not start if you do not intend to end' should be the maxim. If Anson did not have the case or the stomach to accuse Richards and Caborn explicitly, he should have kept quiet. Given what he had told me before the meeting, it was the latter he seemed to lack. Interestingly, without anyone mentioning any names, both Richards and Caborn took umbrage.

Richards's response was to accuse Anson of targeting him. He said he was outraged and would no longer serve. He rose, put on his coat and prepared to depart, protesting that he would keep his resignation quiet so as not to embarrass the bid! No one believed him.

Keith Mills and I both told him to sit down and stop being so unhelpful. He sat, but few believed the problem had been resolved.

Caborn then launched into his 'defence', praying in aid Gordon Brown. Until Martin Sorrell intervened. He is one of Britain's finest international businessmen. Often he shared advice privately rather than offering it in board meetings. On this occasion, however, he could hardly have been more to the point.

Turning to Caborn, he said he was completely 'p***** off' sitting there listening to him 'whinge', which was followed by: 'If you have anything positive to say, say it now.'

Caborn, clearly taken aback, started in about how he was the Prime Minister's envoy. When he stopped for breath Martin brought the exchange to a close with the words 'I think you and we would be better off if you shut up'. Most of the board tried not to look too pleased. David Richards looked very annoyed.

Some time later Triesman told me he had warned Anson in advance not to start the row unless he was willing to finish it. Like a show-jumping horse, Andy baulked at the double gate. Apparently he was worried about negative public relations for the bid. In fact the story of Richards's departure would probably have been a 24-hour wonder, as indeed proved to be the case a few weeks later when he did walk. The issues of Anson's judgement and board membership remained unresolved.

Then the board had another revamp. The Sports Minister left, as did Gordon Brown's envoy (allegedly after further rows in No. 10). Later, Simon Greenberg, ex-Chelsea, became chief of staff. He joined Anson as the bid's executive engine, but without any significant reference to the board.

There was a most unpleasant and little-known corollary to this internal New Labour rumble. Triesman, having taken advice from senior sport administrators, decided to leave the Labour benches in the House of Lords to join the non-party crossbenchers for the duration of the bid. He was anxious that no party-political label should be attached to the bid. The Labour Party leadership was fully pre-briefed.

Shortly afterwards, he started receiving calls on behalf of other Labour MPs from Alan Keen, chairman of the All-Party Parliamentary Football Group, begging this former general secretary of the Labour Party not to desert to the Conservative benches. Triesman told me later he was amazed when the MPs told him that Richard Caborn had been predicting this move. Allegedly he was claiming that Triesman was anticipating the Tories winning the 2010 general election and that he wanted to be well placed if/ when this happened. In Triesman's case, it was being alleged, the crossbenches were merely to be a halfway house. Understandably David is still bitter, and back in his place as a highly respected Labour frontbench spokesman.

Earlier I referred to more than one bid chairman. David Triesman resigned during a dramatic weekend after a Sunday newspaper published allegations about him which he believed left him little option but to go. David phoned me early on the Sunday morning to tell me what had happened. Subsequently I had the privilege of having a long chat with him and Lucy, his wife, over lunch. Both conversations gave me knowledge and insight into the alleged incident, its media-related fallout and why David felt so upset.

On that Sunday, David asked me if I thought he should resign. I replied that probably he ought to leave the bid board but it might be possible for him to remain chairman of the FA. If that was what he wanted then he needed to start talking to his colleagues very quickly; I believed that they would soon be inclined to buy into the alleged incident, rather than support the chairman. Which is what happened.

Some time after that conversation, Andy Anson phoned me. He had already been in extended contact with David Dein, having decided that Dein should be the new bid chairman. Indeed he was planning to convey that message to the FA board at its emergency lunchtime meeting. I had to remind him that the choice of chairman did not lie with him or even the bid board. This was in the gift of the FA board, which would probably not appreciate any attempt to bounce it, nor his obvious lack of loyalty to his chairman. His tone soon became subdued even though he continued to argue his case. He was plainly not interested in, nor seeking, my opinion, so I did not volunteer it.

After further reflection I had a confidential conversation with a friend on the FA board. I suggested that he and his colleagues should not rush to judgement but if, eventually and after careful consideration, they did decide to look for a new chairman then what about Geoff Thompson? Geoff's integrity was well known in FIFA and would be deemed a positive virtue, though sadly, from our point of view, his ability to 'deliver' was less impressive. At least ExCo members would view him as one of their own.

I returned home from church to learn that David had gone. With him, I thought, had gone any small hope our bid might be successful. I am not neutral about what happened to David. He was and is a friend. To me his generosity of spirit and desire to do right were (and remain) virtues which more football leaders ought to have appreciated. And if, occasionally, naivety is deemed to be a sin, then most of us have sinned.

Because the dispute, with its legal ramifications, remains still open, to the best of my knowledge, I do not intend to comment specifically on the newspaper's allegations. This is David's story to tell, or not, as he wishes.

Eventually Geoff Thompson (FIFA vice-president and former FA chairman) replaced David Triesman as bid chairman.

David Triesman and Andy Anson had travelled round the world becoming the recognised faces of England's bid. But recognition is not the same as influence. Our bid was, in essence, a major sales operation when what was needed was an impressive political one – with a small 'p'. Geoff Thompson's face was already well recognised in world football so, in that sense only, the change did not much reduce our momentum.

Apart from the British media rightly deploring the clashing egos, the football world generally appeared impressed by our efforts. At least, this message was repeated regularly in Anson's weekly summaries to the board. Cruelly, I could never quite decide whether or not I was reading *Alice in Wonderland*. The reports were simply too good to be true. What the bid really needed was a well-informed and tightly controlled campaign targeted on impressing the twenty-four voters (eventually twenty-two), persuading them to vote for us and then holding them to that persuasion. To be fair, Anson and Greenberg argued that this was what was happening. I never believed it nor saw compelling evidence to that effect.

In reality what we had was superficial information about the twenty-four but apparently no ability to pull their appropriate levers. We did not set up any sophisticated system designed to check and recheck their real intentions, not least because we did not have the money that would have facilitated setting up such a system. Having neither oligarchs nor oil, we could not compete financially with Russia or Qatar. Campaigning skills and experience plus worldwide access to intelligence existed within the board but were ignored or disdained. One example will illustrate what I mean.

When John Major resigned the leadership of the Conservative Party in 1995, he invited a few of us to form the core of his re-election team. This included gathering and keeping a tally of his support. Handling these 'black arts' was crucial to his success. We had lists of Tory MPs openly supporting John, some who maintained they were 'undecided', and even a few who were generally perceived to be supporting John Redwood MP, all working for us.

All three groups reported on their conversations with Tory MPs. So each day we might hear what an individual MP had said in maybe six or eight different conversations. In those highly political circumstances, nailing true intentions was a serious challenge.

Three hundred and twenty-nine Conservative MPs were eligible to vote. Our final prediction of the result was only two votes in error.

This way of working would have been much more difficult in our sort of bid because of its worldwide nature, but we did not even approximate to it. As a consequence the board was essentially 'blind', so we wound up believing what we wanted to believe. England fans, with no hard information, believed us. Understandably, and regrettably, this heightened their sense of disappointment when the magnitude of our loss was revealed. They were not to know that our campaign had had no hard edge or that it had become blunter after Triesman left.

Triesman told me later he had tried twice to persuade the executives to pursue a more 'political' campaign rather than a 'sales' one. I too tried. We both failed, miserably.

The result of all the team's hard work was a professional and presentationally impressive public campaign, but one which only looked good; receiving a single vote is just plain embarrassing. We simply did not have the knowledge, skill or experience to pierce the voters' weasel words. My constant and often outspoken (but private) criticism of the bid's management, strategy and governance made me very unpopular with the executives. Very. They found me profoundly irritating – or worse (Simon Johnson being the exception). That I might be right never occurred to them. My advice and ideas were discarded as simply unwelcome. This non-executive deputy chairman was sidelined and ignored comprehensively.

Reflecting on my practical uselessness, I offered my resignation to David Triesman. He refused it. After Geoff Thompson had succeeded David, he too refused my resignation even though he had been given chapter and verse about my discontent and 'irrelevance'. Geoff made the executives' life a little more uncomfortable but fundamentally nothing changed.

The honourable thing for me to do was quit. But behaving honourably would also have involved explaining publicly why I was quitting. Triesman highlighted the competing issues when we discussed my leaving. He did not argue against my analysis or judgement (neither did Geoff Thompson). More pragmatically, David was concerned about the credibility of the bid, including how it would be perceived 'if the chairman of the Football League followed the chairman of the Premier League out the door'.

Damaging the bid because I was and felt sidelined was, in itself, hardly an honourable thing to do. It was typically generous of David to add that if we lost the bid some might blame my leaving, pointing as it would to board discord. David emphasised that this would be grossly unfair to me.

My instinct was to go, but in truth I could not discern any moral absolute, even after praying about it. Our son Stephen helped my thinking. Eventually I yielded to persuasion and stayed, resigning myself to offering occasional advice, which I knew would be ignored, and observing from the touchline that was the board table. I did not rock the boat.

After the FIFA inspection visit, the six-month run-in to the vote was largely incident free, apart from those generated by the British media. By this time Triesman had gone and David Dein had joined our efforts. He was travelling the world talking to ExCo members, most or all of whom had been his friends for years. After the result David felt more despondent than anyone else because he believed he had been let down by his so-called 'friends'.

We knew about the proposed BBC *Panorama* programme, which was to raise questions around money handling in FIFA, well in advance. Despite its unhelpful timing a few days before the vote, Simon Greenberg kept telling us its substance was unlikely to include anything new; it would merely rehash history. But even if this were to be true, the possible political damage the programme would do, or would be perceived to do, to the FIFA voters' self-regard could become a real problem. In the event Simon's reassurances to the board proved misplaced.

The programme did include a new document, dated June 2010, which listed allegations of inappropriate money-related behaviour by a number of FIFA members. This evidence was documented and serious but, at that time, largely dismissed or vehemently denied by FIFA.

Anson and Greenberg had insisted on a meeting with Mark Thompson, the BBC's Director General, to complain about the programme (which they had not seen) and to ask for it not to be shown or, at least, not to be shown shortly before the FIFA vote. From my experience of the BBC, I argued strongly against their plan, warning that Thompson would reject any such request outright, thus leaving us in a more difficult position. We would be putting him in a position where he had to say 'no' if he wanted to retain his professional integrity. My advice was again ignored and Thompson did indeed say 'no'.

Anson's public reaction to the programme, that it was embarrassing for the BBC, was silly. He and Greenberg would have been better employed organising a briefing for the twenty-two ExCo members personally, in advance of the broadcast, to mitigate its effect. The letter they drafted later for circulation to ExCo members, which ignored my suggestions, was unpersuasive.

The earlier *Sunday Times* article about alleged corruption did provoke action by FIFA. Two of its committee members were alleged to have offered to sell their votes. They were suspended, reducing the bid's voting electorate to twenty-two. Even during this process the British media was roundly castigated, particularly by Blatter, for ignoring the football and instead being too concerned about inappropriate behaviour and corruption – though the latter was not attributed to the suspended members by the FIFA Ethics Committee's subsequent inquiry. FIFA spokesmen made it sound as if it were the *Sunday Times* that was guilty of bad behaviour for breaking the story. Talk about shooting the messenger.

The British media was turned into a whipping boy by FIFA members who did not want to have to change their dubious financial status quo. This was particularly convenient for the majority who had no intention of voting for England. It gave them an 'excuse' for not doing so.

After more than thirty years in public service, I understand and have defended repeatedly the value and importance of a free media and freedom of speech. This country is among those who lead the world in this aspect of a free society. Of course that freedom can sometimes be uncomfortably exercised and occasionally abused, but to me, defending it is more important than worrying about embarrassing twenty-two egos. I would love England to host the World Cup again but not at the expense of undermining one of the pillars of our freedom.

Persuasive efforts in the final weeks of campaigning by Geoff Thompson and David Dein were rebutted, with FIFA fingers pointing towards the BBC and the *Sunday Times*. 'Why does your media not support your bid?' was the mantra behind which these democratically elected members hid. To be fair, not all of them lived in countries where a free press strengthened their democracies; and regimes inclined towards totalitarianism do not appreciate a free press.

The choreography of our bid presentation in Zurich was rightly hailed as another success, but the voters were not impressed. They wanted meaty substance from the contenders. I was able to form my own judgement on this only because Geoff Thompson insisted his deputy be present.

The Russian Deputy Premier's speech was dismissed by our team as too long, complicated and boring. But he addressed the members' real concerns about Russia – infrastructure, stadia, travel distances and so on – in an impressive and reassuring way. Mr Putin understood what he was doing and what was being done in his name.

When it came to Qatar's turn to present its case, the wife of the Emir cut through the tendency towards Hollywood hype. She asked a pointed, searing question. When did FIFA members think would be the 'right time' to hold the World Cup finals in an Arab country? Despite Qatar's burning heat, the voters got the political message.

For our part, we made legacy claims which simply were not believable and talked about how we would use football to change lives in ways that must have seemed like scratching the surface to those whose lives and countries literally had been transformed by the beautiful game. Our bid was polished, professional and very well received. Sadly its substance was not thought to match its presentation.

Apart from David Magliano, whose CV was enhanced by the presentation he had prepared, three men deserve special mention. David Dein, the bid's International President, should have joined the board long before he did. He was not a favourite with either the FA or, even more so, the Premier League, so he had few friends in high places. Initially he had added conditions to his willingness to serve, perhaps in the hope of re-embedding himself in the FA. Unfortunately these simply provided an excuse to delay his appointment for those who were not his admirers. After he joined us he was tireless. His support and enthusiasm could not be faulted.

Prime Minister David Cameron deserves special mention. His commitment to the bid was impressive – in both time and effort. His speech during our bid presentation was substantive, powerful and easily our best contribution. He probably made those who lied to him about their voting intentions feel uncomfortable (I hope that was the case) but if so he did it with grace and charm. His endeavours were widely praised and appreciated – rightly so.

Finally, Lord Coe was a major force behind the scenes. He has huge credibility in international sport generally. It is a pity his gifts of charm and rational persuasion were not used more widely. But even if they had been we would not have prevailed.

Our team in Zurich was on a high, enhanced by the presence and friendliness of Prince William. It really believed we would win. The general consensus was that Mr Putin's absence from Zurich indicated he knew Russia would not succeed. My contrary interpretation of his absence, that he knew he had already won, was dismissed as typical grumpiness and poor judgement.

I badly wanted England to win and eagerly looked forward to taking my grandchildren to Wembley in 2018. But deep down I never had a sense that this was to be. Within a few hours of the announcement I was getting text messages from friends; sentiments along the lines of 'You were spot on with your earlier World Cup analysis' were fairly indicative.

Any analysis of our bid and the resulting FIFA decisions needs to assess (1) our strengths and weaknesses and (2) FIFA's behaviour.

Our strengths were impressive: organisational experience; passion for football; great stadia; good national infrastructure; compliant and committed government support; a media enthusiastic about hosting; great fans and the worldwide fan base of our Premier League teams. No country received better accolades from FIFA for its bid book and inspection visit.

So why only one vote, apart from Geoff Thompson's? In no particular order: we were seriously underfinanced; we got our strategy wrong; we created management and governance structures which were dogged by conflicting egos and football politics, too much of which stemmed from the senior ranks of the FA; we had little, if any, influence in FIFA; the British media became the ExCo's *bête noire* and the Premier League and its clubs did not flex their considerable financial and sporting muscle sufficiently on our behalf.

On finance, not only did we not receive the Labour government's promised £5 million, but it was only in the dying weeks of the campaign (well after Triesman's departure) that the Premier League started to offer real resources – too little too late. The Premier

League's refusal to offer the bid, say £500,000 from each of its clubs' multi-million-pound central allocation, was a serious disappointment. Nor was there any discernible public effort by them to drive a bandwagon of support politically with big business. Abroad they could have used their clubs' fan base, in the appropriate countries, to seek to persuade FIFA ExCo members. This apathy, or concentration on their own league business, if you will, undermined the idea of England united, on which the bid was built. To be fair, Richard Scudamore talked a good game, but rhetoric was not enough.

Geoff Thompson is an honourable man of genuine integrity. I count him a Christian friend; but not even his best friends would claim that he commands situations, compels support or shapes outcomes. His judgement is usually sound but too low key for the brash world of FIFA football. And he was our one and only national representative among the FIFA elite. He told me he thought he had persuaded some of his friends on the executive committee to vote for us, presumably believing their word. In the event they let him down. Or, to be blunt, they lied to him. Maybe they thought, knowing Geoff's sense of Christian forgiveness, that their lack of morality was relatively risk free.

The fact is, others could and should have joined Geoff in FIFA's structure over the years but they all thought home-based football was more important. They did not attend committee meetings, or had 'better' things to do than undertake generously well-paid trips to Switzerland. Those attitudes need to change if we want to be able to exert more influence in FIFA in the future.

Finally, we were too morally correct to be able to impress ExCo members – but not necessarily too morally correct.

FIFA's behaviour throughout the process was unimpressive, to put it delicately. It had created a strong sense that its judgements would be objectively based on demonstrably fair criteria. This turned out to be nonsense. Seventeen hundred pages of an excellent bid book coupled with outstanding inspection and commercial assessments were supposed to constitute the framework. When the time came to vote, they meant nothing.

As we have noted, Qatar's risk factor assessment was high, though not, of course, when it came to finance. The country was deemed to have insufficient infrastructure, no stadia (except on planning paper) and a temperature which would be around 45 degrees Celsius at game time.

And what notice did ExCo members, including Blatter, take of this risk assessment? None; Qatar got 50 per cent of the votes cast in the first round of voting, ahead of the USA, Australia, Japan and Korea.

After the decision, Blatter suggested changing the date of the finals to January 2022 (without worrying what effect this would have on the European leagues, who would provide maybe 50 per cent of World Cup players) on the grounds that the summer temperature of 45 degrees Celsius would be too hot for players and fans. Too late. What an insult. The projected temperature had not been changed by a FIFA vote.

If, despite Qatar's honourable intention to stick to July, FIFA insists on moving the finals to January 2022, I hope the defeated countries demand a new ballot. In my view they would be entitled to do so. Even the all-powerful FIFA should be bound by some ethical standards.

Only those who have sought democratic election understand the pressures involved. Those who vote can and do put enormous pressure on candidates to make commitments in advance in return for the hope of winning support. Candidates need to be strong. Sometimes it is easier to lie.

When twenty-two men control the expenditure of billions of dollars, the temptations and, perhaps, inducements are probably significant. Some will behave honourably and with integrity. Some will do deals in line with their national agendas. And it must be possible that some will respond corruptly.

FIFA had no real system for the regular policing of its ExCo's integrity, much less a means of insisting on it. So no one knows how much corruption existed. No outsider has the knowledge, information or ability properly to assess the purity of FIFA's processes to sufficient depth. And those on the inside obviously believe it is in their best interests not to reveal. Personally, if I was a member of the FIFA executive, I would want controls and transparency to protect my reputation against defamatory allegations. But, for the most part, FIFA sails on with little sign of concern – all expenses generously paid. Although it is true that a number of the ExCo members who voted in Zurich are no longer football powers because of their alleged 'dubious' behaviour.

Holding simultaneous elections for the 2018 and 2022 finals enabled Blatter, and his ExCo colleagues, to influence the 2022 outcome, which otherwise could have fallen beyond his time in office. FIFA's argument that combining the two votes enhanced their commercial benefit may or may not be true but I do not believe that this was their real motivation.

Having viewed FIFA's pantomime at close hand both before and after the vote in Zurich, I, like others, hope to see procedural changes before attention turns to choosing the 2026 final host. By then England's chances of hosting may have improved under new FIFA leadership – or not. The following two suggested changes to the process would be of general benefit and are not designed to gain England an advantage.

First, making two hosting determinations simultaneously should be deemed to have failed. It beggars belief that FIFA believed there would be no contact or conversations between countries bidding for the 2018 and 2022 finals once the inevitable separation into Europe (2018) and non-Europe (2022)-based finals had occurred.

We, for example, possibly against a strict interpretation of the rules, talked to the USA (and Michel Platini) about making simultaneous announcements that we were ending our interest in the 2022 final and that the USA was withdrawing from 2018. This had the effect of ensuring that the 2018 final would be held in Europe. I think some hoped this show of camaraderie might influence the USA to consider our bid more benignly. It did not.

Spain (2018) and Qatar (2022) allegedly did explore synergy, and for all I know mutually supportive voting, because they saw a potential mutual benefit. From their point of view, choosing to talk was simple common sense. If these or other countries had been bidding for the same final there would have been little appetite to participate in such banned activity. The failure is FIFA's. The way to prevent any hint of alleged collusion in the future, and in the process reduce allegations of corruption, is blindingly obvious.

Most sensible people believe that such a worldwide event, involving so much money, should be handled within a more explicitly objective framework. This would not be hard to achieve. FIFA should set up an independent commission to assess bid books, together with the results of national inspection visits, and to take account of FIFA policy for any particular final, using a pre-published marking system. Bids could then be ranked, with only the top two or three being allowed to proceed to executive committee vote. Such a system would extract greater value from the millions of pounds spent by countries on preparing their bids.

The announcement of these finalists should be made as close as possible to the determining vote. In the intervening period, any contact between a bidding nation and a FIFA executive member should be required to be registered transparently. Bidding countries should also be required to register their lobbyists, and tough conditions should govern contacts and their monitoring.

Discovering an unregistered contact between a lobbyist and an ExCo member should cause both to be given a life ban from football. Discovering after the vote that such a contact had taken place should involve expunging the vote of the ExCo member. The offending country should be excluded from the following World Cup.

This sort of system would quickly create the perception of a squeaky-clean, objective-driven FIFA commanding worldwide respect. Were Blatter to introduce such a scheme he would justify the accolade of using football to enhance the lives of millions.

After Zurich, David Triesman and I reflected on Blatter's speech at the vote ceremony, when he commended the merit of using the finals deliberately to spread football beyond its traditional territory.

We agreed that, if FIFA had announced this policy at the beginning of the process, rather than at the end, as a late defence of 'surprising' decisions, then together we would have proposed to our board and the FA that England's bid be withdrawn. That would have permitted England's £18 million bid money to have been spent on the grassroots amateur game around the country, and in the Football League, not to mention sparing embarrassment to England's football family and some local authorities.

Discerning the greatest weakness of England's bid requires a return to the beginning – to Gordon Brown and his feasibility study.

Feasibility? On what issues did the government need reassurance before any commitment could be made to host an international sporting competition? What were the things Gordon worried we might not be able to do? By the time the FA took the formal vote, 'feasibility' having been established – surprise, surprise – it was seen almost as a technical afterthought. In short, the FA was bounced by a sophisticated politician. I doubt if Gordon ever gave a serious thought to feasibility.

The FA should have conducted its own in-depth feasibility study. I know from numerous private conversations at the time that this was not going to happen; public comment along these lines was certainly not welcomed.

The result was that the FA allowed itself to be bounced in the direction of inadequacy. Maybe the government was ready; the FA was not.

Or, maybe, even the government was not ready, for it was 'Feasibility' Brown who reneged on his promise to give the bid £5 million.

Politicians!

17

Blame the Ref!

Ken Bates is undoubtedly one of football's largest personalities, of this or any generation. He's a man who has been very influential in shaping the contemporary football scene. He was one of the main architects of the decision by the First Division (as it was then called) to leave the Football League to form what was to become the Premier League, taking most of the money-earning power with it – a memory which still rankles with some in the Football League. At that time he led Chelsea. He was also a key figure in planning the new Wembley. It is not Ken's fault that this project overran its fixed-cost contract by about £100 million.

And, as the saying goes, he takes no prisoners.

After leaving Chelsea in the financially enhanced hands of Roman Abramovich, he became the new owner of Leeds United, where he promoted fiscal prudence to try to rescue that club from the financial mess left by its previous board. The roots of their debt lay in their dream of playing in European competitions. Stripped of its dreamy sentimentality, all this means is that they spent significantly beyond their means.

Prior to his Leeds days, Ken's path and mine had crossed only twice. Both times I was a guest in the Chelsea directors' box, where my friend David Mellor introduced me to him. After a perfunctory handshake, Ken, who seldom gives the impression of admiring government or politicians (which, of course, does not make him unique), would make some disdainful comment about what we were doing in government and quickly shift his attention to someone else.

His personal antipathy towards me broke surface in May 2006. Whether this was politically driven or a reaction against the strong governance-based leadership I was giving the Football League, or simply because he did not like me, I do not know. Nor does it matter. We were sitting together at a Championship play-off final in Cardiff's Millennium Stadium. The stakes were high. At full-time either Leeds United or Watford would be promoted to the Premier League, with its untold millions.

Ken was very tense, which was hardly surprising in his circumstances. After about ninety seconds of play, his pent-up tension erupted. One of his players had been on the receiving end of a robust tackle. Trying to be friendly, I said, 'I've seen yellow cards given for tackles like that.' Ken's engaging reply was a memorable moment in my seven-plus years at the League. 'What the f*** do you know? You know nothing about f***** football – you're a f***** Fenian!' I made no audible response but decided Ken wanted to watch the game without social interruption!

Later our paths recrossed big time in one of the most seminal events of my League service. In the process a precedent was set for the way the League delivered proper governance, which enhanced the League's leadership standing in the wider world of professional football.

Quite apart from the precedent set, this story is a good example of the League board's role in 'refereeing' the business and governance relationships of the seventy-two clubs in its charge. Just as, when the referee blows his whistle in a game, the aggrieved party blames the ref, so it is difficult for any club easily to accept that it has broken League rules. Yet someone has to arbitrate – to be the ref.

The issue at the heart of Leeds's behaviour was complicated, especially for those who want only to cheer their team, but so important to football's credibility that it is worth examining in some depth.

When a club goes into administration, the law of the land permits it to expunge its debts by means of a creditors voluntary agreement (CVA). This offers payment to creditors, the amount determined democratically, based on an agreed number of pence for each pound of debt owed. In other words, a CVA can wipe out millions of pounds of club debt – usually at the expense of the businesses and charities, often local, whose services and trade allow the club to function. Too often the taxpayer is the largest creditor. Debt owed to Her Majesty's Revenue and Customs (HMRC) is frequently a low priority to a club which has put itself under financial pressure. Or, even more simply, taxpayers too often pay for the profligacy of club directors, which helps to explain why HMRC is now taking a more robust attitude towards clubs which use it as a sort of 'private banker'. And rightly so.

The League's innovative record as governance referee to its clubs was a 1–1 draw during my chairmanship. On the positive side, with Andy Williamson's help, I negotiated a ground-breaking agreement with Dave Hartnett, who then ran HMRC. Setting aside historic club debt, which each club was to resolve with HMRC individually, we agreed that the payment of national insurance and pay-as-you-earn would be made regularly. Despite the law, clubs who were spending their money on 'football' issues would often delay or skip these payments. And because the League had no knowledge of these private taxation issues, we had no ability positively to influence clubs.

Our deal with HMRC was straightforward. We would persuade clubs to endorse two new League regulations. Firstly, they would authorise HMRC to inform the League's board, but not any club-based director, if a club missed a payment (outside a 28-day grace period). Secondly, clubs would authorise us to impose a transfer embargo on those who fell foul of the new specific requirement to pay this tax on time, until the debt was paid. Clubs always understood football penalties better than financial ones.

HMRC took a hard line on CVAs which did not pay 100p in the pound. Initially, after they lost their protected payment status, they had been willing to let clubs negotiate a repayment against debt. Taxpayers were not amused by the losses they suffered, so HMRC toughened its stance. This was significant because, under the law of the land, any creditor owed more than 25 per cent of the total debt could block a CVA even if a majority of creditors voted for it.

On the other hand, to HMRC's fury, clubs always gave each other 100 per cent repayment of outstanding debt – usually associated

with player transfers. In my view such a practice was and is inde-
fensible. This 'de-risking' of transfer payments drives up the cost
of player transfers and associated agents' fees. It is impossible to
mount any moral argument to sustain these Premier League and
Football League practices, but this cosy arrangement remains,
protected ferociously by both bodies on their clubs' instructions.

I think I raised this 'football creditor' rule three times at FL board
meetings – and argued the case for us to change the policy. Each
time the six club directors rejected any change out of hand.

It is only fair to add that these rules have been successfully
defended in court on several occasions, including a recent judg-
ment. Nevertheless, to this simple Belfast boy, all creditors should
be treated the same. For both moral and good governance reasons,
clubs should change this system.

Reducing clubs' debt to HMRC was designed in part to improve
financial order as well as to lessen taxpayer risk. But it was also to
protect integrity of competition, which is the single most important
consideration for the League as the governance referee. If clubs ignore
debt payment, they free up money to spend on giving themselves an
unfair footballing advantage over the other clubs in their division.

One example of the damage which can be done by the wiping
out of debt by an administration will suffice. In the years of my
chairmanship, clubs going into administration left over £40,000
unpaid to St John Ambulance, whose professional service at games
is crucial. St John was too generous to complain, but to me such
behaviour was just unacceptable.

Before my retirement I authorised a board donation to this
excellent charity to convey our thanks and admiration which, on
the basis of how some clubs had behaved, they might have had
reason to doubt. The amount was over £40,000.

Club debt can be huge. Leicester City shed £50 million of debt,
and that was about ten years ago. Rangers, it is alleged, owed
between £55 million and £130 million (the amount is disputed),
and I am not confident enough to guess what the real amount of
Portsmouth debt was.

CVAs (the pence-in-the-pound figure) are calculated by the administrator taking into account both debt and the remaining assets of the business. Then creditors must agree, by vote, to lose a percentage of what is owed to them if the CVA is to be binding on all. As HMRC too often finds itself in the more than 25 per cent blocking position, it is inclined to use its power to do so, not least because it hates the game's football creditor regulation.

In May 2007, Leeds United FC went into administration and individuals from KPMG were appointed as administrators. Within about one hour they had agreed to sell the club to a group represented by Ken Bates for one penny in the pound. In other words, nearly all the club's considerable debt had been 'wiped out' in favour of those who had been in charge of the club. We were amazed, others were outraged, but apparently this was in line with English law. It was no doubt legal but it felt wrong. Although HMRC, with just less than 25 per cent of the debt, voted against the CVA, it was still approved. At the CVA meeting, it transpired that a company called Astor, which had enough 'votes', i.e. debt, to block any proposed CVA, announced it would only support a Bates bid, even if someone else offered more money to them and the other creditors. Both Ken and Mark Taylor, then the club's solicitor, as directors of Leeds United vigorously asserted that they had no link with Astor.

When a CVA is passed, creditors have twenty-eight days to present a challenge. HMRC waited until the last possible day before doing so.

Shortly afterwards, and without any reference to the League, the administrators put the club up for sale again.

Confused?

We were.

The timing of this extra sale was over a weekend. The administrators, as they were entitled to do, ruled that to be acceptable, any bids had to be unconditional. This seemed hard to us. Less than seventy-two hours made proper due diligence virtually impossible, particularly for new bidders. They were being asked to commit money without any assurance that, under League regulations, they would be allowed by the League to take over the club. The administrators must have known this.

What particularly confused us was who 'owned' or controlled the club during this re-sale process. On the Friday we thought Ken 'owned' the club. Did he still? Or had he handed it back to the administrators to resell? And, if so, at one penny in the pound, why would Ken do such a thing, we wondered.

We tried, unsuccessfully, to have the time available to new bidders extended. We also encouraged the administrators to make available relevant additional financial information to new bidders. Again they declined. To be honest, the board felt a sense of frustration with KPMG but we were assured that it was behaving entirely legally.

By the start of the following week, two new 'facts' had emerged. The Bates bid had risen to approximately 8p in the pound. Astor continued to state that it would only support a Bates bid, even if someone else offered more money to them and the other creditors.

If you understand why either of these facts might have transpired you have the advantage over us. Why would people offer to pay eight times what had already been legally accepted? Or was that initial bid no longer legally accepted? Trying to calm poor public relations seemed a weak explanation. And why would some people refuse the possibility of receiving more money unless they had a link with those already running the club? But Ken and Mark were adamant and we had no basis on which to doubt their word.

If you think this is getting complicated, bordering on the remarkable, you should have been sitting round the board table. We simply did not understand what exactly the administrator had intended to achieve by seeking to resell the club on the 'open' market in seventy-two hours. As KPMG was not legally accountable to the board, our ability to probe its actions or indeed its intentions was limited.

Two of the new weekend bids were unconditional. However, the board remained unclear whether these potential new owners were unconditionally offering to buy a club freely available in the marketplace – or were they buying one which was, in some sense, 'owned' at that point by Ken Bates? If the latter, we were also not clear on what basis the bidding had been conducted – on behalf of Ken or despite his wishes? We never were sure.

On the other hand, the board was clear about its imperatives. Within the constraints of the law, our regulations and board policy was to try to help clubs survive. We were never neutral on that point, despite Leeds's fans' disbelief. Whether such a policy remains sustainable in the long term, and is in the best interests of the League and those of its members who do spend money prudently, remains to be seen. Personally I am sceptical. I fear that only one or more club liquidations will be traumatic enough to force financial prudence to the top of clubs' agenda.

In line with our country's law, the board believed creditors should receive the maximum return possible. This was an important emphasis for creditors, who faced losing a lot of money, and therefore a priority for the board. In our view they should lose as little as possible, which helps to explain why, initially, we were so askance at the prospect of a sale at one penny in the pound.

Unnoticed by most, the League's leadership in 2003 had been far sighted, though it got precious little thanks for its initiative, then or since. At that time, League rules required that if a club in administration failed its CVA, there was no other mechanism to save it. The League had no legal powers of 'rescue' in those circumstances. Given our growing belief that HMRC was hardening its position, clubs were potentially very exposed unless they quickly changed their spending habits, and there appeared little chance of that.

So a new policy was drafted for clubs to ratify. Its terms were simple. In the event of a failed CVA, this new policy gave the board an *absolute* discretion to declare a situation of 'exceptional circumstances', and then an *absolute* discretion to devise a strategy which would allow the stricken club back into the League with whatever conditions the board deemed appropriate, in its *absolute* discretion. This amounted to a failsafe for clubs – but only if the board wished to exercise it.

I had no sense that the clubs, while voting for this new policy, really understood its importance. Instead of seeing it as a possible lifeline to prevent one or more of them going out of business, I think many saw it simply as a small shift in power from clubs to the board. They were right, of course, but without it the existence of at least two clubs playing today – Leeds and Luton – would then have been hugely vulnerable, to put it mildly.

The fans of those clubs became very angry about the penalties imposed on them by the board as a condition of their rescue from administration. In their ignorance and prejudice, most of them seemed unaware that, without the board's earlier initiative and present willingness to save them, their clubs would have disappeared. To most sensible people, the penalties imposed appeared a relatively small price to pay for survival. But in Leeds and Luton the currency was abuse and threats.

The board found itself in wholly new territory, made even more complicated by a proposed legal challenge to the CVA by HMRC, and by Astor's insistence that any CVA outcome had to be a Ken Bates-run club or nothing.

We spent hours exploring various possibilities and depended heavily on outside lawyers. But in particular we were grateful to the League's in-house lawyer, Nick Craig, for his sterling work. The challenge of the whole process reminded me of former conversations with senior civil servants over complex legislation, with lawyers hovering in the wings to ensure we did nothing silly that would invite judicial review.

At times the board's only comfort was the repeated legal assurance that, in the event the administrators sold Leeds to someone other than Ken Bates, he, Ken, and his board would not be in a position to sue the League.

Finally, there was an additional and novel complication to address. Leeds had chosen to go into administration on the last day of the season. The club had decided it could not avoid 'normal' relegation and so would take its ten-point sporting sanction in the current season, where its effect would be non-existent, rather than start the next one with minus ten points. In due course the board had to introduce a new regulation to close this loophole. Clubs voted in favour with enthusiasm.

By the middle of July, certain aspects of the complex muddle were becoming clearer. HMRC was maintaining its legal challenge to the CVA. In its judgement, three creditors who had supported the CVA were ineligible to vote or were allowed too many votes. If the High Court supported HMRC's contention and excluded these creditors then HMRC's percentage debt holding would exceed 25 per cent, thus enabling it to block the CVA. A High Court hearing on the issue was set for September – well after the season's start. HMRC was adamant. No argument anyone advanced would persuade it to change its position.

In addition we felt the administrator was trying to blame the League for the impasse. We had the impression it just wanted us to hand over the club to whomsoever it decided, without regard to our rules, which, of course, did not bind it. I understood the frustration, indeed shared some of it, but rigorously defended our governance.

Amid all this confusion two facts remained. A CVA existed and HMRC's legal challenge was alive and would not be resolved for months. If HMRC succeeded, or if any of the original sale terms were to be varied by the administrators in an attempt to resolve the impasse then we would have had to insist on a new CVA. This in turn would be blocked or challenged by HMRC and, possibly, by Astor if the highest bidder was anyone other than Ken Bates. There was, literally, no realistic end in sight.

Still with me?

Leeds, understandably, wanted us to confirm that Ken Bates was the 'new' 'owner' and to hand them the right to play in the League in just a few weeks' time. They dismissed the pending HMRC court case as sour grapes because the taxman opposed the League's foot-ball creditor rules. While this may have been the true reason, the challenge was nevertheless legally real and had to be resolved. By this time, Leeds's offer to creditors had increased to about 13p in the pound. (Personally I never understood why the offer kept rising, I was just pleased that creditors were to lose less money.) The admin-istrator's weekly costs were, of course, reducing the value of any offer.

The board agreed unanimously, by individual vote, that Leeds could not be readmitted to the League until the board had received definitive assurance from the administrator that all its governance due process had been completed and we had had time thoroughly to assess our options.

Throughout these events I kept reminding the board that our responsibility was not just to the club in trouble. We also had a heavy responsibility to all the other clubs in the League and in particular to those in Leeds's division. They too needed to be treated fairly.

Reflecting on our concerns and the time being taken, the board unanimously decided to make its views public, to the administrator's irritation. That press statement again committed the board to resolving outstanding issues as quickly as possible and hopefully before the start of the new season. It:

- affirmed League rules permitted a club in administration to start a new season.
- sympathised with Leeds's fans' growing frustration and confirmed that best efforts were being made to save the club within the League's regulations. Frustration and threats, however, were not a reason for breaching the League's rules. These belonged to all the clubs not just to the board.
- said nothing about the 'exceptional circumstances' get-out, although it was looming larger in our private conversations.

Finally it became apparent to me that we might make progress only if everyone sat round a table. Ken Bates and his colleagues represented Leeds. Senior representatives of KPMG attended alongside the administrators, who had had to agree to this proposal. And I chaired this 'extended' meeting, with League executives and lawyers in attendance, ready to report to the board, which previously had decided which options would be acceptable to it and which would not.

We met for four hours in the middle of July, sometimes with just us and Leeds in the room. HMRC confirmed by phone that they would continue their legal challenge in court over the CVA. This meant that no conventional progress could be made until, at least, September and probably not even then. Without the board exercising its discretion, Leeds was in big, maybe terminal, trouble. So if we wanted to 'save' Leeds, we would have to accept that this impasse constituted a reasonable basis for invoking the never before used 'exceptional circumstances' provision.

I told the meeting that the board had unanimously agreed, by individual vote and on the basis of legal advice, that 'exceptional circumstances' could be relied upon because, in effect, there was no functioning CVA. Creditors were not being 'allowed' to express their willingness – or otherwise – to accept a new proposed settlement.

Leeds were then told that the board had also agreed there would have to be a price to pay – a penalty – for the use of this escape clause, in recognition of the creditors' importance. I stressed to Ken that our willingness to go down this 'exceptional circumstances' route reflected the board's policy that, if possible, we should try to maintain the League's 72-club structure.

I told the meeting that the board had identified three forms of penalty option: financial, points deduction or relegation to the division below. Leeds rejected relegation out of hand (as if they had the final say!). They were already going down one division and would not accept a second divisional drop. A large fine made no rational sense for a club seeking to shed debt. Which left a points deduction. Leeds agreed that this was the logical option – though unwelcome.

A solution was agreed. The board would exercise its discretion over 'exceptional circumstances' and Leeds would be given a fifteen-point deduction. That number had been agreed unanimously by the board following long discussion during which individual members had floated and supported several numbers, both higher and lower, before settling on fifteen. And we agreed Leeds could appeal the fifteen-point deduction to a meeting of all seventy-two League clubs.

There was one final, crucial condition. The club would have to sign a waiver undertaking not to mount any legal challenge against the League. These proposals formed the basis of the motions put to the clubs' meeting, about a week later, to determine Leeds's appeal.

Clubs were told we intended to invoke the new 'exceptional

circumstances' clause for the first time, were asked to endorse the concept of a sporting sanction being linked to the use of the clause and were asked to accept that the sanction should be fifteen points.

I put the board's case. Leeds used a barrister to put theirs, and the motions were carried by significant margins. In the interests of transparency I had talked Ken, Mark Taylor and their barrister through the motions as well as the meeting's procedure before we started. They said they were content.

In summary, Leeds was saved although it would start the new season with a significant points deduction. And the matter was closed (apart from some hard feelings) because of Leeds's agreement not to mount any legal challenge to the clubs' meeting's democratic decisions.

The end.

Not likely.

A few weeks later Leeds sought to lodge an appeal with the FA. Quite rightly, the FA refused to entertain it. Leeds then sought to challenge the FA on that point (no doubt realising that it had already waived any claims it may have had against the League). Again, the FA showed some resolve and refused to bow to pressure from Leeds.

Then in February 2008, some six months after the appeal to the clubs had been heard, the League was served a High Court writ from Leeds and Barnsley. Apart from the close Yorkshire relationship, no one could work out why Barnsley had suddenly become involved. As soon as they understood the ramifications of their involvement, for example being responsible for half the costs if they lost, Barnsley quickly withdrew.

Despite their signature on the original deal, Leeds's writ argued that the board had no power to impose a fifteen-point sanction and anyway fifteen points was too severe – despite these being the decisions of the clubs' meeting.

Our first dispute about the writ centred on the proposed High Court involvement. FIFA rules, binding on the English FA, require that football disputes are resolved in legal football tribunals, not the courts. Leeds initially seemed reluctant but eventually the League insisted and a tribunal was established. Both parties wanted a speedy resolution before the start of the next season, as did other clubs which could have been affected by what happened to Leeds.

The board's external and internal legal advice was as unambiguous as lawyers ever permit themselves to be. We would win. And, in the unlikely event we lost, legally Leeds would simply revert to the position they had occupied before that four-hour meeting in July when the deal was agreed. That is to say, their future in the League would be 'ended' because there was no alternative 'conventional' solution. We wondered if the club realised that a win would bring them such a poison pill. Or maybe they thought the board could be intimidated into surrender outwith League rules. Fat chance.

So we all embarked on what was called an FA Rule K arbitration. The League nominated Peter Leaver QC to serve on the tribunal panel. Leeds nominated Peter Cadman, and the chairman, agreed by both sides, was retired Appeal Judge Sir Philip Otton. The hearing lasted three days. Andy Williamson, Nick Craig and I were grilled by the Leeds barrister. Andy and Nick were excellent. The board's barrister grilled Mark Taylor. Ken remained quiet, most of the time. The board's minutes, which reflected its thinking and intentions, were closely examined.

The tribunal found in the League's favour on all counts – starting with the binding nature of Leeds's voluntary signing of the legal waiver. We were judged to have acted reasonably and proportionately.

We sent the tribunal findings to our clubs, to the media and to the thousands of people who had written or sent emails (overwhelmingly in Leeds's favour), mainly in the Yorkshire direction! As well as informing people, this communication helped diffuse some of Ken's media broadsides against the board and me personally – an understandable if slightly distasteful diversionary tactic. Apart from welcoming the decisions, I decided not to 'do' the media. After all, Leeds was one of our clubs. Least said soonest mended.

Leeds had to pay the League's costs as well as their own – an exceedingly hefty sum.

I started this story by saying it was and is a case study. If you have struggled to understand the issues, that may be my fault. Or it may be the first case lesson – handling serious football disputes is complicated and demanding and can be a legal minefield.

The second case lesson is the most fundamental. If the board does not defend and protect the integrity of its competitions, no one will. In other words, the board is the ultimate referee. Clubs look out for their own interests. If one of them gets any unfair advantage, it does so at the expense of the other clubs in the League, because the League is a closed system. This includes unfair financial advantage, because that can result in serious on-field disparity, the consequences of which are 'unfair' games which penalise other clubs and fans.

The third case lesson is that there are no easy or cost-free options available to a board determined to referee dispassionately – to govern in the interests of the whole League. Fans are not rational about their teams, nor are they supposed to be. They do not see (or often want to see) the bigger picture. For most, the philosophy of 'my club, right or wrong' is simple and persuasive. That mantra determines how they behave, both at matches and when more serious issues occur.

Sadly, some fans personalise their simple hatreds, on and off the field. When Leeds got to the League play-off final at Wembley in 2008, the League had to organise extensive security for me against the possibility of physical attack by some of their fans. Eventually they and the players settled for fans booing me when I greeted the teams on the pitch prior to kick-off – a somewhat damp squib. Ken Bates behaved with considerable dignity on the day, in contrast to the rude behaviour of at least one of his colleagues.

This case study, this story, throws up two other lessons. The first is about governance. Any government minister, if he or she wishes to progress, learns the importance of rigorous thinking, proportionate behaviour, examining the evidence, speaking carefully and comparing options rather than rushing to judgement. He or she also learns the importance of being careful with the written record, the paper trail.

Throughout the whole Leeds saga, the board handled the problem particularly carefully. Perhaps it was Ken's reputation, the size of the club, the issues at stake or a foreboding that matters could turn legal. Perhaps it was just a strong desire to do the job properly and be good guardians of the League's interests.

Whatever the reason, board minutes were full of references to saying only what was intended; not making any allegedly off-the-record comments; careful and repeated summaries of issues and actions taken, as well as of those still pending; lots of legal advice and much taking of votes by individual polling of board directors – and recording that this was how we had behaved. Decisions to be made were encapsulated in formal motions.

Those minutes were seriously tested by the Leeds barrister, rightly so, and passed with flying colours. Indeed their care and accuracy enhanced the good governance reputation of the League and were the foundation on which our case was built. Thank you Glynis Firth, our Director of Administration and estimable board secretary.

The last lesson reaffirms a fundamental political one. Every leader wants to be loved and being loved is great. But being respected is crucial. And respect sometimes requires people to say no.

In early January 2010, Betty and I gave Ken Bates and Suzannah, his charming wife, dinner in the House of Lords. We had a good evening. Everyone was on best behaviour. It was my hope that Ken would understand (if only a little) that the board's role was to be 'pro' all the clubs and not 'anti' any particular club – including Leeds.

I doubt the Leeds board and fans were sad to see me stand down as chairman. My respect for a minority of its fans remains 'limited', but Ken, however much of a handful he can sometimes be, deserves real respect for the enormous contribution he has made to football. So what if, now and again, he can be flamboyant, edgy, earthy and occasionally just plain rude?

I probably do not have the expressive skills required to explain what 'my' club means to a real fan. It is often a lifelong, passionate commitment and priority; my club, right or wrong, win or lose. Neither criticism nor ridicule makes any serious difference to a real fan.

It is his or her emotions, memories, fantasy, statistics, unexpected delight and despair, hope, experience and expertise all rolled into one. Fans can all pick better teams. And they easily transfer blame for lack of success to the referee and club directors.

Their solutions are simple. Blame the ref – whose birthright and eyesight are regularly questioned (loudly) – and urge directors to pour even more money into that famous black hole which is their club's balance sheet. In this regular, vocal exercise, together with the emotional pressure it generates, they become unwittingly complicit in their club's overspending, with all the negative consequences that can flow from such unsustainable behaviour.

Real fans will travel hundreds of miles to away games, enjoy arguing over pints and pies and feel strongly that it is their responsibility to introduce the next generation to the world's most popular sport. And an increasing minority will continue to enjoy their prawn sandwiches. There may be no law which requires their football club always to exist but any other scenario is unthinkable. And they make sure that everyone knows that this is their position.

A chapter on testing the rules cannot focus only on the story of Leeds United. Other clubs were similarly guilty of forcing the League to act as ref. Luton Town had directors whose behaviour was hard to understand – to put it gently – together with fans who had a serious chip on their shoulders. The club consistently spent money it did not have and the League was not the only regulatory body to take an interest in the behaviour of some of those associated with the club's leadership. Luton fans were virulently of the 'my club, right or wrong' variety, especially when the club was in the wrong. Unfortunately for them, Luton Town had had to enter administration three times in less than fifteen years – not an enviable record. I cannot guess the amount owed to creditors that went unpaid and how much advantage on the field this gave the team against the rest of the clubs in their division. Such unfairness did not seem to bother Luton fans and, maybe, still does not, though it should. Fans of the other twenty-three clubs in Luton's division should certainly have been bothered.

The details need not detain us. The third administration dragged on for a long time. Creditors were sidelined and eventually Luton too had to be deemed to be in 'exceptional circumstances' so that it too could be saved by the League's board. It was given a significant penalty – twenty points – and the FA penalised the club a further ten points. What Luton fans do not know is that I complained bitterly to the FA about their interference, which, I acknowledged, the FA had the legal right to do but which was done without reference to the League. Subsequently Luton was relegated from the League.

In this case, as with Leeds, all the board did was defend the integrity of its competition against repeated Luton attempts to gain unfair advantage through shedding debt. We refereed fairly as between all the clubs. Or, to put it another way, the board saved Luton Town from liquidation when its directors appeared incapable of doing so. While their team was of limited ability, the spirit of their fans was outstanding. To this day it is a given in club and town that their relegation, which was so hard on the club's many real fans, was solely due to the League and its 'ringleader', that villain Mawhinney (you may substitute a harsher epithet – Luton fans did).

This case study too underlines the truth that if the board does not defend the integrity of its competitions, no one else will. And no board acting in this way should ever expect fans to say thank you. Having no knowledge of the present Luton board, my comments relate entirely to my time in office.

Southampton FC provided a different challenge to the ethics of football competition. It had a controversial history of boardroom change and dispute, often at the club's expense; too many directors rowing with each other too often. It too accumulated debt, in part through the building of its new and impressive stadium.

The club's business structure was interesting. Under a holding company there were two entirely separate businesses, one of which ran the club. When, in the view of its directors, the club's debt endangered the whole edifice, the holding company went into administration. By fingering the holding company in this way, they maintained that the club itself was not in administration, thus arguing that it should escape the ten-point sporting sanction.

To the board, this was but another example of that well-known political duck lesson. You know – if something looks, waddles and quacks like a duck it is almost certainly a duck! The board believed the club was in administration but, to referee fairly, we needed supporting evidence before it would be appropriate to deduct ten points.

The club maintained a media barrage protesting its innocence. We appointed forensic accountants to report back as quickly as possible. Their report contained information the board could not ignore – not because it wanted to punish Southampton but because compelling evidence was forthcoming on which action was required if we were to be fair to all the other clubs. The whole process was made more difficult because those who supported the club and/or sought to buy it kept issuing emotional public statements which the people of Southampton probably believed, but which the board had difficulty squaring with the evidence that was accumulating. Lacking our knowledge, public opinion railed against the League.

In April 2009, Southampton FC was penalised ten points by the League board. We said at the time, 'The holding company has no income of its own; all revenue and expenditure is derived from the operation of Southampton FC and the associated stadium company. The holding company is solvent in its own right. It only becomes insolvent when account is taken of the position of Southampton Football Club and the other group companies.'

In July 2009 the club was bought by Markus Liebherr. He installed Nicola Cortese as executive chairman. They accepted the ten-point penalty without complaint or any threat of legal challenge. Today the club has been steered away from choppy financial waters and become one of the best administered in any league. I hope they enjoy playing in the Premier League.

Running the League is not dissimilar to running any trade association. Part of the governance challenge is that none should claim or expect special treatment because they are large, famous or indeed weak. Andy Williamson, the chief operating officer, who has been with the League for forty years, taught the board the importance of this principle. He was our respected guardian of competitive integrity.

Incidentally, it is for reasons of competitive integrity that leagues have occasionally penalised clubs which played weakened teams in competitions. A club may not be too bothered by the thought of losing a particular game, but handing three points or a cup win to a rival is a bonus not shared by the other clubs involved. In other words, the integrity of competition is undermined.

No story about 'refereeing' can or should be complete without reflecting on what happens on the football pitch itself, for dubious morality is not restricted to the boardroom. Each week fans pay to see skill, endeavour, passion, teamwork and bravery. They also get to see too much cheating.

The game really hates that last word, even though, or perhaps because, it is so endemic in the game. Some years ago, fed up with all the on-field cheating in both the Premier and Football Leagues, I wrote an article for the *Daily Mail* condemning this widespread practice – thereby committing one of football's great 'sins'. I actually used the 'c' word several times. Andy Williamson sucked his teeth while reading the draft article and advised me to find a different word for cheating. Richard Scudamore gave me serious earache. He told me I had no business using the word. Doing so brought the game into disrepute. It was not for 'administrators' (his word) like us to express such opinions.

What nonsense.

The game's extreme sensitivity towards the words 'cheat' and 'cheating' is, in my view, a reflection of its sense of guilt. It knows the reality of cheating is obvious and widespread, but it will not seek seriously to stamp out this endemic bad behaviour, preferring instead to deal only with the most blatant cases. (Even then some media commentators will look for excuses for the foul behaviour.) Commendably, an increasing number of journalists now use the word, with critical intent.

Of course the game has a rule book. Indeed, so much of that rule book sprang from our British experience that the UK associations still play a disproportionate role in FIFA's annual review of international rules. The problem is not the rule book; the problem is the game's unwillingness to play by the rule book.

Graham Poll, a very distinguished former senior and international referee, whose opinions would widely be held in high regard, including by me, wrote in the *Daily Mail* (9 January 2012) on the issuing of red cards:

> Sending off a player is a big deal. It changes games and invites a major analysis because – as I have written before – there is so much at stake in professional football. Sending off players for two technical offences, such as removal of shirts or kicking the ball away, really does seem too harsh and only leads to criticism. So, naturally, referees shy away from dismissing players – especially for offensive, insulting or abusive language, even though in law it is a red-card offence.

In sport, as in a political democracy, it is absolutely permissible for anyone to criticise any rule and seek to persuade any governing body to have it changed. But, for me, until change happens, existing rules should be applied. They were not adopted lightly but for a purpose. They were considered to be in the best interests of the game and designed to reflect its best and fairest standards for the benefit of those playing and those watching.

So that old mantra holds good. Play to the whistle – and, in my opinion, the whistle should reflect the rule book.

With that in mind, some of Graham Poll's views are worth further reflection. Sending a man off does or can change games but that truth should be for managers, not referees, to ponder and analyse and, boy, do some managers need lessons in how to – objectively – analyse some of their players.

'There is so much at stake in professional football.' Actually what is at stake is a win, loss or draw and their monetary consequences. The referees' professionalism is supposed to transcend all that. Graham Poll's did. We are not talking about life and death here, nor even a job, food on the table or a roof over heads, but football.

More recently I heard Graham say that good referees deserve more support from the FA disciplinary system when properly and somewhat controversially given red cards are (too often?) overturned. Well said. I agree with him and hope our sentiments are heard in the echoing corridors of Wembley. Referees need supportive encouragement.

The referee's job is not to mitigate offences by deeming them 'technical' or to determine the 'harshness', or otherwise, of the rules. It is to apply them. If they think them too harsh they should lobby the FA and FIFA to have them changed. When they 'shy away' from doing the job they are paid to do to the best of their ability, for fear of criticism, they deserve to be criticised for undermining the rule book and therefore the integrity of competition.

There is another good reason why this should be the case. Given the celebrity status of leading players, who are treated as role models in our society, it is important that no one is seen to be, or even thought to be, more important than the rule book. What are young boys and girls expected to deduce, and then imitate, when they see their heroes' foul-mouthed abuse being ignored by referees – their cheating being treated as of little consequence? To be fair to referees, often they do abide by the rule book. But, as in other aspects of everyday life, normal and appropriate behaviour goes unremarked while the abnormal stands out and demands attention.

PGMO (Professional Game Match Officials) is the quasi-independent body which governs referees in our professional game. It is 'quasi' because the Premier League, the Football League, the footballers' union (the PFA) and the Football Association are all members. It is chaired, at the time of writing, by an experienced football man and a personal friend, Peter Heard – the same one who introduced me to the Football League. PGMO's philosophy appears not to be too complicated. It expects referees to keep the game flowing, not to be too tough, controversial or legalistic and to be consistent in their decision making. (The latter is very important.) They worry about referees being too 'noticed', hence the apparent go-easy impression which, I am guessing, is never pressed on referees as a written instruction. And PGMO monitors referees' progress, ability and willingness to adhere to advice.

As Football League chairman I was never allowed near PGMO (they knew my views!). It is not a secret organisation but its confidentiality exceeds that in any other football activity. And the independence PGMO enjoys means it is not answerable either to league boards or to clubs. When I brought its chief executive to a clubs' meeting, the outcome was entirely unsatisfactory from the clubs' point of view. It simply added to their frustration.

So what is this cheating?

One personal objection will suffice. Other than physically endangering an opposing player, the cheating I find most unacceptable is the deliberate blocking of the taking of free kicks by the refusal of one or more players to retreat ten yards immediately a free kick has been given against their side. The rule book says that not to retreat is a yellow-card offence.

Instead, what we see far too often is a deliberate and often apparently practised effort to prevent the taking, not to mention the quick taking, of the free kick, by the team that offended. Shame on the guilty managers. As a result, the sinned-against team forfeits part of its advantage, with the referee's connivance. In fact the team against which the foul has been given is frequently instructed by the referee not to touch the ball until he has undertaken his walk of shame. Ten yards. Nine metres. After which he lines up the defending players like a primary school teacher in the playground. Then he may choose to ignore the defensive line edging forward to give themselves yet another illegal advantage.

So, in one small but oft-repeated episode, the rule book is treated with disdain. Justice is neither done nor seen to be done. The integrity of competition is not defended. Other clubs in the League are disadvantaged. And, perhaps, worst of all, this practice is now repeated week after week in the youth leagues also. Tell me, how many yellow cards have you seen given for this law breaking? Why do you think that is?

When you add to this the pervasive stealing of yards at throw-ins and free kicks, players claiming advantage they know they do not deserve, or trying illegally to intimidate the referee, the deliberate illegal holding, often wrestling, of opponents in the penalty area, shirt pulling of epidemic proportions, iniquitous 'diving', bad-mouthing referees, the feigning of injury (in an attempt falsely to damage the prospects of an opposing player), you are left wondering why managers do not, and do not even want to, exercise more control over their players and why club directors do not insist that they do. Managers who do not rein in or discipline such behaviour are implicitly condoning the cheating, as are referees who turn a blind eye. And fans are penalised by being deprived of the opportunity to enjoy an emphasis on clean and skilful play.

I commend football journalists each time they condemn such cheating behaviour. One example will suffice. Matthew Syed (*The Times*, 11 April 2012), under the heading 'Culture of cheating makes fall guys of us all', wrote:

> Ashley Young is a good footballer – but he is a far more accomplished diver. They call it simulation, but why bother with euphemisms? There is a more accurate word. Cheating.
>
> There are certainly worse things in modern football. Two-footed lunges that are conceived in malice, for a start; these can often culminate in a player being dispatched to hospital, or put out of action for a season, or even having their career ended. Such hideous tackles can ruin lives.
>
> But diving – well, if it is not becoming more prevalent in English football, it is certainly becoming more portentous … It can change seasons and, by consequence, careers too.

Well said.

I have bluntly debated with Peter Heard the failure of referees to stamp out the illegal blocking of free kicks by issuing yellow cards – to no avail. He remains a friend I admire and respect but on this issue, so far, I might as well have been banging my head against a brick wall. PGMO does not want to know.

I understand their counter-argument. Today, they claim, we have slipped so far from the rule book that trying to 'keep the game moving' can only be achieved by selectively ignoring it. (Of course they use more elliptical phrases to convey this truth.)

A flurry of yellow cards, as the laws require, would lead to player expulsions, they argue. There would be short-term mayhem. So what? Once managers understood that the change in attitude was permanent, they would very quickly force a change of behaviour on their players. And the game – faster, cleaner, fairer – would be transformed for the benefit of the fans. But everyone opts for being loved rather than respected.

Recently I heard a Premier League manager complain bitterly on television about his defender being punished with a penalty for blatantly wrapping his arms around the opposing forward so preventing him from moving. Ridiculous, was his manager's judgement. This happens all the time and penalties are never given. If we are to expect penalties in future then there will be so many that the game will be permanently disrupted. Actually the referee was right according to the rule book. The controversy should have focused on all his colleagues who turn a blind eye to what happens in the penalty box. If they too would whistle by the rule book then this manager, and his colleagues, would soon sort out the behaviour inside the box.

Cheating will never be wholly banished, for we are dealing with human nature, but that is no reason for not making an effort to improve. Were referees to be seen to be always playing to the rule book, rather than mainly doing so, then the blame for the culture of cheating would fall entirely on the players and clubs – and that would be good for the game.

After final whistles, managers regularly criticise referees, often deliberately highlighting a controversial decision they did not like even when the referee was right, to avoid having to dwell on their team's inability to pass the ball accurately, shoot straight or tackle fairly. This simply adds to the 'blame the ref' sentiment, quite unjustly.

Referees are also undermined by radio and television pundits who rely on watching multiple shots of an incident, from a variety of camera angles, and then proclaim the man in the middle in error for an instant decision he had to make in the heat of the moment. Such unchecked behaviour can, totally unfairly, undermine confidence in the referee to the point where the integrity of competition is challenged.

Of course referees make mistakes. They are human. Sometimes they take the blame for mistakes made by one of their assistants. They too are human. But their professional standard is high and most of us accept the need for it to be raised higher. Accentuating the positive in referees' judgement, rather than the negative, ought to be the goal, alongside a determination to ensure that on-field governance is the best it can be. This can never be expected from partisan fans but it ought to be deliverable by managers and allegedly professional commentators, not to mention the PGMO.

One area of the game where serious mistakes do happen should have been addressed years ago. I am pleased to see the FA now finally in favour of installing goal-line technology – to determine whether the ball crossed the goal line. I also happily learn that the Premier League is poised to introduce this technology some time soon. I wish they had both been so supportive when, about six years ago, I wrote to Mr Blatter at FIFA offering to trial this technology for him in the Football League. He never replied or, if he did, the letter got lost in the post. Exactly the same thing happened two years later when I wrote again volunteering the services of the Football League. Then neither the FA nor the Premier League wanted to take the lead.

Still, better late than never. Certainly Mr Blatter's rhetoric has changed. Whether his well-developed instincts have also done so remains to be seen.

Thank you, referees, for doing a difficult job, sometimes an impossible one, without always receiving that element of support which you have the right to expect from the rest of the game. Your integrity underpins the beautiful game – which is why your highest standard of professionalism is always required.

Fans deserve to watch fair games. That was and remains the Football League's commitment, as the governance ref, even if occasionally we made some fans mad at us in the process. Being mad at the ref on the pitch, an inalienable right of football fans watching games, lies beyond the League's ability to fix.

18

Back to the Future

Now that you have read this book you can exercise your own judgement. When you were starting out, I told you, 'The public have a low opinion of politicians generally. They rank them in public esteem with journalists and estate agents at the bottom of repeated polls of public judgement ... Frequently this low regard stems from a commonly held belief that politicians do not give straight answers to straight questions; that they are not honest ... For whatever reasons, politicians are seldom revered ... I hope these stories will help to redress that imbalance – if only by a little.'

Now you can better decide where the balance accurately lies.

I told you, 'Most people have little insight into the ordinary and sometimes extraordinary events which constitute the lives of MPs and ministers. I hope this book draws back the curtain just a little.'

Now you can decide if you are better informed.

I told you, 'I am privileged. Unlike many of my generation, I have stories to tell within two public frameworks. Politics touches all of us in that we each have a right to vote and the responsibility to pay taxes ... Football, on the other hand, is voluntary ... This book's chapters on football are not meant to constitute an in-depth analysis ... of the game. As in the reflections on my political life, they are stories which illustrate how a few of the big issues of the day were handled behind the scenes. In both pursuits, choosing which stories to tell has been difficult. Many good ones had to be omitted. Still, I hope you find these few stimulating and informative.'

Now you can decide if you did.

Finally, I told you, 'It will be clear to all that my experiences are being reflected through the prism of my Christian faith. I realise that my presuppositions will not necessarily be widely shared. But every book reveals something of the author's values. In that sense this one is no different. I can only hope that these stories are a worthwhile read in their own right.'

Now you can decide for yourself what role you think what I believe played in what is recorded here and whether you think that is good or bad, always remembering that all ministers will, indeed must, shape government policy to some degree.

And, who knows, you may even choose to reflect on what I believe.

I do want to stress one principle. My activities in both areas were firmly grounded, were robustly underpinned, by democratic reality. The dictionary defines 'democracy' as 'a political or social unit governed ultimately by all its members'.

Each of us has a constituency vote and, in that sense, a democratic say in how the country is run. Government runs most effectively when 'collective responsibility' is paramount. It was Winston S. Churchill (in 1947, after a second world war) who put democracy at the heart of governing when he said, 'Democracy is the worst form of government except all those other forms that have been tried from time to time.'

For a Christian politician, Churchill gives modern weight to what the Bible teaches. From it we learn that God only ordained three things to be observed and cherished by His human creation – the Church; marriage, one man and one woman together; and government. The latter, as St Paul tells the Church at Rome, was to provide a framework of order to constrain the otherwise instinctively selfish lives of individuals; to differentiate between right and wrong, promoting the former and resisting the latter. Thirdly, government was to act ethically, raising and spending taxes for the common good.

I have Christian friends who need to reflect on this biblical teaching, who are too 'holy' in their thinking, if not their behaviour, to allow themselves actively to help shape our democracy. Obviously these stories underscore my disagreement with their theological interpretation. Politics is not, or at least does not have to be, an ego-driven exercise. Its basis, to be effective, must be the 'common good'.

Maybe Abraham Lincoln had the best turns of phrase to help convey the reality and philosophy of my stories and their emphasis. In 1854 he said, 'No man is good enough to govern another man without that other's consent.' Four years later he expanded this thought in the pressing context of his time. 'As I would not be a slave, so I would not be a master. This expresses my idea of democracy. Whatever differs from this, to the extent of the difference, is no democracy.'

Or, as we Christians put it, God made men and women in His own image – hence human dignity.

St Paul recognised that, left to themselves, men and women will resort to violence to try to resolve difference. So did Winston Churchill when he said in 1951, no doubt with the Second World War again in mind, 'The object of Parliament is to substitute argument for fisticuffs.'

These stories demonstrate that I agree with and know the truth of both observations. I made progress, and sought to lead, by analysis, argument and persuasion, not by 'thumping' people! My tolerance fuse for bullies was short. And the image of a ballot paper in one hand and an Armalite rifle in the other is an obscene perversion of democracy.

The democrats understand that you win some and lose some in life's tussles. Not only is this the way life is, it is also the way life should be. Recognising and accepting that truth enhances leadership, on the one hand, and relationships on the other. And it helps all of us to keep our feet on the ground – to live in the real world.

And the same principle governs sport. It was the so-called father of the modern Olympic movement, Baron Pierre de Coubertin, who said in 1908, 'The important thing in life is not the victory but the contest; the essential thing is not have won but to have fought well.' He would have made a good referee – on and off the field.

In case you think I am becoming too philosophical or, indeed, sentimental, let me remind you of a fact that underpins my stories. I have sat on the opposition benches, the government benches and the government front bench in the House of Commons. I have no doubt which bench is the most desirable, enjoyable and important if you want to effect change for the common good – no matter how much abuse you have to handle in the process.

My preference must be crystal clear. If not, I have failed you. And yet, 'It is an error to believe that the world began when any particular party or statesman got into office. It has all been going on quite a long time.'†

---

†   Winston S. Churchill, 9 November 1951.

Acknowledgements

For many years Betty and I have been privileged to have George and Eileen Carey, the former Archbishop of Canterbury and his wife, as friends. Some time ago we were giving them dinner in the House of Lords when the conversation turned to George's experiences in high ecclesiastical office, and the book he had written.

'Why are you not writing about your role in the country's history?' he asked. I mumbled something about not wanting to break confidences. George was not appeased; quite the opposite, in fact.

'Of course you must protect important confidences,' he agreed, 'but there is much you could say that would be very interesting. You owe it to historians and, through them, to all of us to contribute your insight and knowledge about how the country was run and your particular contribution to that process – which many of us think was significant both nationally and to the Christian community.'

As my mother might have said, he would not take no for an answer.

With Betty's encouragement, that evening spurred me on to a final attempt to interest and inform. Without George this book probably would not have been written.

Any author's name is inextricably linked to his or her book. But no one believes, least of all the author, that he or she is the only reason the book exists. Others play an important role in delivering the final product.

This has been as true of this book as of any other. I want to acknowledge that help and say 'thank you' to:

- Richard Hegarty, John McConnell, David Triesman, Nick Craig and Gavin Megaw for reading chapters and making helpful, insightful and occasionally salutary comments. My wife Betty and PA Judi read the whole manuscript and without exception their suggested changes enhanced its interest level, accuracy and colour.
- My agent, Jonathan Lloyd. His professionalism eased the necessary arrangements for publication and made them appear straight-forward, which any author will tell you is a huge compliment, and relief.
- Iain Dale and Sam Carter of Biteback, for being willing to have confidence in me. They too could not have been more professional, more supportive or more willing to smooth the path to publica-tion. I would also like to thank them for boosting my confidence.
- Ted Olsen (of Chicago), Richard Ormston and Michael Vincent, for having the Christian gift of encouragement.

I am especially indebted to my PA Judi Broadhead. She has guided, humoured and put up with me for more years than she cares to remember, with minimal complaint! She bore the brunt of translat-ing my writing and, at times, jumbled thoughts into a coherent and readable form. I am very grateful and extend my thanks also to her husband John for his patience. Too often this project crashed into their personal time.

Finally, it would certainly be true to say that without Betty's love, encouragement, strong support and balanced common sense there would definitely have been no book because there would have been few if any of these stories to tell. Practically, she too contributed to the final script. But her importance is not encapsulated in one manuscript. Not only has she enhanced my life and made it special, she has acted similarly for our children and grandchildren. That is why this book's dedication means so much. Thank you. As has been the case for the last forty-seven years I am in your debt.

I have been extremely fortunate that so many people have helped me along my journey; I thank them too for adding to my wealth of memories.

✝

In writing the book, apart from the period of the 1997 general election, I have not had any diaries to rely on. Much of the content is based on memory, and in the interests of style I have rendered various conversations as direct speech. I am confident I have not misrepresented the substance of any of these, though in the odd case these may not be a verbatim report. If I have misplaced the odd word I hope I may be forgiven.

Index